Shifting
SUPERPOWERS

MARTIN SIEFF

Shifting SUPERPOWERS

THE NEW AND EMERGING RELATIONSHIP BETWEEN THE UNITED STATES, CHINA, AND INDIA

CATO INSTITUTE
WASHINGTON, D.C.

Library of Congress Cataloging-in-Publication Data

Sieff, Martin.
  Shifting superpowers : the new and emerging relationship between
the United States, China, and India / Martin Sieff.
    p. cm.
  Includes bibliographical references and index.
  ISBN 978-1-935308-21-8 (hardback: alk. paper)   1. United States—
Foreign relations—China.   2. China—Foreign relations—United
States.   3. United States—Foreign relations—India.   4. India—Foreign
relations—United States.   5. China—Foreign relations—India.   6.
India—Foreign relations—China.   I. Title.

  E183.8.C5S5375 2010
  327.73051--dc22

                                                            2009042024

Cover design by Jon Meyers.

Printed in the United States of America.

                          CATO INSTITUTE
                  1000 Massachusetts Ave., N.W.
                     Washington, D.C. 20001
                          www.cato.org

For Debbie
"Couldn't have done it without you, hon."

Contents

Introduction: The Myth of Permanent U.S. Global Dominance

Two vast nations, the most populous in recorded history, are rising, gaining economic and ultimately military power in Asia. One is a democracy; the other is not. The first is India; the second is China.

Americans have historically ignored the former and obsessed over the latter. Currently, the romantic obsession in the eyes of Washington policymakers is shifting from Beijing to New Delhi. But it matters little. Both nations are pursuing their own interests, as organized nation-states have done for many centuries.

But within the Washington Beltway, Republicans and Democrats, conservatives and liberals alike, overwhelmingly buy into the same delusion. They assume that America's "unipolar moment" of global dominance can and will be sustained.[1] Since the terrorist attacks of September 11, 2001, the U.S. military presence has expanded in Central Asia at the very time that some fear the U.S. homeland to be under greater threat than ever before.[2] The need to rebuild the U.S. Army after its grueling deployments in Iraq and Afghanistan may force future administrations to keep U.S. ground forces closer to home. And yet the placement of troops in China and India's strategic neighborhood is consistent with the Bush administration's National Security Strategy of September 2002, issued a year after the 9/11 attacks, and a half year before the invasion of Iraq, which explicitly committed the United States to actively work to prevent the rise of major hegemonic powers that could conceivably challenge unipolar dominance.[3]

The Bush administration, like Clinton's before it, operated in Asia on the assumption that hands-on U.S. leadership in Asia could work. Indeed, the neoconservatives who influenced strategic planning in America's first 21st-century administration argued explicitly that the ancient principle of "balancing," whereby rising nations gang up to first hinder, then block, then topple any would-be continental or global hegemon, is now extinct.[4] They argued that the United

1

States—alone among the great nations of history—had solved the enduring riddle of international relations.[5]

America, so the argument went, had convinced the rest of the world that it had nothing to fear from the United States because it was a benign hegemon; and besides, other nations have no hope of matching American wealth, resources, advanced technology, and power, so why bother?

But India and China in the early 21st century offer timely case studies on why these views are already wrong. In 2003, for the first time in its history, China outstripped the United States as the greatest magnet for foreign direct investment in the world. When President Barack Obama took office in January 2009, the U.S. government was projecting an annual federal budget deficit of $1.2 trillion. China, through its purchase of U.S. Treasury bonds, had helped finance Washington's spending binge and therefore held a crucial credit advantage over the United States, similar to that which 18th-century Britain held over France, and that which the 20th-century United States held over Britain. In each case, once this "tipping point" of global financial and industrial power was reached, it proved impossible to reverse.[6] China began to behave as a country with leverage. As U.S. economic problems multiplied, Chinese leaders became more assertive.

Meanwhile, India, at the very moment when its relations with the United States were flowering as never before, went its own way on myriad crucial and often troubling issues.[7] India retained its more than three-decades-old strategic alliance with Russia. Indian leaders from the Hindu nationalist Bharatiya Janata Party eagerly engaged China in diplomatic and strategic dialogue. And they made very clear that they would not accede to U.S. pressures or suggestions on making any concessions to Pakistan that might conceivably weaken their hold on Kashmir.[8]

In fact, this shrugging off of the wishes of the American global hegemon was nothing new for a major U.S. land ally in Asia. During the two decades that China looked to the United States to protect it from the threat of overwhelming Soviet military power, it steadily expanded its industrial and manufacturing capacity. The tremendous free-market success of China in the quarter century following the great reforms of Paramount Leader Deng Xiaoping did not, however, lead to the inexorable spread of pro-American democratic values and institutions, as many American theoreticians prophesied they would.[9]

The rise of the new middle class in China has certainly been remarkable. McKinsey and Co. estimates that it now numbers 300 million. But that means there are still a billion people in China who have not been brought into the inner circle of prosperity and modernity that the free-market economy generates. That is why Hernando de Soto, author of *The Mystery of Capital: Why Capitalism Triumphs in the West and Fails Everywhere Else*, has made the point that China's prospects for completing its transformation into a free-market capitalist society and thereafter progressing to democracy will be a "race" to bring in a sufficiently large number of those people still outside the system before they turn against it. A violent reaction by those left behind in China's race to modernize could tear down what has already been accomplished.[10]

Even at the height of its global power, the United States could never significantly influence internal developments in authoritarian China. America's influence on democratic India was even more limited. India had been an English-speaking democracy that was committed to the rule of law and the freedom of the press, with genuinely free and overwhelmingly fair elections. Yet this did not prevent it from being an ally of the Soviet Union, and later Russia, for more than 30 years. Delhi had been a leading global critic of Washington's actions for more than 40.

The vagaries and unpredictability of Indian politics confounded Washington. The Bush administration's enthusiastic support for the free-market, pro-American government of Prime Minister Atal Bihari Vajpayee did not prevent its shocking defeat by the Congress Party in the Indian general elections of 2004. When Indians went to the polls again in May 2009, the Obama administration refused to play favorites.

These elections were fair and their results universally accepted. Americans should have been delighted that the largest democracy in the world, a showcase for all Asia, was functioning so well. Yet the outcome of that same open and effective electoral process had in 2004 toppled a government that the Bush team had confidently counted on to advance its agenda of confronting radical Muslim nations and containing China. Democracy clearly did not always guarantee the return of governments amenable to the desires and goals of Washington policymakers.

3

Indian politics held a far more obvious lesson that was also ignored in Washington. Americans simply did not know much about Asia.[11] The actions of the most populous nations in human history could not be explained by the narrow, stereotypical models that some Americans were so ready to impose on them.

This book will argue that the obviously desirable goals of promoting individual liberty, limited government, and peace are best served if U.S. policymakers turn away from trying to influence the internal affairs of China and India. The list of issues on which successive presidential administrations and Congresses in Washington have sought to do this is long. It ranges from advancing human rights and halting nuclear proliferation to internal territorial disputes over Kashmir with India and with China over its occupation of Tibet and dealings with Taiwan.

Washington's continuing pressure on both India and China on these and many other issues had provoked moves toward a Sino-Indian military understanding, possibly threatening a geopolitical backlash in both nations that could prove extremely dangerous to the United States and to U.S. interests in the region.[12] This is the strategic context within which the Obama administration must operate.

The very idea that the United States can and should maintain itself in the long run as the dominant power in continental Asia is a chimera born of the distorting experience of the cold war. Even in World War II, the greatest international conflict that the United States ever fought, President Franklin D. Roosevelt took pains to avoid any significant commitment of land troops in mainland Asia.[13] U.S. grand strategy toward imperial Japan in that climactic conflict was not merely overwhelmingly maritime, it was entirely so. With the arguable exception of MacArthur's Philippines campaign, all the bloodiest battles of the Pacific theater were fought to secure air and sea bases to isolate the Japanese home islands and make them vulnerable to attack.

Even at the apogee of U.S. global power through the second half of the 20th century, no U.S. president of either party, whatever his guiding principles, dared to seek to do more than contain China; none thought it worth the bother to seriously pressure or bully India, even after India grew close to the Soviet Union in the mid-1960s. This was the case even when a large U.S. ground army fought a major undeclared war against China on the Korean Peninsula from the end of 1950 to mid-1953. The aim of that conflict was never to topple the newly established communist regime in China; Gen. Douglas Macarthur was swiftly fired by President Harry S Truman when he fulminated that it should have been. Nor did President Dwight Eisenhower reverse that course when he took office in early 1953. On the contrary, to great domestic acclaim, Eisenhower rapidly settled the Korean stalemate on terms that conceded the survival of communist North Korea. The status quo prevailed but was steadily eroded by China's rising economic and political power.

The last chapter in this book will argue that the U.S. moment in Asia is now over. This is a good thing. Over the past 70 years, establishing and maintaining U.S. hegemonic power in Asia cost well over 200,000 American lives in three major wars: World War II, the Korean War, and the Vietnam War. The last two could have easily been avoided.

Nor can it be shown from the vantage point of the 21st century that fighting those wars to impose U.S.-style political and economic systems on vast sweeps of Asia was in the U.S. national interest, even when they succeeded. One need not wage war to advance the cause of democracy and free markets. It is far more often the case that hostility and distrust provoke a nationalist anti-American, anti-Western backlash. The examples of North Korea and Cuba show that the peaceful evolution of totalitarian and authoritarian regimes into more tolerant and open forms of government is almost never fostered by confrontation, bitterness, and isolation.

The U.S. experience in Asia, within the three decades from the end of World War II to 1975, was in fact a radical reversal of traditional U.S. grand strategy through the first 150 years of the Republic. The United States prospered by generally staying out of the world's wars. Eschewing entanglements in the affairs of others, Americans took full advantage of trade in its most positive and creative forms. In the cold war, however, these priorities were reversed, and the United States found itself fighting two major wars within 20 years— in Korea and Vietnam—while the other nations in Asia prospered from the vast amount of American wealth that poured into both conflicts.

In the early 21st century, American neoconservatives and their intellectual allies still believe that the United States has the power to micromanage Asia, including India and China, and that the more engagement Washington has with either, the more it will be able to exert pressure on the other. But in practice, this is only a revival of the old, oft-recurring American love affair with China. The same kind of idealized, fantasy relationship that Americans such as Henry Luce and Pearl Buck imagined the United States could have with their imaginary vision of China parallels the dream of an ideological superalliance uniting India and the United States in the early 21st century.

On the other side of the U.S. political-cultural divide, many New Deal–style liberals and progressives still believed in the early 21st century that the United States had a moral duty to endlessly lecture and pressure both nations on a host of issues, from protecting China's environment from its own people to enforcing Western concepts of religious freedom on India, a nation whose experience of such things was radically different from anything in the West. In the 2008 presidential campaign, Barack Obama spoke of seeking to force China and other nations to come up to U.S. standards for maintaining independent trade unions and environmental standards, as if this could in fact be done. As with neoconservatives, so with Progressives, the myth of eternal American omnipotence remained an alluring one.[14]

But India and China, like all great nations, have always marched to the beats of their own drummers, as this book will explain. American policymakers up to the late 1990s were extraordinarily ignorant of India's social, political, and economic achievements in its decades since independence. Americans were equally ignorant of India's military power, power that had played an important role in World War I and proved crucial in World War II. And for all the American century-long obsession with the sufferings, hostility, and then friendship of the Chinese people, U.S. policymakers have never been able to play a significant role in fostering the development of liberal political institutions in China, even when U.S. power and interest were at their peak in Asia.[15] How can it be otherwise when that power has already declined in real terms over the past decade?

Two major global developments, both of them highly detrimental to the United States, have already ensured that President Obama and other American leaders cannot throw their weight around in Asia the way that Bill Clinton and George W. Bush clearly wanted to.

The terrorist attacks of 9/11 set the United States on an anguished and complex course of confrontation and interaction with the wider Muslim world, the Arab Middle East in particular. The 9/11 attacks led directly to the war in Afghanistan aimed at toppling the Islamic fundamentalist Taliban government and destroying the al Qaeda terrorist organization there. Although the former was achieved, the latter met with only mixed success, at best.

The sequence of events that followed 9/11 greatly circumscribed the two grand policy initiatives in Asia on which the Bush administration had set its sights: strategic engagement with India and containment of China. Instead, Pentagon hawks who aspired to put China in its place—by, for example, securing the long-term de facto independence of Taiwan—were forced overnight to engage Pakistan as their primary ally in the campaign to topple the Taliban. Suddenly, they had far more immediate and lethal priorities: they needed to hunt down al Qaeda around the world.[16]

Indeed, throughout the rest of Bush's term, the United States became more dependent on Chinese goodwill than Washington arguably had ever been before. The successful toppling of the Taliban regime in Afghanistan in late 2001 was followed by a remorseless, 15-month buildup to war with Iraq, which began on March 19, 2003. The bitter insurgency in Baghdad and elsewhere in Iraq that erupted after the toppling of President Saddam Hussein preoccupied Bush administration defense planners. As a result, the last thing the president and his colleagues wanted was a new confrontation with China. The president's famous inclusion of North Korea in the "axis of evil" in his January 2002 State of the Union address was therefore not followed by stepped-up pressure on Pyongyang. On the signature security challenge in Asia, North Korea's nuclear program, U.S. policymakers had to go through China, the North's great power patron.[17]

The second thing that derailed the Bush administration's grandiose plans in Asia was its evident determination to use the national outrage over the 9/11 attacks to justify the Iraq War. The U.S. plans for Iraq were rapidly derailed, however. They were guided by an assumption that was proved to be totally wrong: that the elite spearhead units of the U.S. Army could go in rapidly, and get out rapidly, with a compliant Iraqi population and democratically elected government accepting their subordination to U.S. policy requirements.

7

Instead, guerrilla war against the United States' occupation forces and its Iraqi allies quickly developed, and by the end of 2006, more than four times as many U.S. troops had been killed in those attacks than in the misleadingly quick and easy three-week war of conquest itself.[18] Initial Pentagon plans had envisioned a U.S. presence of no more than 25,000 troops remaining in Iraq by December 2003. Instead, Iraq became a black hole for the limited resources of the elite and high-tech, but numerically small, U.S. Army.

The decision to launch the war, and the ongoing occupation of post-Saddam Iraq, vastly weakened America's military and diplomatic clout in dealing with both India and China, and with potential adversaries such as Iran and North Korea, as well as the resurgent Taliban in Afghanistan. India produces virtually no oil of its own and is forced to import primarily from the Middle East—especially Iran and Iraq—to feed its great and growing needs. India has had excellent relations with both nations for many years. But paradoxically, those nations were regarded as archenemies by the same Pentagon and White House hawks who wanted to court India. Complex geopolitical realities spoiled the deceptively simple and satisfying grand strategic vision of an enduring U.S.-Indian alliance.

Similar dilemmas of strategic overstretch confronted British military planners and their political overlords in the 1930s as they were torn between defending their homeland against Germany, containing Italy in the Mediterranean, and diverting scarce resources to deter Japan in the Far East. And just as so much of the operational strength of the U.S. Army became bogged down in Iraq after May 2003 fighting the insurgency there, so too was fully 25 percent of the operational strength of the British army tied down by the Arab Revolt in Palestine from 1936 to 1939.[19] Substitute North Korea for Japan, the Iraqi Sunni Muslims for the Palestinian Arab Sunni Muslims, Iran for Italy, and China for Germany, and the parallels are eerie.

In the 1930s, the British Empire was the global hyperpower, just as the United States has been in the two decades since the collapse of the Soviet Union. As has been the case with the insurgencies in Iraq and Afghanistan, the British were taken by surprise by the unexpected intensity and resilience of the insurgency in Palestine from 1936 to 1939. The popular uprising there received a great deal of support from Fascist Italy, resentful of Britain's opposition to its conquest of Ethiopia in 1935–36 and eager to replace Britain as the premier power in the Middle East. Iran has played a similar "on the sidelines" spoiler's role in encouraging and welcoming the continued insurgency in Iraq, even as it has quietly built up its own influence and support among Shiite paramilitary groups in the country. The image of U.S. military invincibility, needed, for example, to deter China from taking unilateral action at some point in the future to bring Taiwan under Beijing's control, has been undermined. Similarly, the continued humiliation of the mighty British army in Palestine, often overlooked by historians, was a significant embarrassment to successive governments in London as Britain faced growing challenges simultaneously in different parts of the world.

The United States enters the 21st century hoping to boost its ties to China financially and India strategically. There are enormous potential rewards for effectively managing these relationships. But the history of U.S. engagement with both nations, especially through the second half of the 20th century, is replete with examples of excessive hostility and demonizing on the one hand, and naive, uncritical romanticism on the other. A prosperous, confident, free-trading 21st-century America, buttressed by wise and lasting strategic relationships with major Asian nations, requires that its policymakers learn from and avoid the many mistakes of their predecessors.

Americans must wake up to the reality that they will have to deal with India and China as equals rather than supplicants—as players rather than playthings. Almost all American policymakers of the Right and Left alike would deny that they think of either great nation in those terms. But their policy initiatives on a wide range of issues from national security to human rights and the environment are widely seen in both Asian nations in this way. There are other—and far better—models to guide decisionmakers seeking to advance the U.S. national interest.

But to successfully apply those models, and create policies that will achieve America's necessary goals of national security and material prosperity, will require a much greater knowledge of India and China and a cautious realism that resists the temptation to lecture and browbeat both nations about their own internal affairs.

1. The Historical Experience of India

India's history of repeated invasion and subjugation from the northwest has motivated a commitment to maintaining a powerful national military force. Today, this manifests itself as a huge standing army and a nuclear deterrent. Indian history over the past thousand years is a repeated tale of massacre, rape, and the extermination of civilizations. The threat has almost always come from the northwest and has usually been Muslim. Fear and enmity toward neighboring Pakistan are therefore far more deeply rooted than in the horrendous mutual massacres and ethnic expulsions and transfers of population that created the modern conflict in 1947.

In contrast to China, India has repeatedly been forced to absorb rich cultures from other origins. These waves of external enrichment were poured onto a polytheistic Hindu religious tradition that by its very nature was eclectic. Hindu India was therefore open to absorbing the most diverse traditions and influences. It found rooms for them in a vast and sprawling house of ideas.

Not surprisingly, when the British started preaching pluralism and democracy, many of the ideas thus transplanted found a wide audience. As the modern history of India since independence has shown, pluralistic democracy proved highly appropriate for a vast, densely populated subcontinent with so many languages, religions, and different ethnic groups.[1]

The British involvement in India began as a straightforward mercantile commitment undertaken for simple profit. From 1757 to 1857, the British exercised power through a London-based corporation, the East India Company. It evolved eventually—at least in the imagination of the occupying power—into a great civilizing mission.[2] From the 1830s on, British technology, then the most advanced in the world, was introduced into India. British educational and philosophical systems and theories were taught in India. The advent of the modern railroad system in the 1840s went hand in hand in that same decade with British educational reforms urged by Thomas Macaulay.

The Struggle for Freedom

The only major domestic upheaval during the 190-year period of British rule over most of India occurred with the Uprising of 1857, as the Indians remember it, but which is, revealingly, still recalled in Britain and the United States as "the Sepoy Mutiny."[3] Following the events of 1857, the British government exercised its rule directly until India became independent in 1947.

The rising was indeed set off by mutinies within the native Indian military forces that the British had raised and relied on for generations. The immediate cause of the uprising of Indian troops, or sepoys as the British called them, was widespread rumors that new cartridges being supplied to the troops had been smeared with beef fat from cattle that was ritually unclean to practicing Hindus. Handling these cartridges was widely believed to break the religious caste standing of the troops who touched them—a matter of the gravest consequences to devout Hindus. The fat in the cartridges was also said to be lard—pork fat—which offended Muslims. Both Hindu and Muslim sepoys participated in the Great Revolt.

There were many, far deeper causes for the rising. And there was a surprisingly modern, 21st-century pattern to them. The rising was a reaction against globalization and modernization that were being imposed by the British on India at dramatic speed. A network of railroads had been constructed across the subcontinent over the previous 15 years. This new transportation system disrupted traditional patterns of commerce. It intensified the competitive advantage that British manufacturers enjoyed in India against Indian enterprises. British regulations to discourage the development of Indian factories that could compete freely against British ones caused social disruption and economic hardship to Indians in the 1850s. Modernization was not allowed to spread in India through the unregulated operation of the free market. It was distorted in favor of British manufacturing interests.

The rising was strongest in central northern India and down toward Rajasthan. It had much less of an effect on southern India and Bengal. Delhi fell to the Indian nationalists. The last Mughal emperor, still Muslim, was enlisted as the figurehead for a largely Hindu military revolt. The war was gruesome on both sides. Hundreds, perhaps thousands, of British administrators and soldiers— and their wives and children—were slaughtered in grisly fashion.

The British retaliated by crushing the revolt using their vastly superior military power with extreme ruthlessness. There were mass executions of captured rebels and suspected mutineers. Even more gruesome, an untold number of Indians were killed by being fired alive out of cannons. The practice was widespread. Most historians estimate the total death toll at several hundred thousand, the vast majority being Indian.

The deterrent lessons were taught and taught well. No serious direct military challenge to British occupation was attempted again for the next 90 years. However, the traumatic lessons of the failure of the 1857 revolt played their part in preparing the ground for Mohandas P. Gandhi's very different nonviolent protest movement of the 1920s and early 1930s. Neither the wave of assassinations of British officials in Bengal before World War I, nor the riotous unrest crushed after the war, significantly dented British control. By contrast, the British lost control of all north central India for months during the 1857 national rising. But in less than a year, they had reestablished full control.[4]

Even at its worst, British repression during the Uprising of 1857 paled beside the self-inflicted wounds suffered by China at the same time. As will be discussed in chapter 2, from 1850 to 1865, the Celestial Kingdom was ripped apart by the Taiping Revolt, the bloodiest civil war in recorded human history, which claimed between 20 million and 30 million human lives. China remained subject to waves of anarchy, civil war, and foreign conquest for another century.

By contrast, India's evolution under the British appeared blessedly stable and steady. By the 1880s, the Indian railroad system was already the biggest and best in Asia. Commerce, within carefully guided and regulated channels, could thrive. British officials imposed high standards for administration and public health. They also vigorously maintained law and order.[5]

However, there was another side to the picture. While offering India modernity with one hand, the British withheld it with the other. They did not allow the Indians to develop any significant modern steel-making or shipbuilding industry, even though up to the late 18th century Bengal was one of the most technologically advanced parts of Asia.[6] Likewise, the great textile industries of the north of England imported Indian-grown cotton and then exported clothes back to India at immense profit for over a century, while colonial officials prevented the Indian states from developing textile industries of their own.[7] Bengal, which had been for more than a millennium one of the richest regions in the world, underwent a slow but inexorable process of decline in the 150 years under British control. These parallel but contrasting legacies of tolerant, liberal political sophistication and state intervention that retarded industrial development continue to shape India's progress even into the 21st century.

Despite the failure of the Uprising of 1857, India never became a passive and pacifistic nation or subcontinent during the period of direct British rule. Popular resentment against the British imperial rule, or raj, repeatedly manifested itself in guerrilla movements. Slowly, the educated Indian middle class developed its own respectable political movement that eventually became the Indian National Congress. Meanwhile, Britain built up Indian military power to serve its own needs.[8] The British proved particularly adept at co-opting recently defeated foes that had impressed them with their martial prowess to occupy niche but honored roles in their own military hierarchy. Generations of Sikhs and Gurkhas took the queen's, and then the king's, salt and served their masters selflessly from Borneo to Beijing and even as far away as North Africa.[9]

The Indian Army, meanwhile, became by far the largest military force within the world-spanning British Empire, dwarfing Britain's relatively miniscule home army. It was used far outside the borders of India to project British power and to impose British interests across half of Asia and even into the Middle East.[10]

Herein lay one of the greatest paradoxes of India's two centuries under British control. The peoples of the subcontinent were subjected to an imperial rule more alien and more radical than anything they had ever known. Under this rule, India's international power became a force to be reckoned with across South and Southeast Asia to a degree not seen since the days of the Mauryan Empire. This power, however, was used in the service of others, not in the service of Indians.

India's British rulers directed this vast military power first from Calcutta and then from the magnificent newly built imperial capital of New Delhi, just outside the fortress walls of the old Mughal capital. They used this power to defeat China in the two Opium

Wars of 1840 and 1859–60. They used it to consolidate the British Empire in Southeast Asia. They used it to conquer Burma. And they even used loyal Indian forces to establish military and naval bases on the fringes of the Ottoman Empire on the coasts of the Red Sea, the Indian Ocean, and the Persian Gulf.

In World War I, Indian Army forces directed from New Delhi conquered Iraq in a long, bloody campaign against tough Ottoman Turkish opposition. It was Indian arms, therefore, that gave Britain its richest stake in the oil wealth of the Middle East.[11]

In World War II, Indian military forces played an even more direct role, even though the scale of the Indian military achievement remains unknown to almost all Americans. Indians were instrumental in the greatest defeat ever suffered by the Japanese army in its history when the Anglo-Indian Army commanded by Gen. William Slim broke the Japanese 15th Army's last great offensive at the battles of Imphal and Kohima on India's eastern border with Burma in late 1944. The victory was a strategic sideshow compared with Adm. Chester Nimitz's central Pacific campaign that led directly to the overall defeat of Japan. But the number of Japanese troops involved and defeated was almost as large as that defeated in Gen. Douglas MacArthur's 1944–45 Luzon campaign.

In short, the British established the traditions of the Indian Army and created the military and national political structures that prepared India for its growth into a global power of the 21st century. But from World War I onward, the power of the British Empire over India was on the wane. The loss of control started with the Montagu-Chelmsford Reforms of 1919. It gathered apace when Gandhi, soon known as the Mahatma, or great soul, launched the first and largest modern nonviolent protest movement in the 1920s. The point of no return was reached, as Winston Churchill furiously but impotently recognized, with the India Act of 1935. That fateful measure set the subcontinent on what proved to be an unstoppable drive toward full political independence.[12]

Gandhi

Gandhi proved to be one of the most seminal figures in modern history. His movement eventually inspired such disparate leaders as Nelson Mandela in South Africa and Dr. Martin Luther King in the United States.

But while his influence is apparent in retrospect, he was an unlikely figure to lead India. He only returned to the land of his birth in early middle age, after studying and qualifying as a lawyer in London in the 1880s and then practicing law in South Africa, where he led a pioneering political protest movement to win political rights for his Indian minority. (He was not concerned about the fate of the black majority.) Gandhi understood from his years of studying law in London how the British legal system worked. Gandhi's extraordinary success in Indian politics was rooted in his cosmopolitan nature. He took the forensic legal skills he had learned in London and his observations of British political life and combined them with the symbols and cultural practices of traditional Indian life.

In this fashion, Gandhi set an example for effective Indian leaders by studying at the greatest institutions of the Western world and gaining the sophistication, polish, and understanding to engage leaders around the world and use their own concepts against them. He learned law and constitutional politics, not guerrilla war and the building of revolutionary organization or totalitarian bureaucracy. He thereby created a revolutionary, though generally nonviolent, participatory mass political movement that the subcontinent had never known before. Gandhi's approach incorporated many of the elements of what modern military strategists refer to as fourth-generation warfare: demoralizing and wrecking the state's management of society and rendering it ineffectual. In fact, many thousands of people died in violent communal riots between Hindus and Muslims in the 1930s and 1940s as a direct result of Gandhi's ostensibly nonviolent activist campaigns.

However, the rosy-eyed legend that surrounds Gandhi, much enhanced by the successful popular movie about him starring Ben Kingsley, obscures both the revolutionary nature of his achievement and the contradictions and ironies that he embodied.

Gandhi presented himself to the world as the exemplar of Indian spirituality, yet he was anything but. The product of upper-caste Indian Brahmin culture, he only retreated to the world of idealized spirituality after he had been supplanted from effective control of the Congress Party he did so much to create, and after he had won all his greatest political battles. He did not become a spiritual romantic until he was a fading political force. His greatest effect was as a political revolutionary of exceptional originality. He adapted

16

Western concepts of political organization, mass participation in politics, and the manipulation of public opinion to the Indian stage. He was the first anti-colonial leader to successfully turn his insider's knowledge of the ruling power's political culture against it. Many would emulate the political-cultural jujitsu that he pioneered.

Gandhi's model of effective leadership for India was dramatically different from the ones that worked in China. As will be discussed in chapter 2, Hong Xiuquan, the spiritual leader of the Taiping, trailblazed the path that Mao Zedong and Deng Xiaoping followed when they ruled China. According to Mao, sophisticated knowledge of the wider world, such as Sun Yatsen and Zhou Enlai had experienced, was a fatal detriment to seizing and retaining supreme power. What was important was to understand the political psychology of hundreds of millions of China's peasants and how to inspire and direct them.

Gandhi, like Hong, Mao, and Deng, certainly understood the importance of winning the support of millions of peasants. "During the two decades from 1920 to 1939 under Gandhi's leadership," Stanley Wolpert writes, the Congress Party "transformed itself from an elite, moderate club to a mass national party representing all of India's regional and national interest groups, capable of mobilizing millions in its revolutionary non-cooperation campaigns."[13] This was the key not merely to his own success but also to the enduring success and surprising resiliency of his Congress Party in the six decades after he died. But Gandhi harnessed the enthusiasm of millions of poor peasants to political ends, not revolutionary ones.[14]

Gandhi was no naive or otherworldly saint who believed the application of nonviolence and the moral superiority it conferred would magically banish the British from India. In his old age, when he was no longer politically potent, he preached his spiritual gospel with as much fervor and zeal as Hong and Mao did their vastly more destructive ones.[15] But in the 1920s and 1930s, Gandhi brilliantly wielded nonviolence as the most effective political tool available to erode the British will to rule India. He showed the British that without making commitments to establish national self-government they could no longer expect automatic compliance from the peoples of India.[16]

Nor was nonviolent an accurate description. Increasingly through the 1930s, mass protests led not merely to brutal British repression but also to ferocious sectarian riots between Hindus and Muslims that took thousands of lives. And it was also true, as Ho Chi Minh in French Indochina bitterly remarked, that if Gandhi had tried nonviolence against the French instead of the British, he would quickly have been dancing with the angels.

Terrorist campaigns had been repeatedly tried against the British in India since the days of the Sepoy Mutiny. (The idea that Indians are inherently nonviolent because they were either spiritually superior or martially inferior to everyone else is a myth.) A guerrilla campaign assassinating British officials rocked Bengal before World War I. It was savagely crushed. After World War I, the British also moved decisively and ruthlessly to repress several disparate violent protests and independence movements from Bengal to the Punjab.[17]

The massacre of protestors at the Jallianwala Bagh, or Garden, in Amritsar on April 13, 1919, was particularly terrible. Popular and violent independence riots had swept the Punjab. On April 10 and 11, 1919, at least five Europeans were killed in the violence in the city of Amritsar. On April 13, British general Reginald Dyer marched 50 armed Indian Army soldiers into the Jallianwala Bagh and ordered them to open fire on a protest meeting attended by some 10,000 unarmed men, women, and children. He had not issued a word of warning. Dyer's troops fired into the terror-stricken crowd that had no way of escaping; the soldiers spanned the only exit. The British admitted to killing 379 people. Indian historians believe the death toll was far higher. The wounded were left without medical attention by Dyer, who hastily removed his troops from the scene.

The massacre gave a huge boost to the nationalist movement across India. But none of the protests, not even the Amritsar massacre, weakened British political control. Gandhi's approach did.

Gandhi mobilized hundreds of thousands of people in dramatic mass protests. In 1926, he organized huge numbers of people in a march to the sea to protest the Salt Tax. It proved to be far more than stunning political theater. Everyone who took part in such mass demonstrations felt they were actively participating in tearing down centuries of British rule in India. It was a form of political activism that could include ordinary village farmers and their wives and children. It did not require literacy, or political sophistication. Yet the people who took part in these mass protests were turned into activists and local leaders of the nationalist movement by their experiences. Gandhi turned an elite, middle-class political organization into a vast, national movement with a grass-roots organization across the rural heartland. The British had never witnessed anything like it in their long history of imperial rule—not even in America.

Rioting produced a number of fatalities, and the nightmare of sectarian strife loomed as India neared independence. Nor did the application of nonviolent principles of protest remove the need for a real national army and police to prevent catastrophic anarchy across the subcontinent once the British left. Nehru had to learn that lesson fast in 1947. For decisively persuading the British ruling class and public opinion to grant full political independence to India, a national movement of mass protests using the rhetoric of nonviolence proved ideal.

Gandhi provided the prototype for Indian political leadership that lasted through the 20th century and beyond. His heirs were cosmopolitan political conciliators and men of two worlds, just as he was, adept at appearing most unworldly when they were in reality being most worldly.

Jawarhalal Nehru, the political leader of Congress in the 1930s and 1940s who became independent India's real founding father, was even more saturated in British upper-class life and culture than Gandhi had been. He was a product of Harrow public school, like Gandhi a skillful lawyer, and equally gifted with charm and words.

However, for all Gandhi's brilliance, guile, charm, and tactical cunning, Indian independence was not granted by wise and generous British philosopher-kings reigning (as they liked to imagine themselves) with Olympian wisdom and foresight. It came amid chaos and blood, screams and tears. The hellish partitioning of two peoples inflicted a trauma that has not healed nearly 60 years on.

The Road to Partition

Who was responsible for the partition of India? Could it have been avoided? Or were the awful massacres and outrages that accompanied partition on both sides inevitable? The subject has understandably transfixed South Asian scholars for 60 years.

The British arguably started the process that ultimately led to partition. In 1905, they divided the province of Bengal for administrative reasons, creating the predominantly Muslim state of East Bengal. But in 1909, the British reversed their decision and reunited Bengal, a move that stirred up Muslim resentment against both the British and the Hindus.

In 1906, the All India Muslim League was founded to promote Muslim political interests in India. At first, it cooperated closely with the Congress movement against the British. In the 1916 Lucknow Pact, the Congress and the Muslim League joined forces demanding greater self-government for the peoples of India. The British rejected the demand. And when the British passed the tough Rowlett Acts or so-called Black Acts through India's Supreme Legislative Council in 1919 to extend emergency security measures promulgated during World War I, the Muslim League again joined with the Congress in opposing them.

The British initially sought to encourage Muslim political organizations as a counterweight to the predominantly Hindu Congress movement led by Gandhi that was trying to force the British to quit the subcontinent. Despite this, Gandhi and other senior Hindu Congress leaders sincerely tried to accommodate Muslim concerns. They failed to do so.

The religious, cultural, and historical divisions between Hindu and Muslim society in India were vast. They always had been. Muslims liked to eat meat, and the easiest way to obtain affordable meat was to slaughter cows. But cows were sacred in the Hindu faith, so the slaughtering of cattle was always a deeply divisive political issue. The old official script of India was a Perso-Arabic one. Hindus wanted to change it to their Devanagari script of Sanskrit. Muslims wanted the national language of India to be Urdu. Hindus wanted to change it to Hindi. In fact, Hindi and Urdu are virtually the same language, though Hindi draws more from Sanskrit, whereas Urdu takes from Persian and Arabic.

As the prospect of full independence drew close for the peoples of India, many Hindus and Muslims came to see it as a zero-sum proposition in which only one community could come out on top. In 1919, Congress called for full independence from Britain. The following year, at the Allahabad session of the Muslim League, Dr. Allama Iqbal called for a separate homeland for Muslims.

In 1931, Lord Irwin, the British viceroy of India (better known by his later title of Lord Halifax, when he was Neville Chamberlain's foreign secretary from 1938 to 1940), gave in to Gandhi's terms, weakening long-term British control of India. The Muslim League was cut out of the process and its leaders felt increasingly isolated.

Although Winston Churchill bitterly opposed the bill and fought hard against its passage in the British Parliament, the Government of India Act passed in 1935. The bill proposed a federal India of self-governing provinces with their own local governments. The British, however, were to retain control over India's foreign policy and defense. The bill confirmed in the minds of millions of Indians that the British were finally going to leave. It gave a boost to Muslim sentiments to create a separate state, rather than come under the control of the majority Hindus. In 1940, Mohammed Ali Jinnah, the founder and leader of the Muslim League, called for the establishment of an independent, sovereign Pakistan. Partition took center stage at last.

The Muslim League might still have been marginalized. The British had distrusted it for a long time and had become increasingly sympathetic to Gandhi. But then Gandhi committed what may have been his greatest political miscalculation.

In 1942, when Britain's fortunes in World War II were at their lowest point and Japanese forces had swept the British from Malaya, Singapore, and Burma, Gandhi unleashed a "Quit India" movement. It caused widespread violence and intercommunity rioting between Hindus and Muslims across India. Alarmed by the protests and the violence, Muslims reacted by flocking in increasing numbers to the Muslim League.

The Quit India campaign also marked a historic turning point in British imperial attitudes toward both the Congress and the Muslim League. The British authorities were furious with Gandhi and the Congress for, as they saw it, stabbing them in the back at their moment of greatest peril. They threw their still enormous resources and political influence behind the Muslim League, which repaid them with loyalty for the rest of the war.

The Muslim League was marginal no longer. With British encouragement, it won power in the Muslim majority provinces of Sindh and Northwest Frontier in the northwest and in Bengal in the northeast.

Gandhi and his colleagues committed a second historic mistake in 1942: they rejected a British proposal to eventually create a complicated, interim government to avert partition after full self-government was established. Veteran British administrators and senior army officers knew the subcontinent well enough to realize that partition would likely lead to catastrophe.

In his own way, Gandhi also tried to avert partition. In 1944, he held a series of negotiations with Jinnah, but the two leaders failed to reach any agreement on sharing power in an independent, united India.

As late as June 1945, the British were not yet convinced of the inevitability of partition. The World War II British governments of Neville Chamberlain and Winston Churchill never expected or planned for it. Besides, Churchill was opposed to granting independence to India anyway.

But Britain after World War II was exhausted. The new Labour Party government of Prime Minister Clement Atlee believed India was a strategic liability and that it should be granted full independence as quickly as possible. At that point, independence did not automatically mean partition. Over the course of his first year in power, however, from the summer of 1945 to the summer of 1946, Atlee came to accept the inevitability of partition in the face of growing sectarian clashes between Hindu and Muslim communities across India.[18]

The Catastrophe of Partition

Atlee appointed a cousin of King George VI, Lord Louis Mountbatten, as Britain's last viceroy of India and charged him with implementing the transition to independence and the partition process that would create the new states of India and Pakistan. It proved to be a catastrophic choice.

Mountbatten was intelligent, charming, and ambitious. He was also shallow, superficial, and vain to a degree bordering on insanity. Worse still, he was incompetent. He had presided over one military fiasco after another, always emerging by virtue of his royal connections, handsome bearing, and gift for flattery and intrigue to rise to new levels of authority and power from which he could unleash even more havoc. During World War II, Mountbatten had lost a Royal Navy destroyer, sunk under him. He briefly commanded the aircraft carrier *Illustrious* until it was crippled by air attacks. He authorized a catastrophic commando raid on Dieppe that cost the lives of a thousand Canadian soldiers without achieving any of its objectives. Only the dropping of the atomic bombs on Japan prevented him from going ahead with an ill-planned amphibious operation to recapture Singapore.[19]

Mountbatten was determined to have the "glory" of bringing India to independence and of doing it as quickly as possible. He was heavily influenced by Nehru, who was having an intense affair with Mountbatten's promiscuous wife Edwina at the time. Mountbatten, curiously, did not seem to mind. On June 3, 1947, Mountbatten issued his partition plan. The plan announced that the partition of the Indian subcontinent between predominantly Hindu and Muslim states would be carried out on August 14. Mountbatten was determined to push through the greatest political and administrative upheaval India had experienced in almost 500 years, transforming the living conditions of half a billion people, and he intended to carry this out in only 73 days.

Throughout the subcontinent, senior and honorable British army commanders protested that the deadline was utterly unrealistic and that no serious arrangements could be made for guaranteeing law and order after they pulled out. Mountbatten would hear none of it. The deadline was met, the partition was enforced, and the British armed forces quit the country. They left behind them the worst violence India had seen in at least half a millennium. The piecemeal way the British gradually conquered India was humane and even idyllic compared with the hell they left behind when they withdrew.

No one knows how many Hindus and Muslims died in panic-stricken mass flights, enforced expulsions, and awful ethnic massacres enforced by mobs, paramilitary groups, and local authorities on both sides. The generally accepted figure is 1 million dead, with common estimates ranging from 500,000 to 1.5 million. But the killing was so widespread and indiscriminate on both sides, and the breakdown of government so complete, that no one will ever really know.

Some 12 million to 14 million people are estimated to have fled on both sides in the chaos.[20] Entire trains of refugees and countless Muslim and Hindu villages were exterminated. Jinnah and Nehru were secular, personally tolerant, and decent men who believed passionately in parliamentary democracy. They had never dreamed they would have to deal with such chaotic violence. If the two men can be faulted, it was certainly not for encouraging the violence but for failing to recognize in advance how bad it would be.

The whole thing was a cruel counterpoint indeed to the traditions and glowing ideals of Gandhi's great nonviolence mass movements of the 1920s and 1930s that had caught the imagination of so many idealistic Britons and Americans.

23

Nehru's India

When it was over, Nehru, the leader of a quasi-socialist governing party, emerged as prime minister of India. The general standard of living in the country was extremely low. The socialist ideals and state nationalization philosophy of the Congress Party impeded rapid economic growth for decades to come.

Postindependence India combined high, soaring public rhetoric on the nation's bright future, with a tough, implacable military approach toward more immediate problems. In 1961, Nehru sent Indian Army forces to snuff out Portuguese occupation of its last little enclave of Goa. He retained control over Muslim-majority Kashmir by military means. India also maintained an effective protectorate over the Himalayan monarchy of Sikkim, strategically located between India and China.[21]

Six decades after partition, the disputed status of Kashmir remains the most contentious issue between India and Pakistan. Hari Singh, the maharajah of Kashmir, had hoped to make his state fully independent in 1947 and wanted to avoid joining either India or Pakistan. He refused to allow a democratic vote, knowing that his predominantly Muslim population would probably vote to join Pakistan. But irregular Azad Kashmir, or Free Kashmir, forces from Muslim frontier tribes flooded into Kashmir. Hari Singh then called on newly independent India for help. He agreed to join India in return for receiving Indian military aid. The terms of the agreement are disputed by India and Pakistan to this day. Indian forces entered Kashmir and forced back the AZK forces in fighting through the rest of 1947. In 1948, Pakistani military forces joined the AZK. India and Pakistan finally agreed to a cease-fire and implemented the Line of Control in western Kashmir, leaving most of the state in Indian hands. It took effect on December 31, 1948. Pakistanis have resented the outcome of this local conflict for close to 60 years.

Like Israel, newly independent India had to temper its soaring hopes for the future with the dark reality of an implacable neighbor, a rival Muslim nation traumatized by its own birth experiences in 1947. Over the next six decades, Pakistan grew into a potentially mortal menace for its far larger neighbor.

It is easy to mock the pretensions and failures of Nehru's India in the 1950s and 1960s. Its economic performance, when compared with Japan's, for example, was dismal. And as will be discussed below, India's foreign policy, based on creating a new "Non-Aligned Movement" among developing countries to stand apart from the conflicting blocs of the cold war, proved ineffective and ultimately absurd.

Nehru also established a long-lasting pattern whereby India insisted on seeing all South Asia and almost all of the former area of the great British raj as being in its sphere of influence. This attitude has been maintained by every Indian government since independence, and it remains a basic assumption shared by the two leading parties in New Delhi today. With the arguable exception of Myanmar, India has intervened militarily in, or has been in conflicts with, every one of its immediate neighbors since independence in 1947. At home, Nehru, despite the ineptness of many of his economic policies, enjoyed some remarkable achievements largely overlooked outside the subcontinent, especially by Americans.

With regard to economic performance, the British were partly to blame for India's slow start. After deliberately holding back India's industrial development for at least a century and a half, the British left independent India with another curse: a passion for socialist economics.

Nehru and his colleagues rejected the free-market, minimal government philosophy under which mainland Britain had flourished in the 18th and 19th centuries. They believed in large state bureaucracies, government planning, and massive, centralized investment in heavy industry.[22] Nehru and his successors in the Congress Party emulated the Soviet Union, pouring huge sums into prestigious heavy industries like steel making and automobiles that were miserably run and failed to give any adequate attention to basic maintenance, cost-effectiveness, market realities, and research and development. As a result, India's economic and industrial development moved with laborious slowness in the 1950s and 1960s.

In foreign policy, Nehru retained India's membership in the British Commonwealth of Nations. The commonwealth grew to become an organization as diffuse and ineffective as a leaking balloon. The mutual membership of India and Pakistan did not prevent them from going to war with each other on several occasions while still remaining commonwealth members in good standing. But in the 1950s and 1960s, in particular, membership in the commonwealth gave India an identity and role in the world.[23]

Nehru was no Mao. Where Mao unleashed 300,000 troops into North Korea at the end of 1950 to fight the United States and snuffed out the independence of giant Tibet, Nehru only used his army to occupy, or liberate, the tiny enclave of Portuguese Goa. But his geostrategic ambitions for India were far-ranging and ambitious, encompassing the Indian Ocean and reaching into Southeast Asia.

As the noted India scholar Francine Frankel explains, "Nehru's ideas of cultural influence and potential dominance of Southeast Asia and the Indian Ocean region appeared as a reassertion of the British imperialist mentality and of an ambition to create a 'greater Indian empire' by dominating neighboring states."[24]

Nehru's greatest foreign policy blunder was his embrace of the Non-Aligned Movement at the Bandung Conference of 1955. India was one of the leading lights of the movement, along with China and Indonesia. But the NAM proved even more bloated, ineffective, and self-contradictory than the British Commonwealth. In October 1962, Nehru's dreams of pan-Asian leadership to be shared with Mao's China came to a humiliating end when the Chinese Red Army whipped Indian forces in a war amid the high glaciers of the Himalayas. It was the greatest national humiliation India had suffered since independence, and the memory of that defeat continues to haunt Indian policymakers to this day.[25]

As will be shown below, the casualties suffered in the 1962 war were relatively light. But in military terms, the scale of the defeat was striking. The Chinese People's Liberation Army could have rapidly overrun Assam, but Mao, in an uncharacteristic act of caution, did not expand the conflict. Having made their political point, the Chinese withdrew their forces from Assam to their original lines, and India has not challenged those lines since.

The shock of the defeat hastened Nehru's death, which came on May 27, 1964. He had certainly not shrunk from using violence to retain Kashmir, enforce partition, and maintain control after independence. And he was not always deterred by international opposition; Nehru's decision to send the Indian Army to occupy Goa in 1961 provoked widespread criticism, the first really unfavorable reaction from other nations against India since independence, but Nehru was unmoved.

However, Nehru's achievements ultimately far outweighed his failures. He was marinated in British progressive values. He established India firmly as a free and fair parliamentary democracy, the largest the world had ever seen. He respected the principles of an independent judiciary and a vast, robust, free press. All these things endured in the 21st century, more than four decades after he died.[26] The strategic alliance between India and Russia, the successor state of the Soviet Union, also endures, and yet U.S. policymakers and pundits remain almost totally unaware of its importance.

The View from Washington

Washington policymakers were not amused when the Indians and Soviets concluded their first treaty in 1966 and a more far-reaching agreement in 1970, but they were not too outraged either. The reason appears to have had less to do with the fact that India continued to go its own way, certainly socialist but still very much free and democratic, than with the remarkable fact that Washington policymakers did not really regard the second most populous nation in the world to be all that important.

Pakistan had always been Washington's favorite. In the beginning, this reflected Anglophile tendencies. Cold war Washington accepted the assessments and prejudices of the British about the wider world, and the Brits favored the Pakistanis. The key figure in setting this pattern toward most of the world was Dean Acheson, President Harry Truman's fiercely Anglophile secretary of state from 1949 to 1953. Acheson admired the "manly" Pakistanis, as he saw them, and despised the Indians. He exhibited similar prejudices toward sub-Saharan Africa, Israel, and the Irish Republic.[27]

Things would certainly have been different if Franklin Roosevelt had lived to decisively shape postwar U.S. policies around the world. FDR loathed the British Empire, especially in India, and wanted to see it liquidated as quickly as possibly. His personal sympathy for the Indian national movement was palpable. He particularly admired Mahatma Gandhi. Through World War II, Roosevelt repeatedly pressured British Prime Minister Winston Churchill—much to Churchill's fury—to speed up the granting of full independence to India.

But for Truman, newly independent India was quickly dismissed as ineffectual, unmilitary, and unrealistic. These stereotypes were reinforced during Dwight D. Eisenhower's presidency.

Ike despised the Non-Aligned Movement, correctly judging that it would prove to be irrelevant. It quickly descended into an echo chamber for Soviet criticism of the United States and its allies. By contrast, as Pakistan's army gained political power through the 1950s, it eagerly consolidated its ties with Washington.

The key figure in both these developments was General, later Field Marshal, Muhammad Ayub Khan. Khan was one of Pakistan's greatest military heroes of the founding period after partition and was credited with having defended East Pakistan (later the nation of Bangladesh) in 1948. Ayub Khan became the first native-born commander in chief of the Pakistani Army in 1951 and defense minister in 1954. With Eisenhower administration approval, he seized power in a bloodless coup in October 1958 and ruled as Pakistan's president for the next 11 years.

Ayub Khan established Pakistan's global political identity as the main ally of the United States in southern Asia. He eased tensions with India by signing the 1960 Indus Waters Treaty to share the waters of the rivers of the Punjab region. Pakistan's industry and agriculture flourished under his rule. He attracted large amounts of development aid from the United States and the nations of Western Europe while maintaining old ties with Britain.

In 1958, Pakistan won Ike's heart by joining the short-lived CENTO, the Central Treaty Organization, that was supposed to stabilize and band together the major nations of the Middle East and South Asia against communism, as the North Atlantic Treaty Organization had done for Western Europe.

But it didn't work out that way. The very act of joining CENTO, and therefore being seen as a U.S. and British puppet, doomed the pro-Western government of Iraq. Iraq's prime minister Nuri e-Saad was torn to bits by a mob in the streets of Baghdad, and the entire Iraqi royal family was slaughtered. That was the effective end of CENTO, though it staggered on as a ghostly presence for some years. Although the alliance itself proved short-lived, Washington did not forget Pakistan's willingness to join in an alliance against the communists.

The Johnson and Nixon administrations might have paid more attention to India's new alliance with the Soviet Union if they had not had their hands full in Vietnam. With their grand strategic position in Southeast Asia secured, U.S. policymakers adopted a relaxed posture toward India. Nevertheless, it is remarkable that even while U.S. policymakers disapproved of India's alliance with the Soviets, they did so little about it. For their part, Nixon and his national security adviser Henry Kissinger used democratic India's tilt toward Moscow as an excuse to embrace Pakistan even more enthusiastically.

They backed Pakistan even when it was mercilessly imposing its rule on East Bengal, killing hundreds of thousands of people there. The Pakistani repression of the East Bengal independence movement, however, provoked Indian intervention, and the most decisive Indian military victory over Pakistan in the three wars they had fought since independence. The conflict ended after Indian forces, supported by the East Bengal rebels, forced the surrender of all Pakistani forces in East Bengal, which then became independent Bangladesh.

Nixon and Kissinger fumed at India's victory and Pakistan's humiliation. But although they could do nothing about that, they still reaped huge geopolitical dividends from their continued close engagement with Pakistan, because Pakistan had developed its own close ties with China. And so Pakistan proved the key intermediary for Kissinger in his secret approaches to China that led to President Nixon's first visit there in 1972.

Nixon's China opening and his success in recruiting China as a U.S. ally was a huge strategic success. Nixon and his successors saw China as a global counterweight to the Soviet Union, then at the height of its power. After China became the key U.S. ally in Asia, India's continuing alliance with the Soviets seemed far less important in the eyes of American policymakers.

The Triumphs of Democracy

The 1971 Indo-Pakistani war and the creation of Bangladesh marked Indian Prime Minister Indira Gandhi's proudest hour. She was Nehru's daughter (and no relation to the old Mahatma), but not even Nehru had ever won so great a victory.

Flush with success, however, Mrs. Gandhi overplayed her hand when she tried to impose a draconian forced-sterilization policy on her own people in an attempt to slash India's birth rate. The conservative rural population of India had loyally supported the Congress Party since the days of Mahatma Gandhi's mass protests for independence in the 1920s. But they were terrified by the fear of compulsory sterilizations. In the face of widespread opposition, Mrs. Gandhi proclaimed a state of emergency. But the crisis only deepened. In 1977, she was forced to call a general election, and for the first time in the 30 years since independence, Congress lost.

Mrs. Gandhi was defeated in 1977 because she lost touch with rural India, the vast country that existed in villages and small towns beyond the sophisticated middle-class cities. "Insensitive lower eche-lon enforcement of [Mrs. Gandhi's government's] strict policy of sterilization for men with two children or more, especially in crow-ded [Uttar Pradesh State] and Bihar towns," writes Stanley Wolpert, "had alienated and terrified millions of peasants who saw 'Madam's Dictatorship' aimed at robbing them of potency and progeny."[28]

In foreign policy, Mrs. Gandhi embraced her role as a leader of a nonaligned nation, in so far as that label still had any meaning. In practice, she enthusiastically supported the Soviet Union. Conse-quently, U.S. policymakers had relatively little time for India in the 1960s and 1970s. Its economy was neither good enough to compel admiration nor bad enough to solicit concern or horror. And when the United States under the Johnson administration mounted a mas-sive food aid operation to help alleviate the threat of famine in India during Mrs. Gandhi's early years in office, it earned Americans no gratitude from India, which was then tilting rapidly into the Soviet foreign policy orbit.

Mrs. Gandhi sounded to U.S. policymakers through the 1970s like a sanctimonious pain in the neck. But she seldom if ever backed up her words with actions that risked any serious reaction from Washington. India, in U.S. eyes through the 1970s, was still punching far below its weight in international affairs. As a result, the nation's truly remarkable and lasting achievements since independence were entirely overlooked.[29]

India's democracy proved real, popular, and long-lasting. The same could not be said of the constitutional arrangements the British left behind throughout Africa, or in neighboring Burma or Pakistan for that matter. India remained stable. There was no serious threat of widespread civil war. The standard of living rose. Famine prevention programs were far more effective than they had ever been during British imperial rule. Major diseases were rolled back.[30]

Nehru's socialist policies might have crippled economic growth and misdirected the nation's resources, but they never led to famine, as Mao's Great Leap Forward did in China. In spite of the socialist policies, India's prosperity increased. Living standards slowly but inexorably rose. Most remarkably of all, they kept pace with and even outstripped India's enormous population growth. Half a century after independence, India had twice the population it had had in 1947—500 million grown to a billion—and average life expectancy had doubled. It was an extraordinary achievement.

Central to that achievement were the agricultural innovations and vastly greater crop yields gained through the Green Revolution. India eagerly adopted the new enhanced-growth wheat and rice hybrids developed by Dr. Norman Borlaug.[31] It also maintained the world's largest and most successful famine prevention program. Famine had been a recurrent experience in British India, even into the 20th century. Once-prosperous Bengal was often afflicted by it; for example, between 2 to 4 million people died of famine there in 1943.[32] After independence, famine threatened in the late 1960s, but emergency relief measures prevented it from actually breaking out, and through the rest of the 20th century, no serious threat of it arose again.

Because the rule of law was secure, property rights were too, even when circumscribed by the overzealous socialist bureaucracy. Meanwhile, the enormous national bureaucracy served as a social safety net, providing jobs and basic income for scores of millions and their families.

Most of all, the resistance to change that is inherent in any genuine democratic system prevented ambitious Indian leaders from emulating any of the mad excesses of Mao in China and throwing the country into ruin. In Mao's China, like Stalin's Soviet Union, any ruler would just order the army and the internal security services to carry out such a scheme and it would be done, regardless of the millions of lives ruined in the process. But democratic India was not like that. This was demonstrated by Mrs. Gandhi's defeat in 1977. Despite her powers of incumbency and control of the armed services, the elections remained free and fair and she was cast out of office.

That election was arguably the defining political experience of India since independence. The threat to democracy had been real. Democratic constitutions had been contemptuously rolled aside in one former British colony after another throughout Africa. There had been plenty of critics and would-be prophets of doom who had claimed that Indian democracy had always been an artificial construct imposed on the majority by an unrepresentative, left-of-center elite, and that it would collapse within a decade or two of the British departure. Eventually, the critics would be proved totally wrong.

The 1980s, however, proved a dispiriting decade for India. The assassinations of two successive prime ministers—Indira Gandhi in 1984 and her son Rajiv in 1989—rocked the nation. Domestic turbulence grew and the economy stagnated. The 1980s also brought a remarkable shift in the global balance of power that weakened India's main ally, the Soviet Union, and strengthened her two main rivals, China and Pakistan.

The Decade of Achievement

In his full five-year term in power, Narasimha Rao, and his finance minister Manmohan Singh, brought the free-market revolution that had swept the world in the 1980s to India at long last. Rao launched a program of gradual economic reform that opened up the Indian economy to foreign investment. Foreign direct investment remained far lower than the hundreds of millions of dollars that had swept into China during the 1990s, but it started a long-term process of economic growth and transformation.

Rao also started to roll back Nehru's old socialist legacy. He privatized inefficient state-run companies that were operating at a loss. Rao's policies appeared as much influenced by Bill Clinton's Third Way as by Ronald Reagan and Margaret Thatcher. He sought to emulate Clinton in leading a traditionally left-wing party in terms of its nation's politics to accept and implement free-market reforms. He reduced taxes and cut back government direct intervention in the economy. When he followed the traditional Congress pattern of investing heavily in public works, he tried to do so by creating a transport and communications infrastructure that would benefit the private sector. Like U.S. President Dwight Eisenhower, Rao used the federal budget to finance a new system of modern highways constructed on a continental scale to facilitate interstate commerce through the nation. Even when he did not feel politically strong enough to slash taxes and dramatically alter government regulations for the entire country, he sought to do so in high-growth areas to attract internal as well as international investment.

Rao's policies transformed India as no prime minister's had since independence. India rode the globalization wave of the 1990s and took advantage of its focus on information technology and communications. The nation's software sector experienced dramatic growth. India's middle class expanded, in numbers and in its spending capacity, and that in turn fueled a new wave of service industries in the cities. Hyderabad and Bangalore led the wave of cities, especially in southern India, that became the focal points of advanced technology and information technology investment and growth. Mumbai flourished as the nation's financial capital and the center of the entertainment industry. More than ever, it became India's New York and Los Angeles rolled into one.

It is important to remember that India's industrial growth during those years was still low compared with China's. Nevertheless, the still-enormous rural population benefited from the prosperity and consumer confidence in the cities. India chalked up several years in a row of 7 percent growth rates. Times were good.

Their strategic posture was also strong during this period, but the Indians overplayed their hand. Like Israel, India had been a de facto nuclear power for decades—in India's case since the mid 1970s. India's nuclear program had been paralleled by that of its historic rival Pakistan. But successive Congress-led governments had chosen not to make their nuclear status explicit. Prime Minister Atal Bihari Vajpayee and the Bharatiya Janata Party disdained such subtleties. In 1998, they conducted five nuclear tests. The results backfired in more ways than one.

The nuclear tests outraged the Clinton administration, whose foreign policy strategists seriously wanted to prevent both India and Pakistan from becoming nuclear powers that could threaten each other, and all of South Asia, with destruction. The Indian nuclear tests triggered congressionally mandated sanctions, dealing a setback to Vajpayee's hopes of rapidly boosting economic ties with the United States.

But far worse was to come. Within days of India's first test, Pakistan announced that it too had tested a nuclear weapon. It would be inaccurate to claim that Pakistan was on par with India in its military technology. India, after all, possessed a major industrial economy; Pakistan did not. In terms of their respective nuclear programs, India's was entirely homegrown, whereas Pakistan relied heavily on outside aid. Islamabad's Ghauri missile systems were bought virtually off the rack from North Korea. China played a shadowy but very important role in facilitating the transactions. Many Indian and U.S. intelligence analysts believe that China also supplied key guidance components to Pakistan's missiles to ensure their accuracy.[33]

Regardless of the source, however, not only did Pakistan now have nuclear weapons and the delivery systems to fire them, but Pakistan's rockets were far more efficient and accurate than India's own. Far from making India safer, the BJP-initiated nuclear tests arguably put her in greater peril than she had ever known.

Vajpayee's government was on borrowed time. After only 13 months in power, the All India Anna Dravida Munnetra Kazhagam, or AIADMK, a Tamil regional party, withdrew its support from his coalition government. The BJP-led government then lost a parliamentary no-confidence motion by a single vote. Vajpayee stayed on as caretaker prime minister pending new parliamentary elections held in the spring of 1999.

The continuing Kashmir conflict with Pakistan had played a key role during the election campaign in May–June 1999. India discovered an elaborate campaign of terrorist infiltration from Pakistan into the mountains of Kashmir. The Indian Army responded with overwhelming force, driving the infiltrators back across the old Line of Control into Pakistan. Although its casualties were heavy, running into the thousands, the conflict was a clear victory for India. And in the September 1999 general election, Vajpayee rode to a sweeping victory at the head of a National Democratic Alliance coalition. He held the office for a full five-year parliamentary term. He became the first Indian prime minister not from the Congress Party to serve a full term of office. India passed another milestone that year when its population officially surpassed 1 billion.

Vajpayee's third government continued along the free-market road pioneered by Rao and Manmohan Singh. Vajpayee enacted more privatization of state-run companies, cut taxes on the middle class, and reduced the budget deficit. These policies attracted increased foreign capital investment and helped India recover from the effects of the 1998 Asian financial crisis.

At the same time, Vajpayee poured public money into ambitious projects to improve the national infrastructure. He wanted to create a modern highway network. And as Rao had done earlier, and as Deng had done in China, Vajpayee encouraged the creation of special investment zones with tax breaks and reduced state regulation to encourage foreign direct investment. By 2003–4, India was posting annual gross domestic product growth of nearly 7 percent.

India's new growth was different from the patchy progress of the 1950s, where Nehru had emulated the Soviets in trying to use state resources to foster heavy industry only to make a mess of it. This time, growth was greatest in capital-intensive, low-labor sectors, especially the new high-tech industries of the information technology "virtual economy." Hindu religious culture, with its emphasis on mathematics, long and complex time cycles, and subtle philosophical concepts, seemed to encourage enterprise in these areas. Indian computer science thrived. Bangalore and Hyderabad became the Silicon Valleys of South Asia.[34]

In the mid- to late 1990s, India started to come onto the geopolitical radar screen of the United States. This development was enthusiastically encouraged by Vajpayee personally, and it was greatly facilitated by the rapid rise of a wealthy and influential Asian Indian expatriate community in northern California in the original Silicon Valley.

For the first time since Indian independence, influential Washington policymakers on both the left and right woke up to the idea that in the post–cold war era, engagement with the largest, English-speaking, parliamentary democracy in the world might be a good thing. The Soviet Union had disintegrated at the end of 1991, and the United States, at least for the moment, was the preeminent world power.

Washington's relations with China, meanwhile, were slowly and inexorably on the slide. The trouble began when China ruthlessly crushed enormous pro-democracy demonstrations in Beijing's Tiananmen Square in June 1989. Economic growth rapidly resumed under Deng Xiaoping and continued under his successor, President Jiang Zemin, but tensions grew between China and the United States over the eventual status of Taiwan. Nixon's First Shanghai Communiqué in 1972 had defused the issue for more than 20 years, but ambiguity over the U.S. commitment to Taiwan could not persist indefinitely. Meanwhile, the U.S. annual balance-of-payments deficit with China rose to historic levels. And still-communist China even started to bury the hatchet with newly democratic Russia. In this changing world, as the United States sought a partner on the Asian continent, people in Washington began to see democratic, English-speaking India as more attractive than China.

President Bill Clinton certainly did. In March 2000, in his last year as president, he took senior cabinet colleagues with him on a state visit to India. It was an enormous success. Vajpayee's vision of a close alliance and mutual partnership—both economic and strategic—between the world's two largest democracies seemed close to realization.[35]

History was now reversing itself. In the early 1970s, India had been out in the cold, viewed primarily, or even solely, as a Soviet ally. Nixon and Kissinger romanced loyal, anti-communist Pakistan instead. In the 1980s, the Reagan administration poured money into Pakistan, building up the secret service organizations of the Pakistani army to funnel aid to Islamic fundamentalists fighting the Soviets in Afghanistan. The Indians were again left on the outside looking in.

But by the late 1990s, when Washington was finally warming up to India, it was Pakistan and Saudi Arabia that seemed dangerously unpredictable in the eyes of U.S. policymakers.

Reagan had enthusiastically encouraged Saudi Arabia to support Pakistan and fund the Islamic resistance to the Soviets in Afghanistan. The Reagan administration had turned a blind eye to other Saudi activities. The Saudis poured hundreds of millions of dollars a year into Wahhabi Islamic fundamentalist schools throughout South and Southeast Asia. The schools provided meals for their students, an important consideration for poor people in impoverished societies. But the schools also turned out hundreds of thousands of graduates steeped in a reactionary interpretation of Islam. This process continued for more than 20 years before U.S. policymakers finally started taking it seriously. Al Qaeda's attacks on September 11, 2001, led U.S. policymakers to focus at last on the process of radicalization that was taking place in Muslim South Asia. Many of the hijackers came from different backgrounds, but the shock of the 9/11 events led Bush administration officials to focus on radical Islamist trends in South Asia as well as in the Middle East.

The effect of this sudden transformation in U.S. policymakers' attitudes toward radical Islam had major repercussions for Washington's policies toward both Pakistan and India. Despite being founded as a direct result of ethnic-community conflict with India's majority Hindus, Pakistan had for its first three decades been a tolerant and stable Muslim society. Slowly at first, but then more rapidly through the 1990s, that changed. Demographics help explain the transformation of Pakistan's political culture. Pakistan had one of the highest rates of population growth in the world. By the 21st century, it was the sixth most populous nation in the world.

Worse yet, the vast sums of money poured into Pakistan during the Afghan war destabilized Pakistani society in fundamental ways. Most significantly, they gave enormous power to Pakistan's shadowy Inter-Services Intelligence agency, the prime conduit for distributing U.S. military assistance to the Afghan resistance. The rise of the ISI, in turn, undermined the secularists and emboldened the radicals in Pakistan.

America had always preferred military autocrats in Pakistan. The favorite was Zia-ul-Haq, who ruled until his American-built C-130 Hercules mysteriously crashed in 1990. After Zia's death, Pakistan reverted to civilian governments and free elections for a few years, but the military and the growing network of extreme religious nationalist political groups, many of them backed by Inter-Services Intelligence officers, were restless.[36]

Democratically elected Prime Minister Nawaz Sharif sought to defuse tensions with India after the 1999 military clashes on the Line of Control in Kashmir, also known as the Kargil conflict. But tensions with the Pakistani military, especially Army Chief of Staff Gen. Pervez Musharraf, remained high. When Musharraf's aircraft was barred from landing safely at Islamabad in October 1999, Pakistan Army troops seized the airport and allowed his plane to land. Sharif, who was believed to have connived to prevent Musharraf from landing, was ousted from power. Pakistan was under military rule yet again. But this time, there was an important difference. These military rulers, unlike Zia and his predecessor, controlled nuclear weapons.

These changes in Pakistan cast an ominous shadow over India at the start of the 21st century. But in most other respects, it was a bright and optimistic time for the giant nation. India was at a new juncture in its independent history. The nation was newly confident and dynamic. Strong trends of economic growth had emerged with the liberalization reforms of the second and third Vajpayee governments. India was making more of a mark for itself than ever before

37

on the international stage. It still enjoyed a stable, warm alliance with Russia, but was now being wooed by the United States. Vajpayee made clear to Washington that he was prepared to respond favorably to this new attention.

India had even embarked on an unprecedented naval construction and acquisition program. This included plans for no fewer than three aircraft carriers capable of eventually projecting Indian power as far west as the Persian Gulf, on which India remained dependent for most of its oil supplies, and as far east as Indonesia, another important energy supplier. India was also planning a fleet of three new diesel-powered submarines capable of carrying nuclear-tipped cruise missiles to provide a sustainable second-strike deterrent capability against any threat of a Pakistani surprise "decapitation" attack.

However, there was an element of trying to "run before you can walk" to all this. For all the real growth, foreign direct investment per year remained a fraction of that of China's. And India continued to trail China badly in the old-fashioned but still crucial economic indices of steel making, auto production, manufacturing, and industrial exports. Continuing bureaucratic impediments and political interference from legislators at both the state and federal levels undermined India's ability to do business, especially with the outside world.

Politically, India's democracy had protected it from civil war, mass repression, and large-scale ethnic or social conflicts, such as had repeatedly convulsed China. From the perspective of the end of the 20th century, the obvious comparison was to China's recent breakneck economic growth while India had stagnated. But sometimes the tortoise does prove faster than the hare—in the long run. India remained tolerant, multiethnic, and multilingual, whereas China was not, and foreign investments in the long term may yet prove more secure in India's democracy than in China's authoritarian system.

What was incontrovertible was that India's democracy had done far better in its first six decades than all but the most optimistic prognosticators back in 1947 could have dared to hope. It was also a rising nuclear and regional power building an impressive naval fleet.

Yet close to home, India faced the potentially appalling menace of a nuclear-armed and politically unstable and unpredictable Pakistan. This was the longest shadow cast over the largest democracy in history as it entered the otherwise shining prospects of the 21st century.

2. The Historical Experience of China

Though Americans have ignored the modern history of India, they have been obsessed by developments in China. Yet they remain ignorant of its internal dynamics and most of its history. This is of even greater importance than in understanding India's case, for the modern history of China starting in 1840 is replete with the most sudden and extreme shifts of policy, both internal and foreign, often triggering regional wars or catastrophic internal bloodbaths.

Although China and India share broad themes in their long-term historical development, they differ in the details. These differences have produced two totally contrasting societies.

Like India, China is the product of one of the longest continuing civilizations on the planet. China's dates back well into the second and probably even the third millennium BC. Even so, the historical traditions that have emerged from this span are far less varied than the extraordinarily rich Indian tradition.

China has been subject to far fewer waves of invasion and far less subjugation and colonization over the millennia than India has. India was regularly overrun by waves of invaders coming overland from the northeast and from Central Asia or the Middle East. Since the 11th century, most of them, except for Timur, have been Muslims. Although China has known conquest and subjugation far less often, the result was always devastating and lasted for centuries.

China, though, has never experienced conquest by Muslim powers. Consequently, it lacks the hatred or fear of major Muslim nations that still dominates Indian statecraft and national security concerns to this day. Until the European imperialist incursions from the sea in modern times, China's conquerors always came from the north, from the Mongolian steppes.

China boasts an advanced civilization at least from the Bronze Age, and there are traditions of a unified nation going back into the ancient past. Some historical accounts tell of the unification of the land after a devastating catastrophic flood that bears parallels to the

Biblical deluge.[1] In the sweep of recorded history, China, like India, was home to competing kingdoms before it unified at roughly the same time as India, around 220 BC.

Dynastic Cycles

For much of the first millennium AD, Chinese history repeated a cycle, at first heroic and inspiring, then depressing, frustrating, and ultimately terrifying. A new dynasty would emerge, reunite the land, and usher in a golden age of peace, prosperity, and remarkable cultural and technological achievements.[2] Bureaucratic sclerosis, inefficiency, high taxation, and general despair and increasing destitution always set in. Wealth repeatedly concentrated in fewer and fewer hands. Eventually, the dynasty collapsed, either from angry internal peasant revolts or at the hands of new waves of lean and mean barbarians swarming in from the Mongolian steppes.

The Manchu conquerors who established the Qing dynasty had no ethnic connection to the Han Chinese they ruled over. The Qing ruled as an arrogant and oppressive aristocracy rigidly divided from the Chinese people by caste, class, and, most of all, race, down to the time they finally fell in 1911. Indicative of their perpetual separation from the people that they ruled, the Qing even made common cause with Japanese invaders in the 1930s.[3]

Qing civilization was militarily formidable and superficially impressive but ultimately stagnant. In the mid-18th century, it spread as far south as Vietnam and into Xinjiang, China's wild west and great border region of Central Asia. The Manchus, like the Romans, were practical and skilled warriors, not generous or visionary culture creators. The beauties of Chinese culture left 17th-century Western visitors breathless, but they were like pressed flowers in a book: dry husks preserved from earlier and more creative eras.[4]

Signs of decay were apparent in the late 18th century when a British delegation visited Beijing to be routinely humiliated by the reigning emperor. But it would take another 60 years before the European powers would apply their vastly superior military technology to inflict a humiliating defeat on the Chinese.

By 1840, the British Empire, and India in particular, had a huge balance-of-payments problem. The British people were already hooked on tea, and the best tea had to be imported from China. It did not come cheap. Nor were the insular Chinese interested in anything that Britain was producing. However, they had a small drug problem. There was only a minor taste for opium in southern China before the British worked hard to market the drug through China's southern ports. China's appetite for the drug grew in the first half of the 19th century.

When the opium trade in China rocketed to unprecedented heights, the Chinese sent a senior official to their main southern port of Canton to clamp down on the trade. The British objected, and the dispute set off the First Opium War of 1840.[5] That conflict initiated the modern history of China and its long struggle to achieve modernization and technological parity with the West.

The First Opium War proved catastrophic for the Chinese. They had never before been up against modern European warships firing advanced cannons and muskets. They had never encountered troops equipped with modern weapons and trained to fight with European-style tactics. The Qing dynasty suffered the greatest defeat of its nearly 200 years of power and was forced by the 1842 Treaty of Nanjing to open its borders to unlimited imports of opium. Under the treaty, the Chinese were also forced to cede control of the territory that became the new British crown colony of Hong Kong.

The defeat shattered the credibility of the dynasty and plunged the long stagnant and decaying nation into crisis. A bizarre new Christian movement—though by any traditional Christian standard, wildly heretical—spread like wildfire and quickly acquired political power. It was called the Taiping, and its leader was Hong Xiuquan, who believed he was the younger brother of Jesus Christ. The first Chinese response to modernity had arrived, and it proved devastating—to the Chinese.[6]

The Taiping fed on accumulated centuries of suffering and peasant grievances in the south and west of China. Hong, a former clerk rejected by the Imperial Civil Service, at first proved to be a brilliant, charismatic leader with a talent for recruiting dedicated and exceptionally able military commanders. In the years from 1850 to 1860, his movement swept southern China.

But Hong was also mad. He believed that he regularly visited the exalted circles of heaven where he conferred with his big brother, Jesus. He was obsessed with bizarre orgies and religious ceremonies. And he brooked no opposition. His followers slaughtered millions of Chinese, leaving famine, disease, and despair behind them.

41

Amid all this, the decaying imperial court in Beijing stumbled into a Second Opium War with Britain and France in 1860, which it also lost. British forces plundered the Summer Palace of the Emperors, one of the greatest houses of art on the planet. Many of its treasures were scattered into the homes of thousands of British soldiers and their descendents.[7]

When the Qing turned their attention back to Hong and his followers, the repression of the Taiping was as awful as their rise had been. When it was over, all southern China lay devastated. Estimates of the death toll range as high as 30 million. It was the most destructive civil war of all time, with a death toll at least 40 times that of the American Civil War, which was being fought at the same time.

The Taiping revolt was also almost exactly contemporaneous with India's First National Rising, which the British called the Sepoy Mutiny, and it had arguably more profound long-term results in the shaping of modern Chinese history than the Indian rising had on that nation's development. Although the Qing remained in power in Beijing for another half century, they were reviled and hated in southern China. The original grievances of the Taiping, and the way they fought their early, highly successful guerrilla war, were remembered in the oral traditions of the peasants of the south. Eventually, these tactics were revived and co-opted by Mao Zedong's rural communist rising in the 1930s.

The successive hammer blows of the Opium Wars, and the Taiping revolt that erupted between them, launched a recurrent cycle of massive domestic upheaval that ravaged China over the next 100 years. It may be too soon to conclude that the destructive pattern has burned itself out.

Throughout the cycles of China's history, periods of civil war and unrest have been followed by periods of peace, recovery, and modernization. This happened after the Taiping revolt. The period lasted 40 years and was presided over by the Concubine Yehonala, who soon took the title of Dowager Empress Cixi. She ranks with Jiang Jieshi (Chiang Kai-shek) and Mao Zedong as one of the three most powerful, important, and ruthless figures to have disfigured the history of modern China.[8]

Cixi's Iron Hand

Cixi was ignorant but shrewd, petty but cunning, distrustful, and uncomprehending of the wider world and remorseless in her quest to grasp and retain power in the imperial court in Beijing. She was a born intriguer. She oversaw the appalling repression of the Taiping. She then presided over modernization—of a sort.

During Cixi's reign, from 1861 to 1908, China lay under the thumb of the European colonial powers led by Britain. They controlled China's finances and dictated her trade through their micromanagement of the customhouses in all her major ports. But Cixi still exercised influence over national priorities. She encouraged technical development overseeing the construction of major railroads across China, and she also boosted Western learning. Thousands of Chinese studied throughout Europe. However, like so many other authoritarian regimes, Cixi wanted the Chinese she sent to study abroad to bring home only technical expertise, not Western concepts of democracy and individual liberty. She continued to mercilessly repress her population at home.

Hundreds of thousands seeking better economic opportunities emigrated from China during her rule, settling mainly in other Asian lands but also as far away as the United States.

This was not a systematic, tidy, and controlled modernization. Nor was it a confident and self-generated one, such as the Meiji emperor ordered and implemented in Japan at the same time. China remained helpless, humiliated, and prostrate on the international stage.

Two national humiliations, happening in quick succession, exposed the wretched state of the Celestial Kingdom. The first occurred when Japan declared war in 1894 and quickly sank what passed for the Chinese navy. Japan then stripped Taiwan from the mainland's control and ruled it firmly but well for the next half century. Taiwan paradoxically was thus spared by Japanese conquest from the horrors of anarchy, civil war, and finally conquest by the Japanese themselves that was soon to be inflicted on the rest of mainland China.

Then in 1900, the first great popular eruption since the Taiping broke out: the so-called Boxer Rebellion. It, like the Taiping revolt, was instigated by a weird new religious cult. Because its participants practiced mystical exercises and martial arts that they believed made them immune to Western bullets, they came to be known as the Boxers.[9]

Once again, bloodbaths swept China. This time, orthodox Christians were the victims. Western missionaries, many of them American, had been extremely active over the previous 35 years since the annihilation of the Taiping. There were many converts. The Christian message of morality, inspiration, comfort, and hope had spread quickly among the Chinese masses. As a result, tens of thousands were cut down by Boxer rage. The anger was a combination of anti-Christian bigotry and hatred, Chinese nativism, and anti-Westernism.

In 1911, revolts broke out against the Qing in almost every province in China. They were supported by disparate sources ranging from American idealists to Chinese secret societies operating within the country and in its extensive overseas diaspora. A veteran exile, Sun Yat-sen returned from the United States and on December 29, 1911, was elected the first provisional president of the Republic of China. The future, he proclaimed, was bright. It wasn't.[10]

The Age of Warlords

Sun, the leader of a circle of liberal intellectuals in Canton, believed that he could instantly and painlessly impose decent progressive values and the blessings of parliamentary constitutional government on an ancient society that had suffered since time immemorial under the harshest of despotisms.[11]

It didn't work. Sun was quickly pushed aside by Gen. Yuan Shih-kai, a career army officer under the Qing who had risen to become their supreme military commander. Yuan agreed to throw the army behind the revolutionary idealists on condition he could rule the country. When Yuan became president, the world rejoiced—prematurely as it turned out.[12]

Yuan was a simple, brutal, and uncomplicated fellow who thought he would have no trouble making himself emperor. In December 1915, he announced that he was going to do exactly that, allegedly because the people demanded it. But things were no longer that easy. For despite all of Cixi's best—or rather worst—efforts, China had changed.[13]

During World War I, Japan had allied itself with Britain and France against imperial Germany, and as a result, it snapped up and inherited Germany's old holdings and interests in China. In 1919, Japan joined with the Western powers in making a new series of 21 Demands for yet more far-reaching concessions, and the Chinese government of the day felt it had no choice but to accede. That proved to be a big mistake.

Modern universities and schools had finally proliferated across China, many of them staffed by missionaries. However, these Christian teachers often found that their pupils had a very different take on the Western values they were taught. Western concepts of nationalism were adopted by hundreds of thousands of frustrated, idealistic young Chinese. On May 4, 1919, this new young generation of angry nationalists rose in fury across China to vent their anger over the acceptance of the 21 Demands.

The protests of May 1919 were unprecedented in China.[14] Like the failed liberal revolutions in Germany in 1848–49, what started as a popular call for more democracy and freedom could be quickly transmuted into a vast nationalist reaction, a revolutionary mass movement, or both.

The demonstrations of 1919 marked the awakening of a new generation of tireless political activists who clashed in their differing conceptions for the future of China. The upheavals that convulsed China for the next 60 years were led by future leaders who emerged out of the May 4 protests.

In May 1923, Sun Yat-sen died. But not before he had embraced another idealistic international movement that, he was now convinced, would rapidly bring China into a new era of peace, prosperity, and happiness where his old hopes for parliamentary democracy had failed. It was called Soviet communism.

But this movement would have to contend with yet another charismatic Chinese leader. Following his last return from exile in 1917 after Yuan's death, Sun became the apparent leader—in reality the titular figurehead—of a new broad coalition of Chinese nationalists and revolutionaries. The real force in the movement was an ambitious young graduate of the Whampoa Military Academy who had converted to Methodism—a career move that proved wise and lucrative for him in the half century to come. His name was Chiang Kai-shek.[15]

Jiang Takes Power

Chiang, now known as Jiang Jieshi, understood about conspiracies and power. He was a prominent figure in several southern Chinese secret societies. He quickly developed an imposing network of military connections. He married the daughter of a millionaire. He was clearly a coming man.

In 1925–26, Jiang put himself at the head of a new revolutionary movement and army that moved up the Yangtze valley and established its headquarters in the city of Nanjing, which he proclaimed the new capital of China. The Western powers were at first terrified of him. Lurid reports in the American and European press portrayed him as the leader of the long-anticipated Yellow Peril who would sweep the white man out of China and inflict wars of international conquest and misery on the world.

It did not work out that way. Jiang was a corrupt and catastrophic administrator and a merciless, cruel tyrant. But he never dared to challenge the major foreign powers. Unlike the dreamy, inept Sun, Jiang proved a shrewd diplomat and became an accomplished power broker. Beneath his martial bravado, he always took measure of the forces against him. He quickly realized that he had no chance of storming the Western compounds in Shanghai, and that even if he did, retribution would come hard and fast.

Jiang therefore cut a deal with the Western powers. A brief, uneasy truce followed, based on the recognition that the full communist onslaught would not come at once. The Western powers had expected Jiang to drive the Western imperialists out of Shanghai and at a stroke create a nationalist state based on socialism. The last thing they had expected was for Jiang to leave the Western enclaves in Shanghai untouched.

Jiang was also brokering deals with established warlords across southern China. In the 15 years after the death of Cixi, China had fallen into anarchy under these petty local power brokers. Most possessed only limited power, but a few ruled provinces larger than most European nations. It was the Dark Ages with barbed wire and machine guns, exactly the opposite of what Sun had predicted and expected. Jiang at first tried to liquidate the warlords, but some defied him, and he found ways to accommodate them. He was not destroying the old social order at all. He was preserving and protecting it. This was not the pure and idealistic revolution the communists wanted.

Worse was to come. On April 12, 1927, Black Tuesday as it is today remembered in the People's Republic of China, Jiang unleashed his

Whampoa-officered army on the urban communists in Shanghai. The ensuing massacre was particularly brutal and sordid. Some 5,000 communists were publicly beheaded.[16]

One young communist firebrand, Zhou Enlai, managed to escape by the skin of his teeth. He would later prove to be Jiang's nemesis, but as of mid-1927, Jiang had won. Traditional, urban-generated Marxist-Leninist communism was dead in China. But something else would soon take its place; Japan's appetite to carve out an empire in China was growing by the day.

Attitudes in the Japanese aristocracy and military elite toward China in the first decades of the 20th century mirrored those felt by many Germans about Russia. They felt contempt for a vast, chaotic neighbor that seemed incapable of political and industrial discipline; this contempt gradually evolved into the harshest form of racism. Also the Japanese, like the Americans after them, were misled by China's vast size and colossal population into seeing it as a great reservoir of potential wealth. Northern China in particular, including Manchuria, became an infernal playground for the machinations of the Japanese military and secret services.[17]

On June 4, 1928, Japanese agents engineered the assassination of one of the most powerful warlords in China, Zhang Zuolin, master of Manchuria, by blowing up his train just before it arrived at the Manchurian capital, Mukden. Three years later, the Japanese used a manufactured incident at the Marco Polo Bridge in Beijing to seize Manchuria, assumed to be the most potentially wealthy region of China because of its concentration of heavy industry and coal resources—the latter especially attractive to geographically small, overpopulated, and energy-poor Japan.

Jiang temporized with the Japanese. As Japanese depredations on China grew, he presented himself as the leader of the Chinese nationalist cause against them, but all along he was far more concerned, indeed obsessed, with stamping out the resurgent communist movement. For a new leader was emerging for the communists of China, one who defied the advice of Joseph Stalin and who even dared to turn Marxist-Leninist theory on its head.

Enter Mao

Mao Zedong was the headstrong son of a relatively prosperous peasant family. Beginning in early 1927, Mao built a rural-based communist movement in his native Hunan Province in south-central China, and then in neighboring Jianxi, turning generations of peasant misery and oppression into a potent force.

Peasant discontent had fanned into wild rebellion and toppled dynasties before. The Ming had arisen from such a movement, as well as the Taiping only 70 years earlier; peasant unrest had propelled the Boxers too. But Marxist doctrine said the vanguard of the revolution had to arise from the oppressed proletariat of the industrial cities.

Jiang had read Karl Marx. He had expected communism to only come out of China's urban areas. He believed, therefore, that his success in crushing the communists in Shanghai should have ended the communist threat forever. This new movement, however, was arising in China's hinterland, far from the big cities, far from the wealthy merchants and propertied interests who had rallied behind Jiang. And it confounded the predictions and plans of Stalin too. From its very inception, Mao's communist revolution was inherently Chinese and, in a sense, pragmatic, driven by domestic forces, not European ideology. Stalin, like American policymakers 15 to 20 years later, was slow to realize what was going on. But he was hardly alone. China's vastness and complexity often confounded the rulers of distant powers.

In January 1932, Chinese nationalist protests against the Japanese in Shanghai escalated, and the Japanese retaliated by sending a trained force of armed sailors, similar to marines, to the city. But this elite force faced unexpected resistance and suffered heavy casualties at the hands of the Kuomintang's 19th Route Army. The Japanese reacted by committing more forces until they occupied most of Shanghai. Jiang still had strong personal ties to the Japanese and did not yet want to fight them. Also, the 19th Route Army posed a potential challenge to Jiang within the Chinese national movement. Therefore Jiang was not averse to seeing it destroyed.

Instead of confronting the Japanese, Jiang focused on crushing Mao.[18] Jiang's repression had cost Mao and his family dearly. For example, in 1930 both Mao's sister and his second wife, Yang Kaihui, were executed by the nationalist governor of Hunan Province. For several years thereafter, Mao himself was forced to live a life on the run. In 1933 and 1934, Jiang launched a series of major operations designed to wipe out Mao's new rural communists. The scale of

48

military operations was enormous, larger than any global military conflict since World War I, yet it attracted little attention outside China. Jiang's forces seemed to enjoy rapid success. Mao, facing extermination, determined upon the kind of bold, big gamble that would become his trademark. He uprooted the entire communist movement and led it on what became known as the "Long March" of 1934 across vast regions of inner China to remote western provinces where Jiang had never been able to establish effective control.

The human cost of Mao's gamble was enormous. Of the 130,000 who left Hunan and Kiangsi provinces at the start of the march, 100,000 died before they could reach the refuge in northern Shaanxi. Of the several hundred women who accompanied the Red Army forces, only 30 survived. But despite these horrific losses, the march proved a brilliant move in more ways than one.[19]

For someone who inflicted more untold suffering on the peasants of China than anyone since the Mongols, and who did so in the name of raising them up after he won supreme power, Mao treated them with shrewd skill and respect during his campaigns in the Chinese civil war. Chinese communist military forces were always tightly disciplined. Rape and murder were punished ruthlessly, and communist troops paid for food and resources when possible. The areas that Mao's forces passed through during their Long March proved lastingly loyal to him during the remaining decade and a half of China's civil war. The contrast with the uncontrolled brigandage and corruption of Jiang's forces was marked. Even the 19th Route Army, which had defied Jiang in Shanghai, eventually went over en masse to Mao's forces.

But Jiang was fooled by the Long March. He concluded that he had wiped out the communists. He soon had more pressing problems. The Japanese, not satisfied with grabbing China's industrial resources in the north, turned their attention to the rest of China. They wanted it all. In 1937, they landed at Shanghai and launched a military drive up the Yangtze River valley to seize the city of Nanjing.

The Rape of Nanjing

After more than a decade of tyrannical power over the most populous nation in the world, Jiang was unable to develop an effective strategy and assemble a significant military force to stop the Japanese. But he was determined to resist Japan's brazen assault.

The campaign was one of the most awful in modern history. Only Operation Barbarossa, the Nazi invasion of Russia four years later, bears comparison with it in the scale, unbelievable ferocity, and wanton cruelty involved. Estimates of the number of civilians slaughtered in Nanjing alone run from at least 100,000 to well over twice that. Scores of thousands of women were raped and usually tortured or slaughtered afterward. Even Nazi diplomats in the city who witnessed the slaughter were aghast. But the slaughter extended beyond Nanjing. The Japanese army had raped and killed on an even vaster scale in its drive up the Yangtze. Some estimates put the total dead during that single summer–fall of horror at three quarters of a million people. A 1996 study using declassified Republic of China archives in Taiwan put the Nanjing death toll at 300,000.[20]

The killing and raping were not typical of the Japanese army. They were sanctioned from the top of the army command. Gen. Iwane Matsui, commander in chief of all Japanese forces in central China, would ultimately go to the gallows after being convicted in the Tokyo war crimes trials.[21] Matsui's aim was clearly to terrorize the Chinese people and break their will to resist Japan. But the atrocities backfired. As Adolf Hitler found when he inflicted the same scale of terror a few years later, inhuman cruelty generates its own reaction. Far from convincing the Chinese people to abandon Jiang, the Japanese only succeeded in doing what had previously seemed impossible. They made him popular.

This was no easy feat. Most estimates by modern scholars put the number of people who were either murdered by Jiang's regime or became unhappy victims of its ineptitude at 10 million dead. And this estimation did not count those killed in the war with Japan. Only Lenin, Stalin, Hitler, and Mao exceeded that butcher's bill in the long list of 20th-century tyrants.[22] Ultimately, Jiang could not be counted on to resist the Japanese after the horrors of their 1937 campaign. As the communists built up strength and influence, spreading out from Shaanxi and Yunan, Jiang deployed his most effective and dependable military forces against them.

China in World War II

After Japan attacked the United States on December 7, 1941, Jiang used his diplomatic skills and influential media friends in America to obtain substantial U.S. financial and military aid under the Lend-Lease program. And yet throughout World War II, Jiang merely went through the motions of waging campaigns against Japanese occupation forces in the Yangtze valley or in Manchuria. By contrast, the communists under Mao waged a fierce guerilla campaign against the Japanese and came to be viewed as the leaders of the national resistance in China.

The British, led by Winston Churchill, were always skeptical of Jiang; besides, they wanted the Lend-Lease aid for themselves. Jiang was even lampooned as "Cash My Check," a Chinese general on the popular BBC radio program *It's That Man Again.*

Franklin Roosevelt was far more credulous about Jiang than Churchill, however. In November 1943, at FDR's insistence, Jiang attended the Cairo summit with Churchill and Roosevelt. Roosevelt sympathized with the Chinese, as with the Indians under British colonial rule. He was favorably impressed with Madame Jiang. Supporting China was popular with Republicans. And FDR also had wildly inflated hopes of what Jiang's armies—so impressive on paper in their numbers—could do.

Gen. Joseph "Vinegar Joe" Stilwell knew better. The old regular U.S. Army officer sent first to advise Jiang in 1942 and then command his land forces as chief of staff of the Chinese army after the United States joined the war against Japan realized that Jiang's regime was an exceptionally corrupt, harsh, and incompetent dictatorship. He knew that ordinary Chinese soldiers, whom he held in the highest regard, were only occasionally paid, miserably armed and trained, and housed in the most wretched conditions. He knew that the officers in Jiang's army were poorly motivated and many simply incompetent. Not surprisingly, Jiang's supporters in Washington worked hard to discredit and undermine Stilwell.

In 1943–44, U.S. air power enthusiast Gen. Claire Chennault, supported by Jiang's China Lobby, convinced Roosevelt that given sufficient heavy bomber resources he could bomb the Japanese out of most of occupied China on the cheap. Such promises were music to FDR's ears, especially as he could spare no U.S. ground forces for China from the campaigns in the European and Pacific theaters.

The result was a disaster. The Japanese, alarmed by Chennault's air attacks, went on the offensive and easily overran Chennault's airfields in eastern China. Jiang's land forces, as Stilwell had warned, proved utterly incompetent and unable to offer even token resistance.[23]

The fiasco would come back to haunt Jiang four years later when U.S. officials considered whether to commit U.S. forces to try to rescue him from defeat at Mao's hands. The successful communist drive to finally destroy Jiang's regime began right after the end of World War II in the Pacific. The Japanese, pulverized by U.S. air and sea attacks as they pulled back from their positions in the Pacific, were also hit by two atomic bombs.

In August 1945, the Soviet Red Army, with U.S. blessing, swept over Manchuria, occupying it in a quick succession of fast-moving armored attacks. The 26 divisions of Japan's Guandong Army in Manchuria could muster only token resistance. Some 600,000 Japanese troops still serving in northern China became Soviet prisoners of war. Hundreds of thousands of them remained in the Soviet Gulag camps well into the 1950s before the survivors were freed.[24] When the Japanese surrendered, they evacuated all of China, including Taiwan.

Mao's Victory

Mao's forces surged to power, filling the vacuum in the regions previously occupied by the Japanese. There was some crude justice in that: the communists had resisted them, and Jiang hadn't. U.S. President Harry S. Truman was soon assailed by frantic pleas for U.S. intervention from Jiang and his American supporters to prevent a communist victory in the world's most populous nation.

It was a pivotal moment in history. The United States could easily have been sucked into a major land war in Asia. Such a conflict would have been on a far vaster scale than either the Korean or Vietnam conflicts proved to be. The risks of Soviet involvement could not be discounted, and in any case proved far greater than in nearby Korea less than five years later. Stalin would resist the urge to send Soviet troops into the Korean conflict. But almost a million Soviet troops were already in northern China after routing the Guandong Army in 1945.

Had Truman heeded the China hawks of 1945–46, he would have had to strip Western Europe almost bare of U.S. troops. Despite the brief four-year U.S. monopoly on nuclear weapons from 1945 to

1949, Stalin's Red Army legions might have been poised to take Western Europe under their control.

Truman, on Stilwell's advice, resisted the calls to send U.S. ground forces to Jiang's aid. The new president also sent the venerable wartime army chief of staff Gen. George Marshall to assess the prospects for propping up Jiang. Marshall returned home vehemently opposed to the idea.[25] To his credit, Truman kept America out of the fight. In December 1948, Mao's People's Liberation Army forces finished destroying Jiang's demoralized legions. Jiang and his entourage escaped to the island of Taiwan, occupied since 1895 by the Japanese and partially assimilated by them until they evacuated it in 1945. (From 1945 to 1949, Taiwan was ruled by Jiang's Republic of China from his last capital at Nanjing.) The largest nation on earth had turned communist.

To the American people, this development came as a thunderclap. Their long-distance love affair with China had overnight turned into a nightmare. It was useless to point out, as veteran China experts and State Department analysts did, that nothing the United States could have done would have turned the tide. It was pointless to argue that Jiang could not have been saved and did not deserve to be anyway. Believing in a mythical monolithic communist movement, American pundits and policymakers failed to discern that Mao was no puppet of "Uncle Joe" Stalin nor even a reliable ally of the Soviets. Much archival evidence from Moscow suggests that Stalin far preferred to deal with a compliant Jiang. When Mao visited Stalin in Moscow in 1949 as part of the Soviet tyrant's 70th birthday celebrations, the tension between them was evident to astute observers, such as Harrison Salisbury of the *New York Times*. As it happened, "Uncle Joe" never welcomed Mao back for a return visit.[26]

Mao inherited control of one of the oldest continually flourishing civilizations and cultures on earth. He was determined to launch a proud new era. As discussed in chapter 1, Nehru took power in India with similar ambitions, but there the resemblance between them ended. After the bloodbaths of the partition war, Nehru kept India stable and at peace for almost his entire 16-year rule. The occupation of Goa, for example, resulted in relatively few casualties for the Indian Army. Mao, by contrast, immediately led China into a new bloodbath. For while Truman had resisted calls to prop up Jiang in 1946–47, he did not hesitate to commit the U.S. Army en masse to South Korea when North Korean forces, armed and trained by the Soviet Union, swept across the 38th Parallel starting on June 25, 1950.

Lessons of the Korean War

The collapse of the South was barely averted by timely U.S. intervention. South Korean and U.S. troops established a defensive perimeter around the port city of Pusan, halting the North Korean drive to the sea. Then in September, in a brilliant strategic move devised by Gen. Douglas MacArthur, U.S. forces landed behind the North Korean lines at Inchon, shattering the North Korean army. U.S. forces, however, did not stop back at the 38th Parallel. Drunk with success, MacArthur plunged on, confident that his forces could also liberate the North from the communist regime the Soviets had maintained there since 1945. Unfortunately, that meant rolling up to the Yalu River, North Korea's border with China.[27]

Mao would have none of this. In December 1950, he sent scores of thousands of People's Liberation Army troops across the Yalu. The Chinese took MacArthur completely by surprise, pushing U.S. forces back across the 38th Parallel.[28] Eventually, and in large part thanks to the outstanding leadership of Gen. Matthew Ridgway, who had replaced MacArthur as the commander of U.S. land forces in Korea, the Chinese drive was stopped and rolled back, but a bloody stalemate punctuated by Chinese attacks continued for more than two and a half years.[29]

This conflict has been misremembered and mislabeled by the American public almost since it happened. But the term "Korean War" could not be more misleading. The conflict was instead a manifestation of the U.S. phobia of international communism, a fear that had sanctioned a full-scale land war not merely with North Korea, whose forces had effectively been wiped out by the fall of 1950 after Inchon, but with China itself. It was, and remains to this day, the only conflict involving direct hostilities between the United States and China.

The war is usually described as a stalemate. Hard-right critics of Truman and his Republican successor, Dwight D. Eisenhower, have gone so far as to accuse the two men of essentially losing the war by leaving North Korea intact. MacArthur even wanted to "unleash," as he and his supporters put it, Jiang's armies from offshore Taiwan back on to the mainland, an adventure which, given the fiasco of their recent defeat, could only have embroiled the United States in an even wider land war in Asia.

In fact, the undeclared and virtually unacknowledged U.S. war with China was a knockout victory—both tactical and strategic—for the United States. For the rest of the century, China never dared to threaten South Korea or Taiwan. Even the immensely wealthy British colony city of Hong Kong survived unscathed. In 1984, China concluded a deal with British Prime Minister Margaret Thatcher whereby Hong Kong would peacefully revert to Chinese mainland rule on July 1, 1997. And so it did. This outcome proceeded so smoothly that it is difficult in retrospect to imagine it ever happening any other way. But it very easily could have.

The defeat that the United States inflicted on revolutionary China in Korea was overwhelming and traumatic. At least 300,000 Chinese troops, and perhaps as many as half a million, died in their useless human wave attacks against overwhelming U.S. firepower and air superiority. Mao's own son was among the dead. In contrast to the French and Russian Revolutions, therefore, any Chinese urge to export the blessings of their own national liberation across the rest of their continent at the point of their bayonets was nipped in the bud—or rather, drowned in the blood—of the revolution's own sons.

Mao and his more cautious successors remained averse to any full-scale conventional war for the rest of the century. Mao kept his frontier war with India carefully limited in 1962, and he ended it as soon as there was any possibility that the United States might intervene on India's behalf.[30]

Mao also managed to avoid a full-scale war with the Soviet Union when tensions between Moscow and Beijing escalated to a dangerous level in 1969. In August 1969, fighting broke out between Chinese and Soviet forces on the border between China's Xinjiang Province and the Soviet republic of Kazakhstan. After a brief lull, tensions rose again in September, but a wider crisis was averted when, on October 7, 1969, China agreed to reopen talks in Beijing on Sino-Soviet border rectification.

The only other war that China waged during the latter half of the 20th century was an extremely brief but violent clash in 1979 when it was humiliated by the battle-hardened North Vietnamese army, fresh from its conquest of South Vietnam. Early that year, some

80,000 People's Liberation Army troops attacked along a broad front on the Sino-Vietnamese border. The Chinese drove over the mountain barrier behind the frontier and eventually captured the Vietnamese city of Lang Son on March 9, but at great cost; the PLA units performed poorly at the operational level and suffered 30,000 casualties.

This miniwar in fact won a significant strategic success for China, but at the cost of a series of bloody and sobering tactical defeats. The Chinese military campaign against Vietnam convinced the Vietnamese to end their empire building in Indochina and eventually to withdraw their occupation forces from Cambodia (where the Vietnamese had, at least, ended the horrific genocide of Pol Pot and his "Killing Fields").

But the conflict also exposed the PLA's many operational problems and weaknesses. China's new Paramount Leader Deng Xiaopeng was forced to launch a long-term drive to reform and upgrade the PLA. China systematically rotated its entire army for periods of service on the Vietnamese border, where soldiers were put through live fire training in combat with the Vietnamese army's infantry that was, at that time, arguably the best in the world. Deng also downsized the PLA by two-thirds after the Vietnamese conflict and pushed through the creation of a far more capable noncommissioned officer class for it.

The heavy casualties suffered at the hands of numerically inferior forces in the 1979 miniconflict with Vietnam had a generation-long effect, deterring China's leaders from risking any more foreign conflicts. Thus were the lessons of the Korean War and its massive casualties revived for at least another 30 years. Not since 1979 have China's leaders risked sending significant numbers of ground forces into combat. This restraint in exerting China's military power beyond its borders was in striking contrast to the violent, ruthless, and reckless policies Mao followed within his own country.

Nevertheless, the Korean War had a number of positive results for Mao's regime. First, and most importantly, it preserved communist North Korea as a defensive buffer between northeastern China and rapidly growing South Korea, a booming free-market economy allied with the United States through the second half of the 20th century. Second, the war united the Chinese people behind Mao. And third, it gave Mao and the Chinese people a confidence in the face of the

West that they had not enjoyed for more than 110 years, since the British defeat of the Qing in the First Opium War. For even if the People's Liberation Army could not drive beyond the 38th Parallel in the two-year stalemate before the 1953 cease-fire, the army of the United States, the most powerful nation in the world, could not drive north of it again either. Mao could correctly boast that for the first time in over a century, China had successfully halted military aggression by a modern Western army.

Americans also carried away many lessons from Korea, some of which were based on a misreading of the events there. The first misperception was that China could always be counted on to fight in a war if it involved its next-door neighbors. Because China intervened on behalf of North Korea, when Korea was traditionally a friendly client state of China's, later U.S. policymakers in the 1960s overestimated the danger that China would intervene in the Vietnam War on the side of North Vietnam.

U.S. policymakers failed to realize what they could have learned by picking up the *Encyclopedia Britannica*: China and Vietnam were historic enemies going back at least a millennium; consequently, the Chinese feared that the huge Soviet involvement in Vietnam was a bid to outflank them to their south. Not until Nixon and Kissinger played their China card in 1972 did this consideration factor significantly into U.S. policy calculations.

Second, involvement in land wars in Asia was a no-win proposition for the United States, even when it was riding high with unlimited military power, industrial resources, and financial wealth. The Korean conflict cost more than 53,000 U.S. dead and led to Truman's political collapse. He had contemplated a second elected term but was humiliated in the 1952 New Hampshire primary. The American people had no taste for tens of thousands of body bags coming home from a war half a world away with no end in sight, whatever strategic rationale might be offered for it (a lesson that remained relevant in the early 21st century). In other words, absent a direct attack on the United States as a clear casus belli, the sweeping popular support for two simultaneous wars waged in Europe and the Pacific that had existed through World War II could not be counted on when fighting limited, regional wars around the world.

As he usually did after a particularly catastrophic setback (and he had many of them), Mao briefly retreated into the pretense of moderation and tolerance. This respite appeared to be a cultural and even political "thaw" along the same lines that Nikita Khrushchev was initiating in the post-Stalin Soviet Union at the same time. "Let a hundred flowers bloom, let a hundred schools of thought contend!" Mao declared in May 1956. He made it the official slogan of his policy of openness and debate in 1956–57. But the "Hundred Flowers" experiment proved even briefer than Khrushchev's thaw, and it was far more mercilessly suppressed. When the movement threatened to go out of control, Mao had the Chinese Communist Party label its most outspoken critics as "bourgeois rightists" and launched a new "Anti-Rightist Campaign." The beginning of this wave of repression can be traced to June 7, 1957, when the *People's Daily* published an editorial, subsequently broadcast to the Chinese people, reiterating the old orthodoxy that public criticism of Communist Party decisions was forbidden.

From Great Leap Forward to Cultural Revolution

In retrospect, it appears that Mao only encouraged heads to rise up in independent thought in order to more easily cut them all off. Within a year, he unleashed the Great Leap Forward. It was his attempt to solve the riddle of modernization that had baffled every Chinese ruler before him. And like its predecessors, it failed miserably.

Mao's particular failure was rooted in his earlier success. He was peasant-born himself and had risen to rule China, like the founder of the Ming before him, by despising the book learning of urban intellectuals ignorant of his nation's teeming rural reality. He held such views despite his being very much an intellectual himself. He had studied at university and conducted serious sociological research. Mao was also a serious and talented poet and writer. His poetry remains widely read and respected today, and his military manuals are of lasting quality and stature.

But these achievements did not lead Mao to value the opinion of experts; on the contrary, as the years passed, he came increasingly to despise them. Since the experts had been wrong so often, surely they would be wrong about the best way to industrialize too? The support of hundreds of millions of Chinese peasants, their boundless enthusiasm, and his own implacable will had carried Mao so far, why should the enthusiasm of all those peasants not solve the problems of industrialization as well?

Mao ignored the lessons of free-market and collectivist socialist industrializations alike. He did not try to strip the land of food to feed the industrializing masses in the cities, as Stalin had done. Instead, he called on the tillers of the land themselves to create his industrialization for him. Ignoring every precedent of industrializing societies, he rejected economies of scale and basic principles of organization. If Huey P. Long had declared "every man, a king" Mao essentially proclaimed, "Every man, his own blast furnace."

Starting in May 1958, Mao launched a new campaign to micromanage agricultural output and boost food production. It was a disaster. In the summer of 1958, Chinese peasants were organized into giant "people's communes." Food production in the harvest of 1958 plunged precipitously. In 1959 it was nonexistent. By the time the enormous experiment had run its course, three years later, at least 25 million people had starved. Based on an analysis of Chinese death rates in the four years from 1958 through 1961, researchers Jung Chang and Jon Halliday concluded that the death toll from the famine was even higher. They put the figure at 38 million dead. This dwarfed the depredations of Jiang and the Japanese invaders.[31]

Still, Mao charged ahead. He ordered the doubling of steel production in 1958, from 5.3 million tons the previous year. Steel, Mao imagined, could be produced anywhere and everywhere. He mobilized 90 million people throughout China to produce in small "backyard" furnaces. The goal was met, but Mao later acknowledged that 3 million tons of the new output was useless.

As the revered founding father of the Chinese Revolution, Mao was too powerful to be toppled outright, but a coterie of more pragmatic, second-tier figures moved the old potentate aside. Led by Deng Xiaoping, one of the most eminent and competent figures in the Second Generation of communist leaders—and one whom Mao had always distrusted for that very reason—the group thought they had put him safely on the shelf. At a conference of 7,000 Communist Party and government officials in Beijing on January 27, 1962, President Liu Shaoqi blindsided Mao with a devastating speech criticizing the Great Leap Forward. "People do not have enough food, clothes or other essentials," Liu said. "Agricultural output, far from rising . . . dropped, not a little, but tremendously. . . . There is

59

not only no Great Leap Forward but a great deal of falling backward."

In response, on January 30, 1962, Mao criticized his own policies for the first time since taking power in 1949. He left Beijing and spent an extended period in Shanghai, which remained a secure party stronghold for him, run by Ke Qingshi. Responsibility for ending the policies of the Great Leap Forward and restoring order and stability in agriculture fell to a triumvirate of Prime Minister Chou En-lai, Chen-Yun, and Deng Xiaoping.[32]

But Mao could never be safely discounted so long as he breathed. With the help of his ambitious third wife, Jiang Qing, he plotted and planned with younger hard-line stalwarts to outflank the elderly moderates. Within a few years, Mao and his supporters were ready to strike. In 1965, Mao called for a Great Cultural Revolution to topple the old, experienced cadres of the party.[33]

It was yet another chaotic bloodbath. Once more, far from emulating the Soviet Union, as conventional Marxist-Leninist theory would have had him do, Mao was following precisely the opposite course. The party bureaucracy that he himself had created over the previous 35 years was now blocking his way. Therefore, he would destroy it. In his old age, Mao was trying to turn back the clock to a pre-Stalin, Trotskyite revolutionary past. Bureaucracy was bad. Revolution was good. He called on a new generation of revolutionaries to destroy the Communist Party itself. Effectively, he set off yet another civil war.

That war raged in greatest intensity from late 1965 through 1967, coinciding with violent student riots across Western Europe and the United States. For a while it seemed as if the entire world was on fire. In China, perhaps a million people were murdered in the upheaval, but scores of millions more had their lives uprooted and destroyed. To be an educated, qualified professional—say a serious scientist, engineer, or administrator—was to guarantee being sent to the remotest collective farms and given degrading and exhausting tasks of manual labor. Once again, Mao squandered the most valuable human resources in China. And the consequences were exactly opposite of those he craved: China's ruler had dreamed that he could modernize his nation and make it an industrial superpower overnight, a generation ahead of schedule. Instead, he set back its emergence as a modern industrial power by 30 or 40 years.

Unlike Stalin, who left behind an institutionalized system of repression that would preserve his legacy for at least a generation,

Mao used the ideology of revolution to destroy the revolutionaries, smashing the institutionalized base of the Chinese Communist Party. But in so doing, he cleared the way for a sweeping, free-market system to be established by his successor Deng Xiaoping. Mao, in effect, ensured the success of a system he abhorred as applied by a man he detested. The Cultural Revolution was a case of a revolution devouring itself.[34]

The Cultural Revolution also traumatized the coming generation of Chinese that was averse toward foreign conflicts. The Cultural Revolution also allowed a stable, conservative, even repressive, society to emerge in a China that was obsessed with economic growth and the building of a huge industrial infrastructure. After the purges and unrest, China maintained a low profile in international affairs. Mao's successors focused on breakneck economic growth at home. And they succeeded.

Mao Turns to America

Mao's one bold move on the international stage during his last decade of life was the conclusion of a strategic partnership with the United States. He agreed to host U.S. President Richard Nixon and signed with him the first Shanghai Communiqué of 1972. U.S.–PRC rapprochement put the issue of Taiwan on ice, at least for another generation or so.[35] This was less of an extraordinary U-turn than it appeared. Mao, it was true, had always fulminated against the United States and the free-market capitalism it embodied. But he had never been the mindless tool or eager partner of the Soviet Union that so many in America had always believed. For Mao, nothing was more important than power, and every principle and adventure on which he staked the lives of his long-suffering people could always be abandoned or reversed in the pursuit of power. In the realpolitik of Nixon and his national security adviser Henry Kissinger, Mao found compatible partners.[36]

He needed them too. In October 1964, China had detonated its first thermonuclear device, becoming the fifth member of the nuclear club after the United States, the Soviet Union, Britain, and France. It was an impressive achievement, especially given China's still meager and chaotic industrial base. It was also a victory for China's engineers and scientists in what turned out to be their race against Mao's own self-destructive drives. Less then two years later, he unleashed the

61

Cultural Revolution that brought all serious scientific and technolog-ical research to a grinding halt for well over a decade.

The Soviets were alarmed by Mao's acquisition of nuclear weap-ons, however. Soviet Premier Nikita Khrushchev had refused to help the Chinese with their nuclear program. In unguarded, bombastic comments, Mao had alarmed Khrushchev with the idea that China might eagerly trigger a global nuclear war, counting on China's enormous population to allow it to emerge as top dog after the United States and the Soviet Union had incinerated each other.[37] Tensions between the Soviet Union and China grew following Khrushchev's de-Stalinization speech to the 20th Communist Party Congress of the Soviet Union in Moscow in February 1956.

Mao believed Khrushchev had made a great mistake. In typically crude language, Mao told the Chinese Politburo: "We must not blindly follow the Soviet Union.... Every fart has some kind of smell and we cannot say that all Soviet farts smell sweet."[38]

But the split between the two leaders only became apparent to the wider world on June 21, 1960, when Khrushchev, speaking to Communist Party leaders from 51 countries gathered in Bucharest, Romania, publicly rebuked Mao's position that a world war was needed for the global triumph of socialism. As historians Jung Chang and Jon Halliday observed, Khrushchev's speech "was tantamount to saying that Mao was crazy and suggesting that co-existence with the West was a better bet than continuing an alliance with Mao."[39]

Thereafter, the enmity between the two giant nations of Eurasia was exacerbated by an ideological dispute over Marxist theory. China maintained that its theory of rural-generated communist revo-lution fitted the new facts of the decolonized third world far better than the Soviet ideology of first laboriously building up an industrial infrastructure from which the urban revolutionary vanguard could be recruited.

But in the end, it all came down to grim geostrategic realities. China with its teeming millions was—or would be, if not for Mao's repeated bungling—a mighty rising force in the world, threatening huge chunks of Soviet-ruled and underdeveloped Central Asia and the Far East where the Russian population was small and increasing slowly, if at all. The Soviets were so threatened by China's rise— Soviet military power had not yet peaked—that they sought U.S. cooperation for preemptive strikes against Chinese military and nuclear facilities. For example, in 1969, Khrushchev's successor Leonid Brezhnev tried to obtain a green light to carry out attacks. U.S. leaders wisely rejected such calls.

The Chinese leadership took this danger seriously, however. In 1969, they publicly ordered the construction of underground shelters throughout China and also a nuclear shelter in the government complex of Zhongnanhai in Beijing. Alarmed by the imminent Soviet threat, even Mao found the Americans the lesser of two evils.[40]

As the Cultural Revolution ran out of steam, Mao maneuvered to preserve his heritage. He named a true believer and loyal party functionary, Hua Guofeng, as his chosen successor. But Mao, like other overbearing tyrants, fell into a familiar trap. Because they cannot bear to have men of real ability around them, they bequeath power to more accommodating figures who lack the skills or the drive to carry forth ambitious plans. Within two years of Mao's death in 1976, Hua was gone too, peacefully toppled by one of the most important and successful figures in his nation's long history, Deng Xiaoping.[41]

Deng's Achievement

Deng appeared an unlikely figure to reverse the fortunes and political dynamics of the entire planet. He was tiny, only around five feet tall. He lacked Mao's charisma and megalomaniacal ambitions. He erected no huge mausoleums. While utterly ruthless when he felt he had to be, especially in suppressing the 1989 democracy demonstrations in Beijing, Deng had no appetite for conquest, glory, or blood. But he did what no Chinese ruler in the 140 years of endless upheaval since the First Opium War had been able to do: he mastered the challenge of modernizing China. He created the political and conceptual infrastructure to unleash an enormous industrial revolution, one of the longest and most successful the world has ever seen.

Deng was a lifelong communist revolutionary. He joined the Chinese Communist Party while still a student in France as early as 1923 and was a founding leader of the so-called returned students who had studied in Moscow. In 1928, Deng led an armed uprising. He participated in the Long March and even served as general secretary of the CCP while still only in his 20s. At the climax of the civil war, he commanded the final assault on Jiang Jieshi's Kuomintang forces in Sichuan and then served as mayor of Chongqing, the greatest city in China's west.

Mao had always disliked Deng; indeed, Mao had purged him from the party three times. On the third occasion, already middle aged, Deng was sent for years into the rural hinterland to labor with his hands as a lowly peasant. His son was thrown out of a window by Red Guard thugs during the Cultural Revolution and was crippled for life. But tiny, ugly, soft-spoken Deng seemed to exemplify Nietzsche's superman: whatever didn't kill him made him stronger.

Deng replaced Hua as ruler of China in 1978, and in the following year he proclaimed his "Four Modernizations." Just as Mao had destroyed the physical infrastructure of communism in China, Deng now completed the job by dispensing with everything that communism had always taught. He allowed the private ownership of property and trade in it. He legalized and encouraged profit making. He welcomed overseas investment in China with open arms. He created special industrial enterprise zones in China's southeastern coastal provinces. Through all the economic liberalization, he made no attempt to democratize China and kept its authoritarian political structure in place. Only a decade later, Soviet thinker Andranik Migranian studied Deng's reforms and proclaimed them to be the model Russia should have embraced when it cast off communism.[42]

Deng's policies worked. Through the early 1980s and the 1990s, except for a brief pause after the Tiananmen Square massacre, overseas investment flooded into China and the economy boomed. In the 1980s, the United States, eager to strengthen China against the Soviets, opened its markets to exports from China.

This Chinese industrial revolution created enormous inequalities in regional and personal wealth and power. According to official Chinese government figures from 2005, 86.5 percent of foreign direct investment in China went to the coastal cities of China's south and east, whereas only 9 percent went to heavily populated rural central China.[43] Coastal China, especially in the south, boomed. Guangdong Province, long known in the West as Kwangtung or Canton, replaced Pennsylvania in the United States and Sheffield or Birmingham in England as the "Workshop of the World." *The Economist* magazine gave Guangdong that title in October 2003. By the beginning of 2003, the *Wall Street Journal* noted that 50 percent of the world's cameras,

30 percent of its air conditioners, and 20 percent of its refrigerators were being produced or assembled in China. According to Chinese government statistics issued in 2006, the nation by then had 4.98 million private firms employing 120 million people with 7.6 trillion yuan (about $950 billion in 2006 dollars) in registered capital.[44]

Deng's achievement was epochal. For the first time in centuries, China was a first-rate power. The real standard of living for much of its population was rising. Estimates of the size of China's middle class varied from 25 million to 300 million, depending on the measurement criteria used. By the end of the 20th century, however, China had indisputably become one of the preeminent industrial nations in the world. And in 2003, for the first time, China surpassed the United States as the leading magnet for foreign direct investment.

Not coincidentally, this period of rapid economic growth was also one of engagement with, and learning from, the outside world. To a degree not seen even under the Dowager Empress Cixi a century before, hundreds of thousands of Chinese traveled overseas to study and work, acquiring high-tech expertise—especially from the United States—in the process.

Where Mao was visionary, Deng was pragmatic. He was the antithesis of the Great Helmsman in every way. In what appeared to be a conscious and visceral reaction to the lifestyle and antics of his predecessor, Deng was obsessively self-effacing. But when Deng's power was threatened, he could be every bit as ruthless as Mao.

The Shadows of Tiananmen

In the spring of 1989, students throughout China gathered in apparently spontaneous mass protests for democracy. The Beijing demonstrations were particularly large. More than a million people camped out day and night in Tiananmen Square, the vast public space in front of the Forbidden City of the old emperors, which Mao had razed to house gigantic communist ceremonial pageants.

The demonstrations were unprecedented in China's communist era, comparable to the May 1919 mass demonstrations 80 years earlier. The crowds were peaceful and good natured, but they posed an implied rebuke to Deng and his heirs. Deng had brought growth and prosperity to China by gutting the sustaining Marxist ideology of the Chinese state, while allowing the Communist Party to retain its monopoly on political power, without any of the old justifications for doing so. The democracy protestors were demanding popular participation in national policymaking and threatening to expose the hollow nature of the regime.

China's leaders feared that the protests threatened their hold on power. They also feared that giving in to the demonstrators would destroy central authority in China and ignite a new wave of anarchy and chaos like the one that had followed the fall of the Qing dynasty. China's leaders could also see the once-mighty Soviet Union disintegrating before their eyes as popular calls for democracy in Russia rapidly gained volume and support. The Soviet Union did not finally fall apart for another two and a half years, but by mid-1989 the process of disintegration was already evident.

Deng and his colleagues at first looked on with contempt and then with horror as Soviet President Mikhail Gorbachev's dalliance with democracy and openness brought down a system that had long appeared more monolithic and stable than China's. Deng was determined not to let the infection of democracy wreak similar chaos on China. All his life, he had seen the human suffering created by the collapse of public order. The tough old communist revolutionary and survivor of the Long March was not about to let humanitarian scruples stand in the way of preventing that disintegration. So, on June 3 and 4, 1989, he unleashed the People's Liberation Army to crush the protests.

The crackdown was brutal and decisive. Thousands died. The world was appalled. China appeared momentarily thrown into chaos. Wild reports floated in the Western media about entire PLA corps taking the side of the students or protecting them against other army corps. Deng was even said to have been thrown into jail or protective custody. The stories proved false. The army remained united and subservient to the civilian authorities.[45]

For all its horror, the crackdown was a success in one narrow sense: it solidified the political authority of the Communist Party. Contrary to the predictions of many Western critics, Deng's economic reform program did not collapse, and the Communist Party regime did not lose public legitimacy or its grip on power. Like the American and French publics after the upheavals of 1968, most of Chinese society was inherently conservative. By and large, the Chinese people relished the remarkable prosperity as well as the peace and quiet that Deng's policies had brought them. In the past, such interludes of peace and prosperity had proved few and far between. During the 28 years in which Mao held supreme power, for example, the Chinese people had not experienced periods of stability and security for any length of time. After Tiananmen, no significant social group in China wanted to risk losing the security and economic gains of the previous decade to return to chaos. Memories of the Great Leap Forward famine and of the Cultural Revolution were still fresh.

So China's national consensus held, and after a brief hiccup, the breakneck economic growth resumed. Gradually, through the first half of the 1990s, Deng handed over effective power to his successor, President Jiang Zemin. Deng's Second Generation of communist-era leaders had followed the Founding Generation of Mao and Zhou. Deng's passing of the torch to Jiang signaled the emergence of the Third Generation of Chinese leaders.[46]

Continuity and Achievement

The transition from Deng Xiaoping to Jiang Zemin was akin to the Soviet Union's transition from Nikita Khrushchev to Leonid Brezhnev 30 years earlier. Jiang retained Deng's economic policies, and China remained a welcoming and astonishingly successful home for foreign direct investment. During the 1990s, China transformed its standing relative to its great rivals: India, Russia, Japan, and the United States.

Neighboring India's domestic development from independence to the early 1980s contrasted very well with China's. As discussed in chapter 1, India had not suffered hundreds of thousands killed in a needless war like that in Korea; it had not suffered a horrific famine like the Great Leap Forward, or the chaos and virtual civil war of the Cultural Revolution; India had not suffered the annihilation of much of its historic art, archaeology, and records such as Mao had inflicted on China. Parliamentary democracy had proved its superiority indeed.

But in the 20 years following Deng's rise to power, the picture was reversed. China became a genuine industrial juggernaut and its centralized, authoritarian state provided a secure and stable environment for the change. In all categories of wealth generation and industrial might, China outstripped India, which was still mired in the endless layers of inept bureaucracy and dreamy socialist values that Nehru had established.

The reversal in China's relations with the United States was even more spectacular. From December 1948 to President Nixon's first visit in 1972, the American public and its policymakers alike had looked on ferociously hostile China with a combination of fear and hatred. These attitudes proved totally misplaced. Americans did not realize how decisively they had defeated China in the Korean War, or how deeply that trauma had been felt in Beijing. China was incapable of directly threatening the United States, and the Chinese were not inclined to do so, either.

A Symbiotic Relationship

The rise of China created a complex new symbiotic interdependence with the United States. U.S. investment, business know-how, and advanced technology were crucial factors in China's industrial transformation. Chinese economic growth was powered by its exports, and the United States was the most important market for them. China still needed the United States. But the United States needed China too. Low-cost Chinese imports helped prevent the inflationary pressures building up in the domestic U.S. economy during the roaring 1990s, and they proved equally important in cushioning the effect of soaring energy prices in the first years of the 21st century.

The net capital outflows from the enormous, sustained, and ever-growing annual balance-of-trade deficit grew so great that by the turn of the century, a very large proportion of U.S. Treasury bonds was held by China's State Bank. In September 2008, according to official figures released by the U.S. Treasury Department, China was the largest foreign holder of U.S. Treasury securities (totaling $585 billion).[47] The United States had become a net borrower from China on a colossal scale.

When Britain became a net borrower of the United States after World War I, the British held onto their global empire for another quarter century or so, but they could not afford to maintain it. After World War II, they rapidly liquidated their colonies in South and Southeast Asia, the Middle East, and Africa between 1947 and 1963.

Similarly, the foundations of U.S. global hegemony were being eroded by China at the very moment triumphal pundits were proclaiming that America's "unipolar moment" after the collapse of the

Soviet Union would inevitably lead to a "unipolar 21st century" of continuing American dominance.[48]

Under Jiang, this transformation in relative economic strength between the United States and China started to cast longer shadows. China's relations with the United States slowly deteriorated through the 1990s, most notably in the Taiwan Strait crisis of 1995, when President Bill Clinton sent a U.S aircraft carrier battle group to the region to reaffirm the U.S. commitment to defend Taiwan. Spurred by this action, China started to use its new wealth to augment its military budget in new, very focused, and—in the eyes of many Americans—ominous directions.

The U.S. Defense Intelligence Agency estimates that in 2006, China's total military-related spending amounted to between $70 billion and $105 billion—two to three times the publicly announced budget. The 2006 *Annual Report to Congress* on the military power of China by the Office of the Secretary of Defense noted, "As China's military expansion proceeds, its military forces seem focused on preventing Taiwan independence while preparing to compel the island to negotiate a settlement on Beijing's terms." Therefore, "evidence suggests the PLA is engaged in a sustained effort to interdict, at long ranges, aircraft carrier and expeditionary strike groups that might deploy to the western Pacific."[49]

A huge annual investment went into building land-to-sea and land-to-air missile sites around the Taiwan Strait, as well as into developing Chinese versions of the Russian Shkval, Klub, and Moskit sea-to-sea missiles that had the capability to seriously threaten American aircraft carriers. The Chinese navy also developed a unique Chinese terminally guided ballistic missile that could be fired at carriers from land bases hundreds of miles away.

The Chinese media, meanwhile, carried open criticism and threats toward the United States. In 1995, a senior PLA general publicly mused that China might be prepared to incinerate Los Angeles if the United States remained committed to the effective independence of Taiwan.[50]

The context of this remark was both a deterrent and consistent with China's "no first use" nuclear policies. The general was sending the message that since China now had the capability to retaliate against any nuclear attack, the United States could no longer credibly threaten the use of nuclear weapons against China itself, despite having done so on at least six previous occasions.

Still, China did not put any significant military investment into force projection, for all its saber rattling about claiming control of the oil-rich waters around the Spratly Islands in the South China Sea. Its prime strategic drive, as judged by where it actually invested in its military infrastructure, remained fixated on eventually reclaiming Taiwan.

Jiang's years in power saw a profound change in China's global posture. It sought no wars and took few risks, but China displayed a new confidence and independence on the world's stage. To the day he died in February 1997 at the advanced age of 92, Deng had generally advocated public deference to the United States, even while successfully pursuing policies at home and abroad that made Chinese leaders feel increasingly less dependent on Washington's goodwill.

China in the 1990s did not need wars to rise in the world. As noted earlier, on July 1, 1997, Hong Kong peacefully and smoothly reverted to mainland control, thereby finally suturing a humiliating 145-year-old wound. The symbolism was inescapable. The ceding of Hong Kong to Britain after the First Opium War had triggered the collapse of China into a century of helpless chaos. Did the city's reversion to mainland rule herald a coming Chinese century of unprecedented global dominance instead? The peaceful reacquisition of Hong Kong and Macau made China stronger. Now only Taiwan, of all the historic Chinese lands, remained to be reunited under Beijing's leadership.

The Shanghai Pact

Less than three years after regaining Hong Kong, Jiang took another giant step, facilitated by Washington's overreaching. On June 15, 2001, recently inaugurated President George W. Bush gave a well-received speech in the Polish capital Warsaw pledging to extend the North Atlantic Treaty Organization through the nations of eastern Europe. He took pains to specifically include the three former Soviet republics of Estonia, Latvia, and Lithuania. The hubris of strategic overextension was striking. The three little states were a national security liability to the United States a continent and ocean away. Without massive U.S. military protection, they were defenseless against any future Russian move against them.

But the Russians were hardly sitting still. On that same day of Bush's speech in Warsaw, an event of considerably more import happened half way around the world. Jiang played host in Shanghai—the city that above all others had embodied prostrate China's century-long humiliation at the hands of the West and Japan—to Russian President Vladimir Putin and the leaders of several of the former Soviet republics of Central Asia. Together, Putin, Jiang, and their Central Asian allies proclaimed the creation of the Shanghai Cooperation Organization. It was, tellingly, Jiang, not the low-key Putin, who insisted on publicly christening it the "Shanghai Pact," after the 1955 Warsaw Pact.[51]

The speeches of Putin and Jiang at the time and thereafter left no doubt about the SCO's purpose. It was to preserve a multipolar world, Sino-Russian diplomatic code language for opposing American unipolar global dominance. In other words, the SCO existed to prevent the United States from becoming the dominant power in Eurasia.

Neither Jiang nor Putin was in the business of openly confronting the United States. Indeed, when al Qaeda terrorists struck the United States a few months later on September 11, 2001, China kept a low profile. Putin went out of his way to aid the United States in toppling the Taliban regime in Afghanistan that had sheltered the Islamic terrorist organization. U.S. Defense Secretary Donald Rumsfeld and his Pentagon strategists used the opportunity to establish U.S. bases in Central Asian nations. China was upset by this development, but Beijing never entertained a direct challenge to U.S. forces in the region.

This proved to be a wise policy. The U.S. strategic position in Central Asia quickly unraveled. Uzbekistan expelled U.S. forces from its Karshi-Khanabad, or "K-2," air base after the fall of the Kyrgyzstan government in the Tulip Revolution of March 2005 alarmed its neighbors about the possible consequences of permitting more democracy, as Washington urged. In 2007 and 2008, the United States and its North Atlantic Treaty Organization allies faced resurgent Taliban forces in Afghanistan. At the same time, the continuing Sunni insurgency in Iraq and the growing power of Shiite militias there forced the United Sates to increase its military commitment in Iraq, further distracting it from Central Asia.

In contrast with the brief American moment in Central Asia, by 2008, the SCO appeared to be there to stay. As security in Iraq deteriorated, the idea that the United States would have the forces to spare to be a major player in Central Asia was clearly absurd, however much Pentagon spokespeople might have protested to the contrary. The more the United States got sucked into Iraq and, indeed, the more Bush administration policymakers pushed ahead with even more ambitious dreams of destabilizing and toppling the governments of Syria and Iran, the less time and fewer resources they were going to have to contest Chinese and Russian cooperation in Central Asia.[52]

China under the Fourth Generation

In 2003, Jiang handed over the presidency of China to another Deng disciple, Hu Jintao.[53] The transfer from China's Third Generation of communist leaders to its Fourth went off smoothly. The following year, Jiang was eased out of control of China's Central Military Commission, his last remaining power base.

Hu inherited a China with major problems still ahead, but its strengths and potential far outweighed its challenges. He faced vast disparities in wealth between the old rural heartland and the amazingly booming industrial regions of the south and along the coastlines. China now had the greatest concentration of heavy industrial capital on the planet. Yet the nation's banking industry, based in Shanghai, was somewhat weak. Although the panic of 1998 was followed by a speedy recovery, China's financial system was still a corrupt mess in the early years of the new century. In contrast to neighboring Japan, the government in Beijing showed little enthusiasm for opening its finances to outside scrutiny.

Meanwhile, communism was stone-cold dead as an ideology, which left a worrying spiritual and moral vacuum in the largest nation on earth. Historically, new religious and philosophical movements had always arisen to fill such gaps, and they had never stayed out of politics. The horrific examples of the Taiping and Boxer rebellions showed what happened when militant religious movements were allowed to metastasize and grow out of control.

Therefore, when the Falun Gong cult swept China in the late 20th and early 21st century, the government of President Jiang Zemin lost no time in trying to repress it. International and especially American human rights activists were outraged. But from the Chinese point of view, the Falun Gong represented a potentially deadly threat. Its combination of martial arts exercises and spiritual values echoed the Boxers, while its apocalyptic view of the coming end of the age bore unsettling parallels to the teachings of the Taiping.

The Boxer Rebellion had shown how quickly China could turn from a peaceful and open society to one that is deadly and xenophobic. The pattern was repeated throughout the 20th century, and it may yet reemerge in the 21st. This was not something that any responsible, historically aware Chinese government could ignore. That is why, through the turn of the century, first Jiang and then Hu cracked down hard on the Falun Gong movement.

But China's remarkable growth and prosperity also fed a proud new nationalism. The nation's huge economic success created what Marxists would have called a tension between the base—a dynamic and rapidly changing economy and society—and the superstructure—an outmoded political order that still wanted to control and centralize, and that had little to offer in managing a 21st-century economy.

There were clear signs under both Presidents Jiang and Hu that the leadership of the Chinese Communist Party sought to reconcile these contradictions by evolving their party in a nationalist direction. But this kind of transformation carried risks of its own. If the party's legitimacy for its continued autocratic control of the nation rested on its nationalist credentials, it would have less room to maneuver and defer the expectations generated by China's rise in global power, especially on the issue of Taiwan.

China entered the 21st century with a far weaker and more volatile, indeed dangerously unpredictable, political system than India. Meanwhile its economy, even allowing for the great and still-growing wealth disparities between its industrial regions and its rural heartland, was far stronger than that of its neighbor. Nor did it face the kind of deadly unpredictable threat from an unstable and unremittingly hostile neighbor that India did from Pakistan.

But like India, China in its strengths and unpredictable weaknesses entered the new century as the sum of its parts, powered by a widespread consensual nationalism and buoyed by an unprecedented wave of prosperity and confidence resting securely on a huge industrial foundation. In the East, the rising sun cast bright rays of hope for the coming day.

3. The Historic Relationship between India and China

To many U.S. policymakers, India and China at the dawn of the 21st century appear as two wildly contrasting giants, both destined to set their very different imprints on the world's stage and both fated to eventually clash. That may indeed be the case in the long term. But in the long term, as John Maynard Keynes famously said, we are all dead. The interaction of India and China over the 60 or so years since both became effectively independent has been a study in contrasts and cautious maneuvering. This chapter traces the historical relationship between India and China and examines how India and China's strategic interests have been interacting, conflicting, and sometimes converging in recent decades.

This is a relatively recent phenomenon. Through the long historical record of both nations, it is surprising how little interaction there has been between these two civilizations. Both were clearly aware of each other from the earliest times, but trade between them does not seem to have been significant until the time of the early Roman Empire, the heydays of the Han dynasty in China and the Gupta Empire in India. Even then, revealingly, India traded more with Rome than with China.[1]

The spiritual effect of India on China proved to be profound, however. The teachings of Gautama Buddha at first took little hold in his homeland, flourishing instead far across Southeast Asia in the centuries after his death. During the Tang dynasty, Buddhism penetrated China and proved to be a lasting and significant force there.[2]

Both great agrarian civilizations were based on the drainage of river valleys and both shared the fear of being overrun by hoards of mounted barbarians from the steppes of Central Asia. That happened repeatedly but seldom to both of them simultaneously. They did share a common enemy in the Huns, who were a serious threat to the Gupta Empire in India and the post-Han regimes in China.

Contacts between the South and East Asian worlds were so sporadic or casual that no serious attempt seems to have been made by either to woo the other. In times of mutual power and prosperity, trade increased between them but remained relatively insignificant.[3]

This pattern even continued into medieval times. Genghis Khan captured Beijing in 1215 at the climax of a campaign that is believed to have taken an incredible 30 million lives. His grandson Kublai Khan completed the conquest of China in 1279 and founded the Mongol Yuan dynasty there. But the Mongols never conquered India, and the Black Death in the mid-14th century devastated them before they could execute another conquest. Half a century or so later, Timur the Lame, known in the West as Tamerlane, conquered India but not China. In the 16th century, the great "gunpowder empires" of the Muslim Mughals in India and the Mongolian Qing in China established their long-lasting domains. In both cases, the indigenous peoples of the two great civilizations were again conquered by familiar oppressors with long warrior traditions.[4]

As discussed in chapter 1, the British were a significant presence in India from the late 17th century. Their conquest of the subcontinent was slow and incremental. Robert Clive's victory at Plessey in 1757 established the British as the masters of India, and the raj was steadily expanded over the next 125 years to include the lands of modern Pakistan and Burma. By contrast, the British and Western European presence in China remained peripheral until the fateful First Opium War of 1840.[5] Even then, the Western powers never established any lasting, formal political control over the Chinese interior the way the Mongols did. The deep divisions between the conservative, isolated, and vast hinterland of China and the industrialized, outward-looking southeastern coastal provinces have continued to the present day.

From 1840 onward, the strategic interaction of India and China was firmly established, and it followed a dynamic exactly the opposite of the one that prevails today. The British used India as the military base from which they repeatedly humbled the Qing and exercised their will in East Asia. India provided most of the troops for both of the Opium Wars of 1840 and 1860 and continued to provide a major share of Britain's colonial armies around the world.

The British were never interested in taking over China, as they did in India. Chaotic 19th-century China was simply not worth the trouble; it was much more efficient to keep enormously lucrative footholds in the crown colony of Hong Kong and the British enclave of Shanghai. The policing of the British Quarter there symbolized the contrasting fates of British India and supposedly independent China as late as the 1930s. Chinese were treated like dirt in Western-ruled Shanghai. Signs in parks barred dogs and native Chinese from entering. Law and order were usually kept by proud Indian policemen, preferably turbaned Sikhs, dressed in the traditional uniform of British "constables" or "bobbies."[6] The message was clear: beneficent British colonialism raised up the Indians far higher in the world than the Qing and their successors could or would do for the Chinese.

The Chinese and Indian independence movements of the early decades of the 20th century looked on each other with favor but little else. Sun Yat-sen and Mahatma Gandhi wished each other well against the common enemy of Western imperialism but did not collaborate in any way. Fitful rhetoric of solidarity was never backed by action on either side. "The nationalist leaders of each country were so immersed in the demands of their own struggle that they had minimal contact with each other," explains Francine Frankel, an expert on Indian-Chinese relations.[7]

As late as World War II, the British Indian Army remained a powerful military force, whereas China's army, for all its vast size, remained mired in appalling corruption and incompetence.[8] Jiang Jieshi's armies continually failed to deliver against the Japanese. In 1943–44, they collapsed when the Japanese army in China went on a rare offensive to conquer Gen. Claire Chennault's airfields in central China. By contrast, the British-controlled Indian Army annihilated the Japanese 15th Army at the battles of Imphal and Kohima in 1944, and then liberated Burma in July 1945.

Even in the hours of chaos before independence in 1947, with Gandhi leading huge new protest demonstrations against the British presence in India at the height of the war, the Indian Army remained loyal to the raj and a formidable military asset. By contrast, Jiang's legions proved useless.[9]

China Takes Over Tibet

Independence came for India in August 1947, little more than a year before Mao Zedong's victorious People's Liberation Army marched into Beijing. But the relationship between the two new titans on the Asian stage started with a dispute over the ancient land of Tibet.

Vast Tibet, landlocked high behind the Himalayas and the Pamirs, had always been effectively self-governing, but in the early decades of the 18th century, the flood tide of Manchu expansion into Central Asia had reached it, too, and Tibet fell under the suzerainty of the Qing dynasty emperors in Beijing. Indeed, the Dalai Lama of Lhasa became the chaplain to the (at least nominally) Buddhist Qing emperor of China.

China had always been a major player in the intrigues around the court of the Dalai Lamas, but its influence in Tibet actually declined in the 19th century. That fact was lost on Lord Curzon, the British viceroy of India. Curzon was convinced that Tibet, backed by the Qing dynasty in Beijing and then still ruled by the Dowager Empress Cixi, posed a threat to British control of northern India. Determined to reassert British authority in the region, Lord Curzon dispatched a military expedition commanded by Francis Younghusband, then only a major but a noted explorer and expert on the Himalayas and Tibet. It proved to be one of the most remarkable military and scientific expeditions in the history of the empire. In a series of battles and skirmishes between British and Tibetan forces, Younghusband rolled back Chinese influence, at least to the satisfaction of the viceroy and his officials in New Delhi.[10] Following the fall of the last Qing emperor in 1911, Tibet enjoyed a brief period of full independence until 1950.[11]

But Mao soon put an end to that. In 1950, Chinese communist forces occupied Tibet. The teenage Dalai Lama, believed to be the 14th reincarnation of the line, remained with his court, but thousands of refugees fled across the highest mountains in the world to take refuge in newly independent India.

Indian Prime Minister Jawarhalal Nehru took no action. Delhi still had its hands full dealing with the wars of partition and their aftermath. Besides, although Nehru had shown sympathy for the Tibetans, he was determined to build close relations with Mao's China. The Indian prime minister dreamed of creating a third power bloc in the world of major Asian nations that was independent of both the capitalist West and the communist East. In 1955, his dreams briefly appeared to come true. In the Indonesian city of Bandung, he launched the Non-Aligned Movement alongside Chinese Premier Zhou Enlai and Indonesia's founding father President Sukarno.

But the honeymoon did not last. In 1959, the Tibetan people rose up against the harsh Chinese occupation that had demolished their monasteries and impoverished their people. The Chinese responded with an even harsher crackdown. The Dalai Lama, then a young man in his mid-20s, fled with his entourage. (He was escorted out of Lhasa by agents of the Central Intelligence Agency.) After an epic journey, they made it to safety in India, eventually setting up a court in exile in Dharamsala in eastern India. Those who stayed behind suffered mightily under the Chinese. Out of a population that never exceeded 7 million, an estimated 1.2 million people died or fled over the following decades.[12]

The events of 1959 had a significant effect on Indian public opinion but only a peripheral one on government policy. However, worse was to come. The border between India and Tibet was now the border between India and China, and it had never been properly surveyed or mutually agreed on. Indeed, Younghusband's 1905 expedition had been sent to lay claim to disputed sections of the territory. The dispute lingered through the 1950s and came to a head in October 1962 when war broke out between the two Asian giants.

India's Humiliation: The War of 1962

The resulting conflict was a nightmarish wake-up call for India. Nehru had neglected the regular army during his first decade and a half in power. Perhaps its stellar performance in the civil war of partition in 1947 had bred complacency. Since that time, the army had succeeded in maintaining a firm grip on most of Kashmir. However, Pakistan was not seen as a serious military threat to India in the 1950s, and Nehru did not view China as a potential enemy. The once-crack army's fighting effectiveness declined due to neglect. Nehru seriously employed the army only once during that decade— to occupy Portuguese Goa.

The war of 1962 was a decisive turning point in modern Indian history. It had vastly less effect in China. In China, the war was overshadowed and forgotten three years later when Mao unleashed the chaos of his Cultural Revolution. But for India, the war was as traumatic in its way as the fall of France in 1940 proved to be for

79

an entire French generation or the surprise attack of October 6, 1973, for Israel at the start of the Yom Kippur War.[13]

The immediate cause of the 1962 war was the still-disputed regions of the Himalayas, another legacy of the British Empire in India. Indians claimed they were just defending their historic frontier with China. But that borderline had been unilaterally drawn by British imperial officials along the so-called McMahon Line in 1897. The Chinese government, then ruled by the empress Cixi of the Qing dynasty in Beijing, was not even consulted. Mao disputed India's claims. Thus did an imperial agreement from the late 19th century between Britain and China eventually lead to military deployments more than 60 years later. These proved to be preparatory moves for the only war between the two most populous nations in the world.

The areas at issue were strategically worthless. But Nehru, convinced of the morality and legality of India's position, boasted publicly that he would not give up an inch of territory. In December 1960, Mao's right-hand man, Zhou Enlai, had made a brief stopover in New Delhi and signaled that Mao was still prepared to accept a compromise agreement to settle the dispute. Nehru haughtily rejected it.

Behind Nehru's bluster was a conviction that China would never dare resort to force. Also, Nehru's relations with the United States were warming on the expectation that they would improve still further when President John F. Kennedy was inaugurated in January 1961. In the first year of the Kennedy administration, JFK gave Nehru informal assurances of U.S. support against China through the U.S. ambassador to Delhi, John Kenneth Galbraith. Nehru, setting an example of high-minded Wilsonian impracticality and incompetence in which too many of his successors also indulged, thought the verbal assurance would be enough and made no effort to take advantage of Kennedy's favorable attitude toward him to conclude a formal alliance with the United States. He lost an opportunity that did not recur for nearly 40 years. It may have been a lost opportunity for the United States too. Apart from preempting the Soviet-Indian strategic alignment that soon followed, an Indian-U.S. strategic alliance in the early 1960s would have given India far more input into policymaking in Washington.[14]

As it was, Kennedy instead inadvertently undermined his own desire to support India. In July 1962, U.S. tensions with the Soviet

Union rose over both Berlin and the looming Cuban crisis. Before those heated up, Kennedy had sought to defuse the dangers of war with China by assuring Beijing he had reined in Jiang Jieshi in Taiwan. The U.S. president wanted to avert any more crises like the confrontations during Eisenhower's tenure between China and the United States over the small offshore island of Quemoy.

Mao, likewise, wanted to avoid running more risks with the United States. The hundreds of thousands of Chinese Korean War dead, including Mao's own son, had taught him how formidable U.S. military power was. Mao did not seek a confrontation in the early 1960s with Kennedy over Quemoy or Taiwan. He did not respond immediately when Indian forces had started to try to dislodge People's Liberation Army units from positions along the Sino-Indian frontier claimed by China. However, he countered India's moves by deploying Chinese heavy artillery to the Himalayan fronts.

The artillery redeployment in response to India's incursions along the border took months. The nearest Chinese railheads to the attack positions against India were 1,200 miles away from the Chinese coast across the inhospitable 15,000-foot-high vastness of the Tibetan plateau. Mao might well have prepared far longer, amassing larger forces and launching a more ambitious and wide-ranging invasion than he did. He was not a man given to half measures: he built a career by launching one spectacular gamble after another. But as it turned out, within three months of reaching his own understanding with JFK and starting the redeployment of Chinese heavy artillery and supplies west, the perfect opportunity to attack a suddenly isolated India came, and Mao took it.

On October 15, 1962, the Kennedy administration received definitive proof that Soviet missiles were being deployed in Cuba. By October 19, Radio Moscow was reporting large U.S. Navy maneuvers in the Caribbean that appeared to be the preparation for a full-scale U.S. invasion of Cuba. Three days later, President Kennedy appeared on television to announce the U.S. naval blockade that had already begun. The great crisis of the Missiles of October, the most dangerous moment in the entire 44-year history of the cold war, had begun.

It appears very unlikely that Mao and Khrushchev coordinated their actions before the missile crisis and the Chinese attack on India. Soviet and Chinese relations were at an exceptionally low ebb in the autumn of 1962. Kennedy's response to Khrushchev's placement of missiles in Cuba took the Soviet leader totally by surprise. He had misread Kennedy as a weakling at their fateful summit in Vienna, Austria, in June 1961. Given that Khrushchev had not anticipated, let alone deliberately planned, the missile crisis, there was no way that Mao could have either. But once that crisis erupted, Mao was already in position to take full advantage of it.

On October 20, 1962, the day after the missile crisis was announced to the world, Mao unleashed the PLA on India in a war at the top of the world. Preoccupied with Cuba and the threat of global thermonuclear holocaust, Kennedy could not come to Nehru's aid. India was on its own.

The Indians were taken totally by surprise. They had no heavy artillery in their forward positions and did not dream that the Chinese had. Their tactical intelligence was nonexistent. The Chinese achieved concentration of forces and a clear superiority in the disputed Himalayan region. That gave them the opportunity to sweep down from the mountains and threaten to overrun parts of northeastern India.

In the Ladakh region to the north, the embattled Indian forces gave a good account of themselves. At first, on the Sela front, it looked like it would be a tough fight for the Chinese too. However, the Indians' only major land battle experience as an independent nation had been in their generally successful war with nascent Pakistan, in which they occupied and retained most of Kashmir in 1947–48. Since then, the Indian Army veterans, many of whom had served during World War II, had basically been in the business of scattering small-scale tribal opposition. The Indian Army was also remarkably poorly equipped. It still had British Empire–era .303 Enfield rifles. Some of its troops went to war wearing tennis shoes. By contrast, the PLA, for all its primitive tactics and lack of modern hardware, was a real army, organized and coordinated as such.[15]

The commander of the Indian 4th Corps in the Sela area, Lt. Gen. Brij Mohan Kaul, was a favorite of Nehru's and owed his promotion to his skill at flattering the prime minister and Defense Minister Krishna Menon. Like Nehru, Kaul came from Kashmir. During World War II, he had commanded a drama troupe to entertain the forces fighting the Japanese and had never seen combat. As the Chinese attacks developed, he had a health crisis—subsequently diagnosed as a panic attack.

During his incapacity, Kaul resigned and was replaced by an able commander, Lt. Gen. Harbax Singh, a weathered veteran of the old Anglo-Indian 14th Army that had soundly defeated the Imperial Japanese Army at Imphal and Kohima in 1944. As the Chinese surged to envelop the Indian positions in Sela, Harbax Singh did not panic. He remembered, and imitated, British Gen. William Slim's determined stand against repeated Japanese attacks in that earlier conflict.

However, General Kaul recovered and insisted on retaking command. Ignoring Harbax Singh's calm counsel, Kaul ordered a full-scale retreat. That retreat quickly became a rout, beginning the greatest military humiliation in the independent history of India. After the Chinese broke through the Indian positions, they threatened to sweep down into the plains of Assam. There was panic in the regional center of Tezpur. Thousands of people fled the city across the Bramaputra River.

The Indian Army, for all its deficiencies in equipment, combat doctrine, intelligence, training, and strategic preparedness did not want for either bravery on the part of its soldiers or for highly capable senior command officers, once Nehru and Menon swallowed their pride and reached out to find them. Lt. Gen.—later Field Marshal—Sam H. F. J. Manekshaw, replaced the disastrous Kaul as commander of 4th Corps and quickly stabilized this force's positions. "Gentlemen," he told his officers at his first command conference, "there shall be no withdrawals." The Indians rallied and held.[16]

They could have done even better. India's ace in the hole was its tactical air superiority. After a face-to-face meeting with Mao in 1958, Khrushchev had decided that the Chinese leader was an uncontrollable madman, and he took care to prevent China from being equipped with state-of-the-art Soviet aircraft. Therefore, at the time of the war with India, the Chinese People's Liberation Army Air Force was equipped only with obsolete, Korean War–era MiGs. By contrast, the Indian Air Force's frontline combat fighter was the British Hawker Hunter, no longer top of the line but still a first-class aircraft and vastly superior to anything the Chinese could put up against it.

The Indians could have emulated British and U.S. combat tactics in 1944–45 and used their air superiority as flying artillery to neutralize the Chinese superiority in conventional artillery. The Chinese supply lines across Tibet consisted of long convoys of slow-moving porters and mules. They would have made rich bombing targets. But Nehru panicked. He feared major Chinese attacks on eastern Indian cities like Calcutta, despite the fact that the only planes in the Chinese inventory capable of flying such distances were aging Soviet-supplied Ilyushin Il-4 bombers.

In addition to the technological edge enjoyed by the Indian Air Force, China had only two airfields in Tibet that were suitable for launching bombing operations. The Indians, on the other hand, had inherited from the British a whole chain of first-class airfields across Assam that was initially built to deal with the Japanese. The Hunters operating from these fields would have made short work of any Ilyushin bombers striking against civilian targets, and any such Chinese attacks would have been limited to conventional munitions; China was still two years away from successfully testing its first nuclear weapon.

Indian Air Force planners assured Nehru that his fears were almost certainly groundless. But Nehru and Menon, in addition to starving the Indian Army of funds and promoting incompetents like Kaul to key positions within it, had also failed to create any effective infrastructure for strategic decisionmaking. India did not yet have a National Security Council. The prime minister and defense minister were improvising. The 4th Corps had received a severe defeat. They did not heed the levelheaded advice of their air chiefs about the uses they could make of their air superiority. And like British Prime Ministers Stanley Baldwin and Neville Chamberlain in the 1930s, they continued to fear that the bomber would always get through, even in the face of all the accumulated evidence that it would not.

Mao had had enough too. He had achieved his primary aim: by beating the Indians in conventional combat, Mao had shown he was top dog in the Himalayas, establishing China as, apart from the Soviet Union, the number one military power in Asia. China had seized and held 33,000 square kilometers of territory. Indian resistance in Assam was stiffening under General Manekshaw's leadership. And most important of all, the Cuban missile crisis was almost over. On November 20, Mao unilaterally declared a cease-fire. It was arguably the only time in his long career that he knew when to stop and did so without bringing some far greater disaster upon himself and his country.

Mao's deescalation was well timed. On November 23, President Kennedy authorized a massive airlift of U.S. supplies to India. It came too late to reverse the tide. India had already lost the key battles, along with small but humiliating chunks of its territory. Mao established a de facto line of control that has functioned without any military challenge from India for more than four and a half decades and that both nations now agree must be the basis for any future border demarcation. But the U.S. assistance helped stave off still more humiliating losses.

What is most remarkable about the Kennedy airlift is how quickly it was forgotten in both India and the United States. For Americans, the 1962 airlift to India became just an asterisk in the endless procession of impressive U.S. Air Force logistics achievements. The Indians resented the United States for not being there when it counted. U.S.-Indian relations soured. JFK's assassination a year later was rapidly followed by the U.S. plunge into Vietnam. And Kennedy's successor, Lyndon Baines Johnson, had no time for the largest democracy in the world—his Asian obsession was Vietnam.

India Turns to Moscow

Relations between India and the Soviet Union were another matter. The Soviet Union had been courting India from the mid-1950s. Nikita Khrushchev authorized extending foreign aid and armaments to nations in the Bandung Non-Aligned Movement, of which India was one of the Big Three leaders along with China and Indonesia. By 1966, Nehru's successor, Lal Bahadur Shastri, and Alexei Kosygin, who succeeded Khrushchev as premier of Russia, found common cause in containing Mao's China.

The Johnson administration, with the State Department's best China experts gutted a decade before by Sen. Joseph McCarthy's anti-communist witch-hunts, was blind to the switch. Johnson and his key advisers failed to recognize that the Soviet Union and China were not a unified monolith threatening all of Asia; rather, the two communist countries were bitterly at odds and could have been easily played off against each other.[17]

The Indian Army bounced back from its defeat at the hands of the Chinese. Only three years later, in 1965, the Indian Army demonstrated its continuing superiority over Pakistan in a second round of hostilities over Kashmir, and in 1971, it knocked Pakistan out of the ring in the war to liberate East Bengal—soon to be Bangladesh. At a tactical level, the hard lessons of the 1962 debacle had been

learned. Nehru's successors did not repeat his bungling micromanagement of military affairs.[18] But the humiliation of 1962 had many
far-reaching results on the Indian side. It was predictable, perhaps,
that the war seems to have been taken far more seriously by the
Indians, who lost, than by the Chinese, who won.

Nehru took the defeat personally. He died in 1964, and he seems
never to have overcome the national humiliation combined with the
destruction of his dreams of India and China marching together in
harmony. His successors turned their attention to matters of international power and diplomacy that he had neglected. What use was
the Non-Aligned Movement if its two greatest nations could go to
war against each other? Shastri abandoned NAM idealism in favor
of traditional realism and balance-of-power policies in international
relations. The Tashkent Declaration of 1965 pointed the way to the
1971 security treaty between India and the Soviet Union.[19]

It can plausibly be argued that the United States drove India into
the Soviet camp. U.S. policymakers, especially in the Eisenhower
administration, favored conservative, Muslim, and fiercely anti-communist Pakistan. They may have inherited this in part from British
policymakers, who had come to regard Indian Muslims as more
loyal to them than the majority Hindus. Meanwhile, Nehru's socialist
policies at home, and high-minded Non-Aligned rhetoric on the
international stage, grated on realpolitik policymakers in Washington obsessed with their global containment chess game against the
Soviets. Pakistan was recruited into CENTO, the Central Treaty
Organization that Eisenhower and Dulles envisaged as a Middle East
and South Asian version of the North Atlantic Treaty Organization to
prevent the Soviet Union from expanding southward. With Pakistan
firmly in the U.S. camp, and China turned unexpectedly threatening,
there was nowhere else, it seemed, for a suddenly isolated India to
turn except Moscow.

The feeling was mutual. The wounds of the 1958 Sino-Soviet split
were still felt in the Kremlin. The Soviet Union's new masters, Communist Party General Secretary turned President Leonid Brezhnev
and his prime minister, Alexei Kosygin, wanted to show that they
could do better at Asian power politics than the man they had
toppled, former Prime Minister Nikita Khrushchev. Recruiting the
second-largest nation on earth into their camp—and the former
keystone of the British Empire to boot—was just the thing for them.

At a time when Soviet leaders seriously contemplated the possibility of a preemptive war against China—and when they feared Mao's well-documented unpredictability—having a huge power on China's southwestern flank was a major strategic asset.

The Indo-Russian alliance certainly served its purpose for Delhi. China was clearly superior militarily to India, especially after it detonated its first atomic bomb in October 1964. India would not match this feat for another 33 years. It was therefore reassuring to know that if China launched any new attack on India, the Soviets would use it as a pretext to threaten Beijing. Pakistan, ironically, improved its relations with China at exactly the same time and for exactly the same reason: to ward off India. The continuing enmity between India and Pakistan therefore served to keep the pattern of alliances in continental Asia predictable and stable through the end of the 20th century. These patterns ensured that so long as the United States remained strongly supportive of Pakistan, India would retain its close strategic ties to the Soviet Union, and later to Russia.

Through the 1970s and 1980s, Indians looked on China as a potential menace, but one that the alliance with Moscow protected them against. Still, the humiliation and trauma of the 1962 war cast long shadows. Even in India's hour of greatest military victory, its 1971 liberation of Bangladesh from Pakistan, Prime Minister Indira Gandhi and her military advisers were concerned that China might intervene on Pakistan's side.

That was where the strategic alliance with the Soviet Union proved its value. China was still enfeebled by her Cultural Revolution, and China's leaders had been alarmed in 1969 when a border dispute with the Soviet Union raised the specter of war. It later emerged that Brezhnev seriously considered a preventive war against China at that time, and he might even have gone ahead with it had U.S. President Richard Nixon not headed him off.[20] China was feeling weak and encircled, and the military rise of India, and the ease with which it dispensed with Pakistan, added to China's fears about being surrounded. "The worst possibility," Chinese Prime Minister Zhou Enlai admitted to Nixon when they met in February 1972, was "the eventuality that you would all attack China—the Soviet Union comes from the north, Japanese [sic] and the U.S. from the east, and India into China's Tibet."[21]

Therefore, even as Indians basked in the glow of their 1971 victory, Indian leaders were not tempted to emulate China's catastrophic political or economic programs. Even after Mao died and Deng Xiaopeng took over, India was preoccupied with its own internal concerns through the 1980s. Delhi was therefore slow to pick up on the significance of Deng's far-reaching reforms.

China paid even less attention to India after establishing its military supremacy in the 1962 war. The Chinese certainly had no fear of India after that, whereas their fear of the Soviets was very real indeed. Through the 1960s, the Soviets had gained influence in North Vietnam, China's traditional enemy to the south.

Through all this time, U.S. policymakers viewed India as a distant, insignificant appendage of Moscow.

The 1970s: India's Decade

Just as the 1970s were a decade of introspection for China, the 1980s were for India. There was a remarkable degree of reverse symmetry between the two nations during those years. Indian national confidence was riding high after the 1971 defeat of Pakistan and liberation of Bangladesh. A cover caption of *The Economist* magazine in London after the 1971 war captured the mood; it called Indira Gandhi "Empress of India."[22] A few years later, India's reliance on the Soviet Union and defiance of Nixon and Kissinger appeared justified, first when Nixon fell in the Watergate scandal in 1974 and then when the victorious North Vietnamese Army conquered South Vietnam and forced an ignominious last minute U.S. evacuation from the South.

Circumstances were far different in China. Even when Mao's worst excesses abated, the old master manipulator remained as powerful, inaccessible, and unpredictable as the most capricious Manchu emperors in the old Forbidden City. He finally died in 1976. No one had done more to create a united China after the previous century of failure; and no one had done more to keep that united China miserable, impoverished, and paralyzed.

Given the state of affairs following Mao's death, Chinese leaders didn't give much thought to competition with India. Beijing had tried to flex its muscles to put the newly assertive Vietnamese in their place in 1979, but the gambit backfired and the battle-hardened North Vietnamese dealt a humiliating tactical defeat to the People's Liberation Army.[23] China did achieve its strategic goals of forcing Vietnam to act with much more restraint and caution throughout

Indochina in the following decades. That clash was far more significant than the West appreciated at the time.

The communist world remained split, with the Soviet Union continuing to support Vietnam. The sweeping, ignorant assumptions that had propelled Lyndon Johnson, Robert McNamara, and McGeorge Bundy into committing half a million troops to prop up South Vietnam in 1965 had been exposed as nonsense. China and the Soviet Union remained bitter enemies; so too did Vietnam and China.

Defeat at the hands of the Vietnamese reinforced Deng's cautious instincts toward the wider world—and his determination to build up China from scratch. It also strengthened his desire to retain at least one of Mao's later policies: strategic cooperation with the United States to protect China from the Soviet colossus. If even the Vietnamese, exhausted after three and a half decades of continual war against the French and the Americans, could stop the PLA in its tracks, what might the Soviet Red Army do? As Henry Kissinger observed in his conversations with Zhou Enlai, being patient and taking the long view come easily to Chinese leaders.[24]

Consequently, India had little to fear from China militarily through the 1980s. Still, the rapid and then continuous success of Deng's enthusiastic application of American and British free-market policies shook the confidence of Indian business leaders and intellectuals through the decade. A profound transformation was beginning to occur: for more than 125 years since the Taiping rebellion of the 1850s, India had been a vastly safer and more secure country to live in for its hundreds of millions of inhabitants than China. Even the First National Uprising of 1857 and the millions of dead from Britain's bungled withdrawal and partition in 1947 were on a far smaller scale than the killing going on in China at the same time. For all of Nehru's socialist fixations and economic daydreams, the standard of living of the Indian people, especially the "real India" of the hundreds of thousands of rural villages, remained stable under him and his successors. There was no repetition of the Bengal famine of 1943 that had been caused by British incompetence. Indian famine relief and prevention were the best in the third world. Even though China had thrashed India in the 1962 war, educated, middle-class Indians had good reason to be complacent when they compared their relative progress with China's lack thereof.

1980s: China's Decade

In the 1980s, that changed. Independent India had never seen anything like the crash industrialization of China's coastal regions. Indians marveled at the hundreds of millions of dollars in foreign direct investment that transformed Shanghai into the most important financial center of mainland Asia. Even the traditional socialist arrogance and complacency of the Congress Party was dented. After Rajiv Gandhi succeeded his assassinated mother as party leader and prime minister in 1984, he put India on the path toward reform and high-tech development to try to loosen the stranglehold of state controls and micromanagement of private enterprise.

India's long-entrenched bureaucracy—the heritage of the British Empire and the decades of socialism that followed it—frustrated Rajiv. He was new to the business of government. Like so many visionaries and dreamers, including his grandfather Nehru, he had no real conception of how the free market worked and how wealth was produced. But he was at least stumbling and striving in the right direction.[25]

Nevertheless, the 1980s were the crucial swing decade when China finally outstripped both India and the Soviet Union in sustained economic growth and when it built the capital and fiscal infrastructure to create a true global-scale industrial and financial colossus. Deng reversed the entire dynamic of Chinese history since 1840, indeed, since the time of the Ming. He transformed the long-term strategic dynamic of China's relations with India as well.

Through the late 1980s and thereafter, other events increased Indians' sense of geopolitical disquiet. First, Rajiv Gandhi sought to emulate his mother's success in playing nation builder and arbiter of conflicts in East Pakistan/Bangladesh by inserting India into the Sri Lankan peace process. He paid for his hubris with his life.[26]

With the approval of the Sri Lankan government, India sent troops to enforce a compromise peace agreement. But the separatist Tamil Tigers fiercely opposed the peace deal and resented the deployment of Indian troops on the island. A Tamil suicide bomber assassinated Rajiv in 1989, only five years after his mother had been shot dead in her own garden by her Sikh guards. The Nehru-Gandhi dynasty appeared to have come to a tragic end. India had lost two prime ministers, cut down by assassins drawn from India's fractious minority community. Was the great Indian experiment in pluralistic, consensual democracy breaking down? Was India falling apart?[27]

The loss of national confidence caused by the two assassinations came while China was far outpacing India in economic growth. This disparity fed the growing sense of doubt about how well the democratic system was working. Was democracy the wrong choice for generating economic growth and prosperity? Some Indians began to wonder whether the Chinese had the right idea after all. Would pragmatic authoritarian tyranny succeed where Mao's ideologically driven communism had failed?[28]

The Soviet collapse at the end of 1991 was another sobering development for Indian geostrategists. For two decades, Indians had rested securely under the protection of the Soviet Union. But the disintegration of the Soviet Union, combined with the economic rise of China, taught Indians that the balance of power in Asia had profoundly changed.

Rajiv Gandhi's successors showed much more energy and enterprise in reforming economic policies in the early 1990s than they did on diplomacy and grand strategy. Finance Minister Manmohan Singh initiated many of the free-market reforms that prompted steadily increasing growth in the high-tech private sector. Later coalition governments led by Prime Minister Vajpayee of the Bharatiya Janata Party to a great extent benefited from, and took unearned credit for, reforms that Singh and his Congress Party colleagues had initiated.

The Erosion of India's Influence

On the international front, however, the later Congress Party governments drifted through the 1990s much as Rajiv Gandhi had through the 1980s. India had quietly supported the Soviet invasion of Afghanistan in December 1979. The Muslim mujahideen who fought the Red Army to a standstill there were Hindu India's traditional enemies as much as they were Moscow's. China and the United States had both responded to the Soviet occupation of Afghanistan in December 1979 by funneling aid to the Muslim guerrillas through Pakistan. That proved to be highly advantageous for Pakistan's longtime ally China. And while it eventually backfired catastrophically on the United States, the short-term effect would result in the end of the Soviet Union.

The Afghan war had ominous developments for India, too. In the two decades after the Soviet invasion of Afghanistan, Pakistan became a very different and far more dangerous nation from India's point of view. It had made steady progress toward the development of nuclear weapons. Pakistan's main intelligence service, the Inter-Services Intelligence agency, became the beneficiary of hundreds of millions of dollars in covert U.S. and U.S.-approved Saudi aid flowing through Pakistan to finance the mujahideen. The ISI became a secret state-within-a-state. Its leaders developed far more extreme and potentially anti-Western sentiments than the regular Pakistani army, with its proud British-inherited traditions. The inner soul of Pakistan's military was moving from the cricket pitch to the madrassah. All that augured ill for neighboring India in the long term.[29]

India never sought to break out of its alliance with post-Soviet Russia. Relations were consistently warm into the 21st century. Russia remained the natural mainland Asian counterweight to rising China. However, Russia on its own was no longer enough. Indian policymakers started to consider seeking better ties with the United States.

Anti-American attitudes within the Congress Party remained strong. However, no Congress leader of the 1990s embraced anti-American sentiments with the same fervor that Indira and Rajiv Gandhi had. And a new party was finally rising to challenge the old Congress orthodoxies on foreign as well as domestic policy. When Vajpayee and the BJP took office in 1998 for an extended season in power, they were only too happy to embrace the United States and other surprising new partners as well.

Vajpayee and his defense minister, George Fernandes, took the geopolitical challenge of China far more seriously than Indian leaders had since the days of Shastri in the mid-1960s.[30] In its newly defiant, post–Tiananmen Square posture under Deng's successor President Jiang Zemin, China was a far more confident and assertive power. In the days of China's so-called Third Generation leadership, the caution imposed by old Soviet threats and the humiliation at the hands of the Vietnamese in 1979 slowly but steadily receded into the mists of the past.

This new China was not afraid to even confront its old strategic ally, the United States. It rattled rockets over the Taiwan Strait in 1996. It aggressively sought to extend its influence in Southeast Asia.[31] Beijing stepped up its relations with Thailand and Burma, now called Myanmar. That greatly alarmed Indian strategic planners. Under Fernandes, Indian geostrategists and defense planners started to talk about the dangers of encirclement by China in the same way that German strategists before World War I had railed against encirclement by France, Russia, and Britain.[32] One allegation often aired in the South Asian press was that China had started, or was preparing, to build naval facilities in the Coco or Andaman Islands. India's naval chief of staff declared in October 2005 that such Chinese installations did not exist, but the rumors persisted.[33]

Sino-American Strains

The Clinton administration had had its share of headaches with China, though it never gave up the hope that warm relations could somehow be revived. Clinton's commitment to free trade, keen economic intellect, and vast political skill had prepared him well to reach out to Chinese leaders. However, he was unable to mount a major and sustained courtship of China. For example, the Chinese were furious about the widespread popular support for the Dalai Lama and his exiled Tibetan leadership in America, but influential groups on both the right and left of the political spectrum limited Clinton's options. Human rights activists wanted to pressure Beijing concerning the future of Tibet. Others called for religious freedom, especially for Christians in China. Domestic politics also accounted for Clinton's unwillingness to support Beijing's Three Gorges Dam project. The Chinese saw the project as essential for meeting their electrical power needs and interpreted the widespread criticism by American environmentalists as simultaneously hypocritical and part of a diabolical plot to slow China's growth and keep her weak. In general, therefore, coming to terms with Jiang and the Chinese would have involved grasping too many thorny issues that Clinton preferred to leave undisturbed, and it seems unlikely that Clinton, had he chosen to confront the domestic political pressures, could have improved Sino-U.S. relations.

The challenges on the Chinese side were equally formidable. Chinese leaders recalled the great Tiananmen demonstrations with horror. They recalled how quickly Gorbachev's democratizing and free media experiments in the Soviet Union had been followed by the disintegration of that vast state. They were determined to prevent a similar breakdown in China. Nicholas Kristof and Sheryl Wudunn explain that Deng "feared for his country as much as he feared for his power base. Deng grew up in a China torn apart by warlords and foreign invaders, and he had lived through famines, civil war, and attacks by marauding guards in the Cultural Revolution. By some accounts, his father was beheaded by bandits in 1941. All this bred in him a primal fear of chaos."[34]

Thus, many factors prevented Clinton or Deng from moving boldly to renew close strategic ties. Far broader changes in the relationship would occur after Clinton left office. In January 2001, a new administration took over in Washington, far different not just from Clinton and his internationalist Democrats but also from the cautious old Republican realist-internationalists that had dominated previous GOP administrations.

Ambitious and bold neoconservatives who enjoyed the support of Vice President Dick Cheney and Defense Secretary Donald Rumsfeld influenced policymaking in George W. Bush's administration. At first, the Bush team appeared prepared for confrontation with China. Led by Deputy Defense Secretary Paul Wolfowitz in the Pentagon, they were eager to embrace democratic India as America's new strategic partner in Asia.[35] But just as Robert McNamara and his acolytes missed the obvious evidence that the Soviets and the Chinese were already far apart by the 1960s, Wolfowitz and his allies failed to see that China and India were disinclined to confrontation with each other.

China's priorities in fact were the exact opposite of what they had been in the lead-up to the 1962 India-China War. In 1962, Mao had taken advantage of an easing of tensions over Taiwan with the United States to move his heavy artillery eastward in order to teach India a lesson in the Himalayas. But in the early 21st century, Taiwan was at the center of China's preoccupations and looked certain to stay there. Since taking power in the spring of 2000, Taiwanese President Chen Shui-bian had steadily led his island of 23 million people in the direction of de jure as well as de facto independence from the mainland. An increasingly confident and nationalistic Beijing leadership repeatedly made clear they would never tolerate this, and they backed up their threats with a substantial military buildup.[36] Hoping to deter U.S. aircraft carrier battle groups from operating in the waters around Taiwan, China deployed close to a thousand short-range ballistic missiles and medium-range ballistic missiles aimed at Taiwan.[37]

It was no coincidence that while this buildup was going on, Beijing's attitude toward India markedly improved. China also became a noticeably more affable and cooperative partner in the annual regional forum of the Association of South East Asian Nations. It took China just 10 years to establish generally warm relations with the nations of ASEAN after a long period of tension; from 1990 to 2004, China's trade with ASEAN countries rose by an average of 20 percent annually.[38]

In 2002, to the initial surprise and great relief of the ASEAN member nations, Beijing started taking a much more friendly and cooperative tone on the hot-button dispute over control of the Spratly Islands. These tiny islands hold a strategic position in the South China Sea and are surrounded by an oil-rich seabed that has made them a bone of contention between China and several ASEAN countries. But in a remarkable diplomatic change of course, Beijing accepted a multilateral approach to address that issue.[39] It seemed that the Chinese were clearing the decks to be able to concentrate on Taiwan, the only remaining area of traditional Chinese territory not yet reclaimed from what the Chinese call "the Century of Humiliation" from 1842 to 1949.

The Sino-Indian Thaw

New Delhi had plenty of reasons of its own to want better relations with Beijing. That was as true under Vajpayee and the BJP as it was under Congress-led governments. For all his tough talk, Vajpayee was an old-fashioned parliamentarian who led a coalition government. He never contemplated abandoning India's traditional alliance with Russia even while he successfully improved relations with Washington. He had even sought improved relations with Pakistan under its last civilian government, and he may have believed that by improving relations with China, he could get Beijing to restrain Pakistan.[40] He visibly basked in every small gesture from Beijing, hinting at better relations and seeking to increase the low volume of trade between the two nations. Although Fernandes loudly and often proclaimed the need to recognize China's long-term hostility to India, Vajpayee only smiled and refused to act on his defense minister's ominous warnings.[41]

Relations between Delhi and Beijing became even warmer when Congress regained control of the Union government after its surprise victory in the 2004 elections. The new government under Prime Minister Manmohan Singh rapidly revived an old initiative of Rajiv

Gandhi's from the 1980s. Singh surprised Beijing and Islamabad by unilaterally suggesting that India, Pakistan, and China should harmonize their nuclear strike doctrines. The initiative went nowhere at first. Pakistan and China were obviously reluctant to put these cards on the table with India. But Singh's overture served notice that the new Indian government would not passively play a role as Washington's puppet. The new Congress government was not about to cut off its highly useful ties to Washington, but it was not prepared to confront China at America's bidding either.

The Bush administration should have learned this a year earlier when it asked Vajpayee to provide Indian troops to join its "coalition of the willing" in Iraq. Vajpayee appeared at first to entertain the request, but there was strong opposition to it from the Congress Party. Senior army officers were divided. Vajpayee finally decided against the idea.[42]

However, even before the Congress Party regained power in 2004, there were clear indications that India was not anxious to make a bitter enemy of China. For example, in June 2003, Indian Prime Minister Vajpayee traveled to China. During this visit, Beijing offered to recognize Sikkim in the Himalayas as part of India, something that it had not done before. Soon after, the two countries also agreed to elevate discussions on their remaining differences over the border in the Himalayas to the political level and agreed on "guidelines and principles" to help finally resolve the dispute.[43]

Even Defense Minister Fernandes, the Vajpayee government's China-basher-in-chief, dramatically changed course. In a February 2004 speech, Fernandes admitted that in the past, "I had qualified China as a 'potential threat number one.'" But, he continued: "There has been a very positive tenor in the Sino-Indian relationship. . . . The future prospects, in short, are promising and both countries have reiterated this determination (to improve bilateral relations) at the highest political level on both sides."[44]

Commenting on Fernandes's remarkable change of mind, analyst C. Raja Mohan noted: "The dramatic expansion of bilateral trade and economic cooperation in the first years of the millennium has created a different template for bilateral relations. From $200 million in the early 1990s, bilateral Sino-Indian trade shot up to $5 billion in 2002 and touched $7.5 billion (in 2003). It is expected to touch $10 billion (in 2004)." But this was just the beginning; Fernandes in his lecture foresaw a rapid increase in the volume of trade to $20 billion a year.[45]

Then he went even further. He acknowledged that India, like China, was consolidating its "bilateral relations with the United States, the European Union, Russia, and Japan," but then added, "none of these relationships are to be construed as zero sum." In other words, as Mohan noted, "India will neither join the U.S. to contain China nor align with Beijing in a bloc against Washington."[46]

Fernandes had closed his remarks, "We must ensure that whatever be [sic] the nature of the military profile that China and India acquire in the near future, this must be managed in such a way that there is no mistrust or needless anxiety." He added, "Individually and together, such capability must be seen as contributing to regional and global stability." Mohan commented with considerable under-statement, "It is not often that India has said that Chinese military strength could be a stabilizing force in the region." And that wasn't just one analyst's interpretation. As if to underscore the point that India was taking a more benign view of China's growing military power, Fernandes even initiated a series of joint naval exercises with China following Vajpayee's Beijing visit.[47] The lessons for U.S. policymakers to take from Fernandes's comments are clear. First, when even one of the previously most hawkish figures toward China at the highest level of the Indian government expresses his commit-ment to long-term peaceful coexistence with China, that position needs to be taken very seriously in Washington. Second, India's strategy of avoiding confrontation with China—and even cooperat-ing with her wherever possible—is embraced by both the nationalist BJP and Congress–United Progressive Alliance.

To be sure, there were still problems in the Beijing-Delhi relation-ship. For example, Fernandes acknowledged what India still regarded as its "deficit of trust" with China over Beijing's relationship with Pakistan. But if this remarkable change could occur even under the Hindu-nationalist—and traditionally anti-Chinese—BJP, how much more could be expected when the traditionally pro-Chinese Congress Party returned to power? And sure enough, after it took power in 2004, the new government of Manmohan Singh accelerated the warming of relations and strategic dialogue with Beijing that began under his BJP predecessor.

Mohan noted that Prime Minister Manmohan Singh's new govern-ment had a "Nehruvian political color." The times could now prove far more favorable, Mohan suggested, "for the realization of Jawaharlal Nehru's vision of Asia as 'the area of peace.' . . . Today, regional integration and great power harmony provide India a positive setting to pursue Nehru's ideas on Asian unity and an 'Eastern Federation.'"[48]

Such a reversion to the hazy nonaligned dreams of Bandung could be a recipe for yet another rude awakening for India on the lines of the 1962 war, or even worse. But there is no doubt that the idea of India joining China to lead a pan-Asian bloc still has some traction in the Congress Party political establishment. U.S. policymakers, therefore, need to recognize that India remains nonaligned and is determined to retain its strategic alliance with Russia as it seeks, at the very least, coexistence with China.

The Asian Dimension

The momentum toward a longer-lasting Indian-Chinese rapprochement found support in unexpected places. Mohan noted that Japan's ambassador to India, Yasukuni Enoki, had even suggested at a New Delhi press conference a few weeks earlier "the development of a strategic triangle among India, China and Japan."[49]

Although the Indian government responded to Enoki's comments with, in Mohan's words, "a big yawn," no one could really ignore the importance of deepening relations between India, China, and Japan. China had replaced the United States as Japan's largest export market. Greater China, meanwhile, including Taiwan and Hong Kong, had become India's third-largest trading partner behind only the United States and the European Union.[50]

For its part, the Chinese government reacted favorably to Enoki's suggestion. The official *People's Daily* newspaper welcomed the Japanese ambassador's remarks, and the English-language *China Daily* ran a piece arguing the case for such a triangular relationship.[51] From China's point of view, when seen in the context of an anticipated showdown with the United States over Taiwan, promoting such a triangular axis in the short term made a great deal of sense. It would ensure that a safely neutral India was not tempted to take advantage of China's preoccupation with the United States to launch mischief of its own, whether seizing Himalayan border territory or encouraging some popular rising in Tibet.

The Indians had shown no signs of such revanchism, but the Chinese knew all too well how Mao had taken advantage of President Kennedy's preoccupation with Cuba to launch the 1962 war and humiliate India in what had previously been seen as an unimportant theater.

Also, the more talk there was about a trilateral axis, the more Japanese leaders might be tempted to loosen their own ties with Washington in order to stay out of the line of fire if the confrontations over Taiwan should ever lead to a war between the United States and China.

Feng Zhaokui of the Japan Research Institute of the Chinese Academy of Social Sciences argued that Enoki's proposed triangle was no pipedream. By 2004, India, China, and Japan together already accounted for 20 percent of the world's total gross domestic product. Precisely because they were at different levels of economic development, they had the potential to cooperate constructively rather than act as rivals. Japan's population is aging, and ultimately shrinking. As a result of rising prosperity, which tends to reduce birth rates, combined with draconian birth control laws from the 1970s, China is projected to begin growing older in the next decade. Therefore, by 2020, India may well have the largest working and consuming population in the world.[52]

Feng, an influential Chinese expert on Japan whose articles are published in the official *People's Daily*, further argued that India, China, and Japan, as major importers of oil and gas, could begin to cooperate on energy security. Feng noted that "China-India naval maneuver[s] were an indication that the two countries [did] not see each other as an imminent threat," and he anticipated that the two could work together in "protecting sea-lanes, guarding the maritime chokepoints, combating international terrorism and checking piracy on the high seas."[53]

Such a rosy vision still appears far off, but Feng hinted at why China was so eager to dangle this particularly enticing carrot before the eyes of policymakers in Tokyo and New Delhi: "No party should subordinate itself to acting as a chessman for a non-Asian superpower to contain others." In other words, Feng continued, "Neither India nor Japan will dance to your tune in order to contain us, Mr. Wolfowitz."[54]

Issues in Common

One does not have to posit the rapid creation of some supersized Asian axis to see why China and India may work together far more harmoniously than some Washington armchair strategists imagine possible, which is why some scholars are taking Sino-Indian trade and warming diplomatic ties seriously.[55]

India and China are both rising, confident nations determined to maintain their sovereignty. Both are mindful of long historical nightmares, whether colonial or anarchic. Both nations are determined to uphold their sovereignty against the many globalizing and extragovernmental forces that did so much to undermine the viability of other nation-states in the closing decades of the 20th century.

The two countries have other shared interests. First, they both oppose any attempt by the Untied States to use the Kosovo precedent to intervene in the internal affairs of nations accused of persecuting minority populations. They also have an interest in preventing nongovernmental organizations, especially those backed by the United States, from pursuing human rights agendas that infringe on their sovereignty.[56]

The Kosovo precedent, in particular, caused equal alarm in New Delhi and Beijing. India remains determined to retain control of Kashmir. It has also faced violent guerrilla movements over the past two decades from the Tamil Tigers who assassinated one prime minister; the Sikhs, who assassinated another one; and the Maoists, who are a spreading threat in northeastern India. China remains on guard against movements to restore Tibet's independence and to radicalize the Muslims of Xinjiang.[57]

Indian analysts Surjit Mansingh and C. V. Ranganathan have observed that China and India share an

> attachment to traditional concepts of absolute sovereignty ... especially on matters relating to territory and security. Neither is amenable to external interference on military and arms-related matters; both oppose external inspections and interventions elsewhere, especially if undertaken without benefit of [United Nations] validation. Their resentment of Western intrusiveness and hypocrisy, as on the subject of linking trade issues to social causes, is loud and insistent.... Both are highly defensive against the West on the issue of human rights.[58]

The implications for policymakers in Washington are profound. The era of economic globalization has fostered nationalist, protectionist, and potentially xenophobic responses in both China and India.[59] Those attitudes appear to have played a significant role in persuading large numbers of voters from the rural villages to support Congress and its allies in the 2004 Indian general election. In China, given the extreme nationalist reactions in the heartland experienced over the past 150 years, the responses to globalization could prove to be considerably more dramatic.

India and China share strikingly similar positions toward the World Trade Organization on issues of labor and environmental standards. Environmental issues also seem to draw the two giants closer together. Both nations remain heavily dependent on coal for electrical power generation, and both are building still more coal-fired power-generating plants. That poses a potentially serious problem for neighboring states, notably Bangladesh and Nepal. But it poses challenges on a global scale as well. The two nations are committed to continued industrialization and have a shared interest in resisting any effort to impose limits on carbon dioxide (CO_2) emissions, as the Kyoto Protocols would have done. Any serious international effort to control global CO_2 emissions, however, must include India and China. Between them, as of 2005, they accounted for 23 percent of the world's energy-related CO_2 emissions into the atmosphere, and their share of total output was projected to increase dramatically in coming decades.[60]

The Cautious Giants

The bottom line is that India and China both face major security challenges in their own backyards over the next few years, and neither great nation appears disposed to alienating the other. They both have more pressing concerns. For India, the immediate strategic threat is from its nuclear-armed next-door neighbor, Pakistan. Relations between these traditional enemies are always tense, and that tension is exacerbated by the continuing Muslim guerrilla insurrection in Indian-controlled Kashmir.

But even if the Kashmir dispute could be amicably settled between Islamabad and New Delhi, the rise of Islamist extremism in Pakistan has thrown that country's long-term stability into question. As long as that continues to be the case, India will continue to seek good relations with China for two reasons. First, India wants to use Beijing's influence to restrain Islamabad. Second, as long as India has its hands full with Pakistan, Indian leaders will not want to run the risk of confrontation along a second front with China.

China's overriding strategic concern is also clear: blocking any drive to establish Taiwan as a permanently independent sovereign nation and eventually reintegrating Taiwan into the People's Republic. The United States' continuing desire to protect Taiwan stands in the way of that goal. But the huge investment China has made in building up its missile forces in the Taiwan Strait makes it clear that China's leaders believe that someday they may have to challenge American power in a limited conventional war around Taiwan.

However, no one has been able to figure out a way to keep any Sino-American war over Taiwan "limited." Unlike the Korean and Vietnam conflicts, it would be fought on Chinese territory and involve direct U.S. attacks on the Chinese homeland, which the Chinese have promised would be answered in kind. It is, therefore, fortuitous for both the Chinese and Americans that Taiwanese President Ma Ying-jeou, who succeeded President Chen in May 2008, pledged to launch negotiations to create a process for resolving the question of Taiwan's relationship to the rest of China.

Nevertheless, as long as the scenario of a full-scale conflict with the United States over Taiwan remains a possibility, China will continue to give priority to avoiding any significant conflict with India. Chinese leaders probably also see warm relations with New Delhi as a necessary precaution against any Indian temptation to attack or threaten Pakistan, for example, if and when China is preoccupied with the United States over Taiwan. (The key point here is not that Indian policymakers may seriously entertain such ideas: There is no evidence that they do. It is that Chinese policymakers may attribute these ideas to them.)

The strategic environment in the early 21st century is therefore nearly the exact opposite of what it was at the time of the India-China War of 1962. Then, China's leader Mao Zedong was able to turn his back on Taiwan and concentrate his forces at the other end of China, when they attacked India from Tibet. He took advantage of the sudden preoccupation of the United States with the Cuban missile crisis to launch his strike. Today, China has been working hard to resolve its remaining Himalayan border disputes with India in order to free up its forces to concentrate on Taiwan. Might they act while the United States is distracted, say, by a military campaign against Iran? The possibility cannot be ruled out.[61]

4. The United States and Engagement with India

As noted in the introduction, U.S. policymakers from both major parties neglected engagement with India to a remarkable degree throughout the second half of the 20th century. The contrast with China could not have been more striking—or revealing. There, enterprising Yankee traders had pushed hard for generations to open a door into China for American goods. At the beginning of the 20th century, Secretary of State John Hay was obsessed with the issue. Pearl Buck and Henry Luce led a China Lobby that had a huge effect on American public opinion in the 1930s and 1940s. After World War II, the China Lobby, backed by conservative Republicans, urged unlimited support for Jiang Jieshi against Mao Zedong. This policy could have propelled the United States into a major war in the heart of Asia that U.S. conventional forces could not hope to win. Policymakers in the Truman administration wisely rejected such a course, but the backlash from the "loss of China" to communism in 1949 transformed U.S. domestic politics and facilitated the rise of Sen. Joseph McCarthy.

On the other hand, when India, still a stable democracy, embraced the Soviet Union as its main strategic ally in the mid-1960s, America did not even bat an eye.[1] Yet the Soviet-Indian alliance proved to be one of the most enduring and significant great-power relationships of the last third of the 20th century. Indeed, that alliance has recently been renewed, and it remains one of the few lasting strategic verities of Asia. The alliance appears unaffected by Russia's growing partnership with China and the United States' engagement with India.

Americans were not totally unaware of India, of course. But until the very end of the 20th century, they saw it only through a series of pacifist stereotypes. Mahatma Gandhi's popular nonviolent movement, popularized by *Time* and *Life* magazines in the 1920s and 1930s, inspired those stereotypes. Decades later, the huge success of the Oscar-winning movie *Gandhi* (1982) reinforced the pacifist view in the American imagination.

Generations of U.S. policymakers were blind to the vital role of the Indian Army in extending the British Empire across Asia from the Persian Gulf to Beijing. Also invisible was the part the Indian Army had played in World War I and in later pacifying Iraq.[2] Likewise, the American public was almost totally ignorant of the role that the British-controlled Indian Army played in the North African, Italian, and Burmese campaigns of World War II.[3]

Nor did American policymakers note at the time, or remember later, what the Indian Army did to restore order from the chaos following independence in 1947. In fact, independent India inherited from the British, and maintained, one of the three largest armies on the Asian continent, along with the Soviet Red Army and the Chinese Communist People's Liberation Army. (Indeed, the Indian Army had decisively defeated a large Japanese field army in Burma in 1944, something neither Jiang Jieshi's Kuomintang Chinese nationalist armies nor Mao's Red Army ever did.) India's military prowess automatically made it a huge player in southern Asia from the moment of its independence. But from the American perspective, it was the sweet, pacifist Gandhi image that stuck.

President Franklin Roosevelt had been a great admirer of Gandhi, and he supported the idea of ending the great colonial empires, especially in Asia.[4] Had he lived, FDR almost certainly would have supported Britain's postwar Labour government in its bid to quit India as quickly as possible. As early as 1942, he was infuriating Winston Churchill by urging him to speed up plans to give India total independence—a policy that Churchill loathed and rejected.[5]

At the root of the American misconception of independent India was the fact that India's real power in the world had been hidden under the British "Union Jack" for hundreds of years. Far from erasing these inaccurate and condescending perceptions, the history of independent India for decades served only to reinforce them. The pattern was set early. Dean Acheson, President Truman's last and longest serving secretary of state, was an ardent Anglophile, and his strategic judgment was clouded by racism.[6] He had critically underestimated the Japanese in 1941 as Franklin Roosevelt's assistant secretary of state for economic affairs when he championed an economic embargo, including on crucial oil exports, against Japan.[7] It

106

is clear that Acheson never dreamed the Japanese army and navy would prove capable of sweeping across East Asia and the Pacific as they in fact did.[8] As secretary of state, Acheson focused first on Europe and then, by force of circumstance, on communist China and the Korean War. He never bothered to give much, if any, thought, to India.

Acheson's blindness toward India provides a salutary lesson to U.S. policymakers in the 21st century. When dealing with a nation of such huge population and strategic influence as India, it is essential to maintain serious and cordial bilateral relations even when the nation in question resolutely refuses to join any coherent U.S.-led global bloc of powers.

Nor was the Acheson era the only missed opportunity to put U.S.-Indian relations on a more secure and intimate footing. John F. Kennedy's presidency was, as we have seen, a frustratingly brief window of opportunity for serious and constructive engagement between the two powers. The warm personal relationship and mutual respect between Kennedy and Nehru should serve as a positive example to President Barack Obama and Secretary of State Hillary Clinton of how personal ties between leaders can open up strategic and diplomatic opportunities that had previously not been thought possible.

The Kennedy experience should also teach Obama administration policymakers the value of heeding the advice and experience of senior U.S. officials and diplomats with records of achievement from previous administrations. For example, John Kenneth Galbraith, Kennedy's ambassador to India, clearly understood how a major Western nation waging a land war in Vietnam would alarm India by reviving fears of neocolonialism less than two decades after the country had won its freedom. Here again, an understanding of the historical experience that shaped the outlook of leaders in other nations is essential to winning their trust and cooperation today.

The Legacy of Vietnam

Kennedy's successor, Lyndon Baines Johnson, did not benefit from Galbraith's advice.[9] Meanwhile, Nehru had died in 1964, though it is doubtful that Johnson would have given him the same respect as Kennedy had he lived. Once Johnson succeeded Kennedy, the die was cast for a more interventionist U.S. policy in Southeast Asia.

Within a few years, Johnson committed hundreds of thousands of American troops to defend South Vietnam.

The decision was taken with remarkably little consideration of the traditional relationships and rivalries in Southeast Asia. For example, the long-standing, bitter competition between the Vietnamese and Thai peoples for supremacy over the contiguous land area of Southeast Asia should have factored into American decisionmaking. But at the time of the Vietnam War, most Americans saw Thailand as just another domino. There was, it seems, no serious discussion or even awareness in the Kennedy, Johnson, or later Nixon administrations that historic rivalries in the region might provide an effective barrier to the further spread of Ho Chi Minh's communist ideology. Nor has the almost complete failure of Vietnamese communism to take root in Thailand since the fall of South Vietnam received sufficient attention from U.S. policymakers and scholars.[10]

The Indians knew better. They were horrified by the foolish American leap into South Vietnam. The U.S. involvement reminded the Indians all too acutely of how recently they had thrown off their own British colonial masters. The struggle for independence against a major Western colonial power was still a recent, vivid memory for the Indian leaders who succeeded Nehru. It was disquieting to them to see the United States establish what appeared to be a long-term presence in another Asian nation.

The fall of President Sukarno of Indonesia and his replacement by President Suharto in 1967 also alarmed Congress Party leaders and policymakers in New Delhi. They believed that the Central Intelligence Agency was heavily involved in the coup that moved Indonesia, the most populous Muslim nation in the world and the strategic giant of Southeast Asia, from the Non-Aligned Movement into the pro-American camp.[11] The transformation was accompanied by a ruthless purge of the Indonesian Communist Party, which devolved into a bloody massacre of ethnic Chinese on the island of Java. The exact death toll is unknown. Estimates run at half a million or more.[12] These events in Indonesia had their effect on the U.S.-Indian relationship. Nehru and Sukarno had been close allies in the Non-Aligned Movement. The fall of Sukarno and the terrible bloodbath that followed fed the fears toward U.S. policies throughout Asia.

As U.S. troop numbers in South Vietnam grew, and as Indonesia fell under the control of the pro-American Suharto, the Indians turned not to Washington but to Moscow as their protector and strategic counterweight to China. The process began not long after new leadership emerged in Moscow in October 1964, with the bloodless coup that toppled Khrushchev. He was replaced by Communist Party General Secretary, later President, Leonid Brezhnev and by Premier Alexei Kosygin. The new Soviet leaders moved quickly to establish strong strategic ties with India. Kosygin endorsed the historic Tashkent Declaration that ended the brief 1965 war between India and Pakistan. The declaration was followed by serious diplomatic discussions between Moscow and New Delhi that brought quick results. In 1966, the two nations signed a security treaty. It remains in effect, in an updated version, more than 40 years later.[13]

The new strategic partnership between India and the Soviet Union gave New Delhi a clearly defined role in the world. The ties of the British-led commonwealth became less significant to Indian leaders. Although Nehru's daughter, Indira Gandhi, carefully avoided serious conflict with the United States, Britain, or any other major Western nation after she became prime minister in 1965, Indian leaders and diplomats often criticized U.S. policies in South Vietnam. Mrs. Gandhi herself regularly expressed sympathy for anti-colonial guerrilla movements around the world. She showed special favor to Palestine Liberation Organization Chairman Yasser Arafat.[14] However, India ultimately paid a steep price for Mrs. Gandhi's anti-colonialist rhetoric. India's relations with Washington remained extremely poor for the next quarter century.[15]

Ill will toward India united both major political parties in the United States. First, Mrs. Gandhi's anti-colonial policies and her criticism of U.S. support for South Vietnam angered Lyndon Johnson and his fellow liberal Democrats. Similarly, they ensured the enmity of the Republican president Richard M. Nixon and his national security adviser Henry Kissinger when they took control of U.S. policy in 1969.

Nixon and Kissinger demanded active diplomatic support for their policies in South Vietnam from their allies—support Indian leaders would not give. In any case, Nixon and Kissinger ignored India and were obsessed with recruiting China into an anti-Soviet alliance. The whole of their global diplomacy during Nixon's first term of office was focused on courting China, and Pakistan—China's natural ally and counterweight against India—was the obvious bridge between Washington and Beijing.[16]

Nixon and Kissinger played the global chessboard of nations as a zero-sum game cast in Manichaean black and white. Within this "with us or against us" mentality, Muslim Pakistan—whose ruling circles and, especially, its powerful, quasi-political military elite were still cast in their attractive veneer of British culture—became one of the good guys. Their historic enemy India, clearly socialistic, moralistic, and ever carping at the United Nations about America's involvement in Vietnam, while securely allied to the Soviet Union, became one of Nixon and Kissinger's enemies.

India's position was further compromised by China's rise. In American eyes, China appeared compliant and ready to learn American ways, even though this assessment would prove to be too optimistic. For Washington policymakers, letting India slip into the Soviet camp in the mid-1960s had not affected the global balance of power. But winning China over to the U.S. camp in 1972 was an historic achievement. A Soviet Union bounded by independent, assertive, and hostile China on its east and a U.S.-backed North Atlantic Treaty Organization alliance on its west was suddenly less terrifying. The red juggernaut that had once seemed unstoppable had been contained. China was essential to that equation. India was not.

It was a striking comment on the primacy of great power realpolitik thinking in both Moscow and Washington that the Soviet Union never tried to destabilize democratic India with its free elections, freedom of the press, and independent judiciary. It did not mind India remaining democratic so long as it was also a reliable ally. U.S. policymakers, Republican and Democrat, were happy to court China at the same time, even though it remained totalitarian and communist.

Decades of Differences

Through the 1970s, American policymakers remained blind to a great geopolitical irony. The democratic India they dismissed as ineffectual proved itself to be a more formidable military power than ever. It wiped the floor with Pakistan during their 1971 war, forcing Pakistan to leave its eastern region, which became the independent nation of Bangladesh.[17] In a military campaign lasting only a few weeks, Indian forces achieved a lasting geopolitical change on the map of Asia. Even with Soviet support, it took Ho Chi Minh's

Vietnamese communists 20 years of relentless struggle to accomplish the far more modest goal of unifying Vietnam. Yet few, if any, American policymakers saw India's victory as worthy of note, let alone emulation.

Through the 1960s and 1970s, Indian policymakers seemed equally uninterested in drawing closer to the United States. Prime Minister Lal Bahadur Shastri had set the ball rolling toward the creation of the Soviet-Indian alliance during his brief premiership following Nehru's death in the mid-1960s. But it was Nehru's own beloved daughter and confidante, Indira Gandhi, who maintained the alliance with Moscow and the estrangement with Washington for almost two decades.

Mrs. Gandhi was simultaneously a study in continuity and contrasts from her legendary father. She was, as he had been, a graduate of Oxford University. But she had not experienced, as he had, decades of persecution by British colonial authorities. And while she embraced the basic political and social beliefs and foreign policy strategies of her father, she had a very different personality.[18]

Where he was charming and diplomatic, she was confident, forceful, and abrasive. Where he saw America and India as fellow great democracies sharing the best of the British political heritage, she saw the United States as an arrogant capitalist-imperialist oppressor. Nehru was sympathetic to the young state of Israel as a fellow young democracy that had snatched its freedom from the jaws of British imperialism. He also saw Israel's development programs in the Negev Desert as holding useful lessons for India. By contrast, Mrs. Gandhi embraced Yasser Arafat and his Palestine Liberation Organization, seeing Israel as the tormenter of the Palestinians and as America's most loyal and lethal ally. Not coincidentally, energy-starved India increasingly needed to stay in the good graces of the major oil-producing states, including Iraq and Iran, who were Israel's and America's enemies.[19]

Therefore, even if American presidents in the 1970s and 1980s had wanted to seriously engage India, they might well have found no takers in New Delhi. This remained the case after Mrs. Gandhi was assassinated in 1984. Rajiv Gandhi, her son and successor, was even more hostile to U.S. ideology and policy than his mother had been.[20] Except for a short Democratic interlude under President Jimmy Carter when U.S.-Indian relations warmed briefly, none of the four Republican presidents from Nixon through George H. W. Bush seriously engaged India.[21]

Beginning in late 1979, America had another reason to embrace Pakistan at India's expense: Pakistan became a crucial conduit through which the United States funneled aid to the mujahideen, the Islamic and tribally based guerrillas fighting the Soviet Red Army in Afghanistan.

The Soviet invasion of Afghanistan in December 1979 rapidly proved to be at least as big a strategic misjudgment for Moscow as the U.S. charge into the paddies of the Mekong Delta 15 years before had been for Washington. Reagan and his advisers were quick to take advantage of the Soviet error. They set up Central Intelligence Agency–run funding and supply lines through Pakistan. Throughout the 1980s, billions of U.S. "black budget" dollars (clandestine funding that did not appear on any financial reports presented to the U.S. Congress and the American people) flowed into and through Pakistan. The immediate benefits of this arrangement were clear to Pakistan's military strongman at the time, President Mohammad Zia-ul-Haq. India could not and would not dare to provoke a war with Pakistan so long as it was protected by the great might of the United States.[22]

During the Reagan and first Bush presidencies, it was easy for U.S. policymakers to ignore India entirely. Rajiv Gandhi maintained his mother's loyally pro-Russian stance and continued her policy of close ties with Iran and Iraq. The Indian economy remained in the doldrums and was therefore insignificant to the United States.

In American popular culture, India remained through the 1980s and even into the 1990s, the land of maharishis and yoga—a place for stoned hippies to wander around, and for sensible conservatives to ignore. And so through most of the 1990s, policymakers in Washington continued to ignore India. Washington is routinely obsessed by nations that should rationally be dismissed as tiny and obscure— think of the endless Irish troubles or the Israeli-Palestinian strife— while there are major nations with large populations and vast potential wealth, such as Brazil and Nigeria, that receive far less attention.

Yet under the radar screens of the American media and the main Washington think tanks, epochal changes were taking place in Delhi. During P. V. Narasimha Rao's premiership from 1992 to 1997, a huge high-tech sector rapidly grew up in southern India around the cities of Hyderabad and Bangalore.[23] India was also training large numbers of highly educated professionals who took advantage of the opportunities offered by the booming global economy of the 1990s to emigrate to the United States. Middle-class, enterprising, well-educated, and alive to the opportunities of the high-tech world, these overseas Indians were identified by Joel Kotkin in his book *Tribes* along with the overseas Chinese, the overseas British, and the Jews as among the most dynamic entrepreneurial quasi-tribal ethnic groups that were transforming the world's global economy.[24] Many of them became significant figures in California's Silicon Valley. In the closing months of his second term, President Bill Clinton decided to pay a state visit to India. Clinton's boldness toward India was so visionary that he could not bring his own colleagues with him. None of his senior cabinet members seemed to grasp what he was trying to do.[25]

Clinton's Initiative

Clinton came to believe that India's democracy could serve as a political role model for the nations of Asia—more positive from a U.S. perspective than China's authoritarian system. He had been interested in South Asia for decades. As a student at Yale University, Clinton had participated in the popular protest movement to free Bangladesh at the height of the Pakistani army's ferocious repression there. Many years later as president, he wanted to showcase Bangladesh as an example of successful democracy in the Muslim world. It certainly didn't hurt that large natural gas deposits discovered in the Bay of Bengal were a potentially attractive investment for U.S.-based energy corporations.[26]

Clinton wanted to be a practical idealist about third-world investment. Even as the so-called boy governor of Arkansas, he had tried to popularize and generate American support for the Bangladesh-based Grameen Bank, which opposed the huge quasi-socialist construction development projects so beloved of World Bank officials during the disastrous tenure of Robert McNamara. Clinton's enthusiasm for Grameen's strategy of spreading microloans around rural areas in third world nations helped build his credibility as an international statesman when he was seeking the presidency. And he was serious about it.[27]

Clinton was also passionate in his belief that the rising tide of the information technology (IT) revolution would lift all ships. He was anxious to ease immigration restrictions on Indian computer programmers and software engineers to come to the United States. Clinton had warm ties with Indian-American entrepreneurs. During his presidency, the Indian-American community, especially those living in California, became significant financial supporters of the Democratic Party. Critics in India initially worried that the emigration of skilled workers to the United States would boost the U.S. economy at India's expense. But by 2005, India was turning out so many IT professionals and software engineers that it had expertise to spare.[28]

Clinton was eager to develop U.S. economic ties with India, but on strategic issues he gave priority to trying to avert a nuclear arms race between India and Pakistan. His State Department team worked hard, but unsuccessfully, to persuade successive Indian governments to abandon their nuclear program. In fact, it was during Clinton's presidency that India stopped even giving lip service to nonproliferation policies, conducting its first nuclear weapons tests in 1998. But so long as U.S. policy toward India gave priority to preventing India from becoming a nuclear military power, no real strategic engagement between the two nations was possible. Clinton also wanted a far closer economic partnership with India, but Americans were not ready for that either, and Clinton could not persuade them. Even so, while Clinton's March 2000 state visit to India proved to be far stronger on symbolism than substance, it was also a huge success. Wherever he went, Clinton was greeted by large and enthusiastic crowds. Indian press and media coverage of his visit was rapturous.

But it was all for naught. The American leader was in the final months of his presidency and enjoyed only moderate support at home. He was not in a position to effect truly significant changes in the U.S.-Indian relationship. Not long after his visit, India quietly nailed down sweeping agreements on weapons purchases and nuclear development with its old great power ally Russia. In substantive terms, nothing had changed in the U.S.-Indian relationship, but in terms of mutual perception, a lot was beginning to.

Bush Seeks an Ally

Far broader changes were soon to follow. In January 2001, a new administration took over in Washington. George W. Bush's foreign and domestic policies were a dramatic departure from Clinton's. His policies were also very different from those of the cautious old Republican realist-internationalists who had dominated previous GOP administrations.

The new administration's national security policies were shaped by a bold and ambitious agenda to transform the map of Asia to America's liking. The last such opportunity had come in the early 1970s, when China emerged to balance Russia. In the early years of the 21st century, with the Soviet Union a fading memory, Bush's new national security team concluded that the United States needed a counterweight to China—and it saw India as the perfect nation to play that role. In particular, National Security Adviser, later Secretary of State, Condoleezza Rice was eager to include democratic India along with Russia and China as the major powers on which the United States should focus its engagement.[29] Another senior Bush administration official, Paul Wolfowitz, had long maintained that the containment of China in the first half of the 21st century might well be as difficult to achieve as the containment of imperial and then Nazi Germany in the first half of the 20th.[30] He asserted that China's gravitational pull would draw South Korea, Japan, Indonesia, Vietnam, and even Taiwan into its orbit—unless India and the United States built a strong working military relationship. Inherent in this argument was the belief that a strong U.S.-Indian alliance would attract other Asian nations that would seek the alliance's protection as the best guarantee of their continued freedom and security against China and other potential threats.

The cautious, pragmatic Republican foreign policymakers from Nixon through Ford, Reagan, and the first President Bush valued strategic balance and reliability among allies above any U.S. ideologi cal commitment to spreading democracy around the world. The new neoconservative ideologues, led by Wolfowitz, were a very different breed. They apparently believed, despite the evidence of World War I and many other conflicts before and since, that democracies rarely went to war with each other. This faith in so-called democratic peace theory led Bush policymakers to believe that democracies would naturally prove more loyal and lasting allies to the democratic United States than autocratic and authoritarian regimes.[31] President George W. Bush appeared the most committed member of his own administration to this view, and he made it the theme of his second inaugural address on January 20, 2005.[32]

115

In the Middle East, this neoconservative faith in the virtue of democracy propelled Bush policymakers toward their war to topple Iraqi President Saddam Hussein in March 2003. In South Asia, it led them to embrace the right wing–nationalist government of Prime Minister Atal Bihari Vajpayee.

The precipitating event that may have served to deepen U.S.-Indian relations during the Bush administration was the terrorist attacks on September 11, 2001, when the two countries intensified their intelligence-sharing and military cooperation. But U.S. officials were careful to maintain close ties with Pakistan, the traditional U.S. ally in the region. They needed Pakistan's support after 9/11 to project their power into neighboring Afghanistan and to topple the Taliban regime that had supported Osama bin Laden and al Qaeda. Bush administration officials were also worried about what would happen to Pakistan's nuclear arsenal if Pakistani President Gen. Pervez Musharraf's regime collapsed. All these issues served to constrain the Bush administration and make it cautious in dealing with Islamabad. They shared India's concerns about what was happening in Pakistan, but they were unwilling to cut ties with Musharraf.

Bush strategists also believed that a relationship with India, similar to the one Nixon and Kissinger forged with China, would do more to avert either conventional or nuclear war on the subcontinent than would the pious exhortations of arms-control treaties. An India that would look on Washington as its protector against China, the thinking went, would be far more likely to heed American calls for restraint in the development of nuclear weapons. In Pakistan, too, where U.S. influence had been declining, the Bush administration believed that American calls for compromise would have more impact if U.S. support for Islamabad against Delhi could no longer be taken for granted.

To the Pentagon planners pushing strategic dialogue with the Indian government after January 2001, India appeared to share their interest in secure oil supplies and in preventing radical Islamists from amassing too much power in South and Central Asia.[33] In short, the Bush planners were confident that their geopolitical interests coincided with those of New Delhi. They also believed that an alliance with democratic India would be easier to maintain in moral and ideological terms than the rough accord with authoritarian China.

Dealing with a Nuclear India

Bush policymakers were not overly concerned, as Clinton's had been, with India's successful drive to develop its own independent nuclear deterrent, a program that culminated in a successful test in the summer of 1998. Far more than liberal Democrats, or for that matter many internationalist Republicans, the neoconservatives around the second President Bush were skeptical of global nonproliferation initiatives. India had officially become a nuclear power with its successful tests in 1998. The long and tedious negotiating process between Indian government officials and the Clinton administration failed to persuade India's leaders to forgo their weapons program. However, it did break the ice between top U.S. officials and a new generation of Indian diplomats and policymakers.

President Clinton therefore had the opportunity to build on the stronger diplomatic ties that had been established during the course of the unsuccessful nuclear nonproliferation negotiations with India. When Pakistani forces invaded the Kargil region of Kashmir, setting off a short but fierce war in 1999, Clinton consulted Vajpayee at the same time that the U.S. president was holding talks with Pakistan's prime minister, Nawaz Sharif. Vajpayee and his colleagues were impressed by Clinton's conduct of the negotiations. This created a positive climate in New Delhi for Clinton's state visit in 2000. The experience from the Clinton years, one that the Bush policymakers did not consider, showed that a great power will pursue controversial policies, no matter how much governments in Washington or elsewhere may disapprove of them, if they believe that such policies are essential to their national security.

The failed nuclear negotiations and the successful brokering of the Kargil crisis revealed another key lesson of international diplomacy: If you can maintain warm relations even when you disagree, it can open the door for far more far-reaching cooperation down the line. Thus, India's 1998 nuclear tests, while straining relations with the United States in the short term, prepared the way for the strategic dialogue of the Bush-Vajpayee era that continued with Manmohan Singh's government after it was elected in 2004.[34]

The 1998 Indian nuclear tests also impressed those who would shape U.S. foreign policymaking under Clinton's successor. George W. Bush and his advisers did not hate or fear India. But they did respect military strength, and the successful nuclear tests certainly displayed India's military potential. Bush saw Vajpayee's India as the clear rival to China. The degree to which Beijing and Delhi had good reasons for avoiding direct confrontation was not so clear to U.S. policymakers. But as this book documents, India and China have been taking serious steps to improve relations and reduce tensions for over a decade.

The belief that India might join with the United States in confronting Iraq and Iran was even more ill considered. India had maintained excellent relations with Iran and Iraq through the governments of Indira Gandhi, Rajiv Gandhi, and Narasimha Rao. Because India had the largest Muslim minority population in the world—150 million people—any Indian government, especially one led by nationalist Hindu parties, had a crucial interest in easing Hindu-Muslim tensions rather than stoking them.[35]

The Bush planners, eager to topple Saddam Hussein's government in Iraq, paid no attention to how their policies might threaten the regional balance and stable oil prices that were prime Indian strategic concerns. Bush administration officials in early 2003 spoke privately about their confidence that global oil prices within a year would fall to around $20 a barrel as the petroleum reserves of a peaceful Iraq came on line. Instead, in April 2006, oil prices were well over $70 a barrel and Iraq was in chaos. By March 2008, the price topped $100 a barrel for the first time. By July 2008, it was over $147 a barrel.

These higher oil prices hurt India, arguably more so than they do the United States. Both countries rely on nitrate fertilizer for their agriculture, but India's high-yield crops developed during the Green Revolution are particularly dependent on exceptionally high concentrations of nitrates. Oil is essential for the processing and production of such nitrates.

Nevertheless, there was a strategic honeymoon, especially as it related to common concerns over international terrorism.

The Impact of 9/11

Before 9/11, the neoconservatives believed they could safely ignore Pakistan and, if necessary, bring it to heel, through the overwhelming combined power of the United States and India. This was consistent with their desire to hang tough toward China—President Bush had described China as a "strategic competitor"—while building up their relationship with India as a counterweight.[36] At first, however, he and National Security Adviser Rice wanted simply to avoid conflict and controversy with China and therefore did not immediately seek to revive or expand the U.S.-Indian relationship.

After the terrorist attacks of 9/11, the Bush administration's relations with the Vajpayee government in India could have been expected to get even closer. And in some respects they did. In November 2001, Vajpayee visited Washington to great fanfare and approved a dialogue of strategic cooperation. The Bush administration eagerly responded. The benefits to India were great, the risks negligible. Both nations had good reason to take the threat of terrorism extremely seriously.[37] But in other respects, the post-9/11 world led to increasing strains in the new relationship. At no point did Vajpayee, for all his pro-Americanism, even hint at ending the strategic alliance with Russia. On the contrary, on his watch the Russian-Indian security treaty was renewed. Continued tensions between Washington and Delhi vividly demonstrated how simplistic it was to assume that the two huge English-speaking democracies were smoothly fated to be intimate global partners.

The sticking point was undemocratic Pakistan. America's urgent need to project its power into Afghanistan, and to maintain it there following 9/11, made the United States more dependent on Pakistan's goodwill than it had been before the terrorist attacks. The Taliban had only survived in power in Afghanistan thanks to the quiet support of the military and the Inter-Services Intelligence that ran Pakistan. The United States enlisted the full cooperation of both Russia and Pakistan to deploy its military into the heart of Central Asia to topple the Taliban, and Washington remained nearly as dependent on Russian and Pakistani forbearance seven years later. Indeed, by all appearances, the United States needed Pakistan a lot more than Pakistan needed the United States. At least, that is what Pakistan's ruthless military leader President Pervez Musharraf, who had seized power in a coup in 1999, believed.[38]

The Bush administration treated the Musharraf government with kid gloves. It felt that it had to. There was no way U.S. intelligence and Special Forces could operate with impunity in Pakistan without Musharraf's support, grudging though it might have been. Musharraf, at least, was not an open Islamist extremist. Further, he presided over a nuclear-armed nation, the first in the Islamic world. Pakistan's arsenal was sufficiently large and dispersed that some bold strike by U.S Special Forces to secure or destroy it would almost certainly fail. For Bush, Musharraf became the only game in town.[39]

The Indians were not amused. Eager to maintain good relations with Musharraf, the Bush administration even started to sound suspiciously like its predecessor in proclaiming the need for compromise and self-determination to solve the Kashmir issue. Given that Kashmir remained 90 percent Muslim, there was no doubt that Kashmir would eventually rejoin a now-nuclear Pakistan.

So long as Vajpayee was prime minister, strategic engagement between Washington and New Delhi moved ahead, despite growing frustrations among senior Indian officials over what they regarded as the one-sided nature of the intelligence-sharing relationship. Indeed, India's intelligence chiefs viewed Vajpayee's enthusiastic courtship of Washington first with skepticism and caution, then increasingly with resentment. Indian generals and spymasters privately complained that they were giving Washington their best intelligence on al Qaeda and on Pakistan's support of Islamist extremists, but getting nothing substantive in return. They were frustrated by Bush's continued inability to hold Musharraf accountable for Pakistan's failure to hunt down the al Qaeda leaders believed to be holed up in their country. Bush even accepted at face value Musharraf's assurance that the notorious nuclear proliferator Professor A. Q. Khan had been acting on his own, and not on behalf of Pakistan's ruling establishment, in his dealings with rogue states around the world.[40] Even worse, whenever the Bush administration wanted good headlines to show that it was winning the war on terror, the Indians worried that the leaking of their top-secret information to the U.S. media was compromising their security.[41]

Vajpayee's Fall

Had Vajpayee remained in power, he might well have continued to stew over the growing frustrations that his pro-American policies were causing, but he did not get the chance. He was swept out of office in the March 2004 general elections. In a development that took U.S. policymakers and Indian pollsters equally by surprise, the Congress Party, led by Rajiv Gandhi's widow, Sonia Gandhi, was back in power.

Vajpayee was devastated. The result was totally unexpected. The elections had not been necessary. He had called them six months ahead of schedule, confident of victory and expecting to exploit the continuing economic boom and peace moves with Pakistan to expand the parliamentary majority of the Bharatiya Janata Party and its coalition partners. But he had miscalculated. The result stunned Indian political pundits and the world. Opinion polls had not reached thousands of rural villages and, therefore, failed to anticipate the flood of votes that swept aside Vajpayee's BJP. The old prime minister accepted the verdict of the voters with dignity and grace. "My party and alliance may have lost, but India has won," he said. It was a sobering lesson on the limits of globalization and the comfortable assumptions among many in Washington who took for granted that economic reformers would always win democratic elections.

The economy proved to be the decisive issue, but not in the way Vajpayee had anticipated. Gross domestic product growth was expected to reach 7 percent in the 2004 fiscal year, but this growth did not significantly benefit the urban poor or the hundreds of millions of peasants across rural India. Productivity was also rising, but only within the Westernized, high-tech, urban economy, which did not translate into more job opportunities or higher wages for the unskilled poor.

Indian analyst Sultan Shahin noted this phenomenon and estimated its political effects more than three months before the general election: "Many people doubt that the good performance is anything more than statistical jugglery and media hype. After all, farmers have continued to commit suicide, not to speak of the privations of the one-third of the population that lives on less than a U.S. dollar a day."[12]

Vajpayee's economic achievements were real and built on a solid foundation laid by his predecessors. In the mid-1990s, following Prime Minister P. V. Narasimha Rao's economic reforms, India's gross domestic product growth registered a steady increase every year from more than 5 percent in 1992–93 to almost 8 percent in 1996–97.

In Vajpayee's six-year term of office starting in 1998, he succeeded in attracting hitherto-unprecedented levels of overseas investment into India. Foreign exchange reserves, which in the crisis of 1991 had dipped to $2 billion, rose during Vajpayee's years in office to 50 times that level. By mid-February 2004, the magic barrier of $100 billion in foreign direct investment was breached. India was flush with foreign money.

Vajpayee could even boast of impressive engineering and public works projects. His proudest was the so-called Golden Quadrilateral, a network of highways and expressways linking the four major metropolitan centers of Delhi, Bombay, Madras, and Calcutta. But these things benefited the already-booming "haves" of India's growing urban regions. They did not bolster his support among the great majority of Indians who counted themselves among the "have-nots." As Shahin noted, "The feel-good factor is limited to the urban middle class, many of whom are potential BJP voters."[43]

Indian commentator Mani Shankar Aiyar, who was to become petroleum minister in India's new Congress–United Progressive Alliance government, put his finger on the contradiction that would undo Vajpayee's—and Washington's—apparently shrewd calculations. "The problem is the participants in the economy constitute only a fraction of the population," he noted. "And even of that fraction, those at the top end of the spectrum stand to benefit far more than those at the lower end."[44]

Under Vajpayee, wealth concentrated in the hands of the few to an unprecedented degree. Vajpayee had not started this process; it had been happening during the Rao–Manmohan Singh reforms too. The trend seemed to accelerate, however, during Vajpayee's years in power. Yogendra Singh, emeritus professor of sociology and development at Jawaharlal Nehru University in Delhi, concluded that by 2004, 3 percent of the Indian population enjoyed a standard of living that was 57 times higher than 40 percent of the people. He told an American reporter, "The sudden emergence of the urban middle class and the stultification of the poor and lower middle classes have resulted in an alienation, a resentment" from the rural and urban poor.[45]

Even Vajpayee's 7 percent projected growth figure for 2004 was far less than it appeared. Nor was it unprecedented. The expansion came after a time of drought and hardship, especially in rural India, so it was in many respects a return to a previous equilibrium rather than a breakthrough to new levels of prosperity and development. Also, the 7 percent figure was more than 50 percent below the annual growth from 15 years earlier, the previous time the Indian economy was rebounding from a period of recession caused by drought and reduced agricultural output. In 1988–89, India, for the first and only time in its independent history, achieved a double-digit growth rate of 10.8 percent in gross domestic product. That was 3.8 percentage points more than what it achieved during the year before Vajpayee called his general election. In other words, India's agricultural economy was recovering, but not as spectacularly as the prime minister thought. And it was recovering largely because of better weather conditions' contributing to higher agricultural output, not because of government reforms.[46]

Even more important, the 2003–4 recovery did not create a proportionate surge in jobs for the most populous and poorest sectors of the population. It was a painful paradox familiar in the United States and Europe. Economic growth fueled by investment in capital-intensive, high-tech sectors benefited the economy in the aggregate and directly boosted the educated middle classes with modern skills. Hundreds of millions of people have been lifted out of poverty by the free-market policies of Indian governments over the past decade and a half. Vajpayee's reforms certainly contributed to this process. But although the circle of those who benefited in India was far wider, this was not widely perceived among the poor. For large sectors of India's population, job growth still did not exist in any real sense.

Also, McKinsey and Company estimated India's middle class in 2007 as still numbering "only" 50 million, although it projected a more than 1,000 percent growth over the next 12 years to 583 million by 2020.[47] That figure would suggest that the "trickle-down" and "multiplier" effects of increasing middle-class confidence and growing consumer spending would have a minimal effect in a society of 1.1 billion people. A middle class of 50 million people is less than one-third the figures of 150 million to 200 million that have often been loosely cited in press accounts to argue that India's middle class today is already larger than the populations of Germany, France, and Britain combined (200 million). It isn't.

But that was not the only miscalculation pertaining to India's economic development. Vajpayee and the political strategists of the BJP in New Delhi had misjudged the sentiments of hundreds of millions of Indians. With Vajpayee's departure, the prospects for recruiting India as a major strategic ally suddenly became far more uncertain for the Bush administration. For her part, Congress Leader Sonia Gandhi lost no time in emphasizing the continuity in crucial policies between the old government and the new one. For example, she assured India and the world that New Delhi would continue the ongoing peace process with Pakistan. But Washington had its doubts.[48] The great elephant of Southern Asia was no longer invisible to American policy planners. But it was not the docile, obedient, and predictable giant they had assumed it would be. Over the next year, U.S. policymakers were to learn that lesson in no uncertain terms.

5. Confrontation with China?

Upon taking control in January 2009, the Obama administration was tempted to lecture the leaders of China on a wide range of issues, following the pattern documented in previous chapters. At the same time, Secretary of State Hillary Clinton recognized the crucial importance of the Sino-American relationship by including a visit to China on her very first overseas trip. Like his predecessors, Obama was forced to strike a balance.

This prudence reflects an unassailable reality: confrontation between the United States and China would be disastrous for both nations. But to avert such an outcome, it is necessary to understand the repeated cycles of dramatic swings in Chinese domestic and foreign policies documented in this book. The American response to the wild extremes of modern Chinese history has been to oscillate in turn between naive rose-tinted idealization of developments in China and extreme demonization. Both tendencies need to be resisted: that is the first fundamental lesson that U.S. policymakers must draw from the historical record. The second lesson is that there are always going to be major political changes in China that will take policymakers completely by surprise.

Drifting Apart: Clinton and China

Consider, for example, the uneven trajectory of Sino-American relations over the past few decades. From 1948 to 1972, it was hard to find a single U.S. commentator who would dare prophesy that the hostile communist China would ever become a friend of the United States, yet so it proved. In the 30 years from the first Nixon visit through the turn of the century, most Washington pundits became convinced that China would always remain a friend or at least dependent on and subservient to U.S. wishes.[1]

That delusion was held as much by liberal Democrats who wanted to "do good in the world" as by supposedly hard-nosed Republicans who prided themselves on being "realists." The Republicans, after all, were the architects of the Sino-American special relationship. President Richard Nixon and his national security adviser Henry Kissinger had planted it with Mao Zedong, and it had blossomed under Deng Xiaoping and Ronald Reagan.

The roots of this bipartisan love affair with the Chinese were as much economic as philosophical. The GOP had close ties to the giant U.S. aerospace and high-tech corporations that had flourished by selling technology and expertise to China during the 22-year honeymoon under Deng and President Jiang Zemin.

The Democratic administration of President Bill Clinton had its share of headaches with China. Policymakers privately recognized the steady and apparently inexorable cooling of relations with Beijing. They never gave up the hope that the trends could be reversed. However, neither Clinton nor either of his two secretaries of state, Warren Christopher and Madeleine Albright, was ever prepared to display the visionary boldness of a Nixon and seek to negotiate a constructive reassessment of the Sino-American relationship with Beijing.[2]

The issue was not urgent enough for them. Clinton preferred to focus on domestic issues when he could. To the extent that he had idealistic dreams, he hoped to be a great peacemaker between Israelis and Palestinians in the Middle East, or between the conflicting factions of Protestants and Catholics in tiny Northern Ireland. Clinton was by temperament optimistic and generous. He preferred to view the world as a garden of emerging democracies and growing prosperity, with ancient conflicts getting resolved, rather than as a jungle of new emerging threats. He viewed China's sustained economic growth as a force that would mellow the most populous nation on earth rather than transform it into a more formidable foe. Clinton and his second secretary of state, Madeleine Albright, believed that democratic values were the wave of the future on the Asian mainland.

But China's leaders remained authoritarian and at least nominally communist. They recalled the great Tiananmen demonstrations with horror and saw how quickly President Mikhail Gorbachev's democratizing experiment in the Soviet Union had been followed by the disintegration of that vast state. They were determined not to repeat this in China.[3]

There were many points of tension between the United States and China. Concerns over the environmental impact of the Three Gorges

Dam, for example, reflected the vast cultural divide between the political leaders in Washington and Beijing. Clinton certainly did not want confrontation with China and sought to avert one at every stage. But nevertheless, the gap between Washington and Beijing grew during his term of office.[4]

The most serious period of tension between the United States and China during the Clinton era came in July 1995 when China responded to what it regarded as moves toward full de jure independence by Taiwan by test-firing missiles in the Taiwan Strait. In response, Clinton ordered two U.S. aircraft carrier battle groups to the region and tensions subsided.[5]

It was the modern version of the old 19th-century British Empire approach of "sending a gunboat"—but far less cost-effective. It is difficult and expensive to send an 80,000-ton nuclear-power aircraft carrier with 5,000 sailors on board, plus all its protection ships, to discourage such behavior.[6]

It was also a lot more dangerous. The troublemakers on the fringes of the British Empire might attack a gunboat or two, or threaten some British missionaries. But China at the end of the 20th century possessed nuclear-tipped, intercontinental ballistic missiles. A Chinese general made this point none too subtly when he threatened to obliterate Los Angeles. In 1996, Lt. Gen. Xiong Guangkai, then deputy chief of staff of the People's Liberation Army and head of the PLA's intelligence service, issued an implicit nuclear threat, telling U.S. officials not to interfere because Americans "care more about Los Angeles than they do." The context of General Xiong's remarks could have been intended as a deterrent, and it was consistent with China's "no first use" policy on nuclear weapons. But it also made clear that China was now a world-class power, and other nations, including the United States, would be expected to respect her as such.

As noted above, the Bush administration took office in 2001 with the intention of keeping Sino-American relations stable but on the back burner. However, an unexpected incident in the first few months of the new administration had a sobering effect on U.S. policymakers.

In April 2001, a Lockheed Martin EP-3E electronic surveillance aircraft was forced to land on China's Hainan Island after it collided with a Chinese fighter jet. The plane had been operating in international airspace but was harassed by the Chinese pilot. In the ensuing collision, the pilot of the Chinese fighter was killed. The crippled U.S. aircraft made a successful landing and none of its crew was killed or injured.

Beijing was furious. The incident threatened the most serious rupture in Sino-American relations since the Taiwan Strait confrontation five years earlier. Secretary of State Colin Powell succeeded in defusing the crisis. But it helped create an atmosphere of distrust between Beijing and Washington.[7] Probably the most significant long-term effect was the priceless intelligence bonanza it gave the Chinese. The plane itself, with its treasure trove of state-of-the-art surveillance electronics, fell into Chinese hands and was carefully studied before being returned to the United States. In political-diplomatic terms, the incident appeared to be profound at the time, but it was quickly overshadowed by the catastrophe of 9/11.

The North Korean Conundrum

Washington soon had a smaller but more immediate menace to confront in Northeast Asia. In his second State of the Union address, his first delivered after 9/11, President George W. Bush singled out three states as the "axis of evil." Two of them, Iran and Iraq, were in the Middle East. The third, North Korea, was on the border of China. It was the same place where, less than 50 years earlier, U.S. and Chinese forces had been locked in mortal combat.

U.S. policymakers had long been concerned about North Korea's drive to develop its own nuclear weapons and missiles to deliver them. In 1994, the Clinton administration negotiated an agreement with North Korea under which Pyongyang agreed to submit its nuclear facilities to international inspections.[8] However, in October 2002, the Bush administration accused North Korea of operating a secret program to produce highly enriched uranium, in violation of the 1994 agreement. North Korea denied the allegations (they were almost certainly true) and reacted by expelling United Nations nuclear inspectors stationed there and then reactivating a mothballed nuclear reactor.

In January 2003, North Korea formally pulled out of the Nuclear Non-Proliferation Treaty. Pyongyang spent the next three years busily enriching uranium. On October 9, 2006, North Korea claimed to have carried out a successful, underground nuclear test. The U.S. Geological Survey and Japanese seismologists confirmed an underground earthquake, magnitude 4.2 on the Richter scale, consistent with what could have been a small nuclear explosion. In February 2007, North Korea finally agreed within the six-party talks framework to dismantle the Yongbyon nuclear reactor that was capable of producing weapons-grade plutonium and to list all nuclear weapons-grade material. And more than 15 months later, North Korea released a declaration stating that it was not engaged in uranium enrichment or any proliferation activities.[9]

The North Korean nuclear issue lingers, however, yet another major challenge that the Obama administration inherited from its predecessor. President Obama and Secretary of State Clinton took office in January 2009 prepared to offer Pyongyang additional concessions in return for a resolution of the nuclear issue, but it was unclear how the increasingly hawkish North Korea would respond. The ongoing North Korean nuclear dispute echoed the disheartening experience that Clinton administration negotiators had had with India and Pakistan in 1998. When a nation determines that its national security requires nuclear weapons, it is extremely difficult to prevent it from acquiring them.

George W. Bush's treatment of North Korea differed greatly from previous American presidents toward other aspiring nuclear weapon states. Republican and Democratic administrations alike took care to maintain, and even boost, their relations with Pakistan and India, for example, even as they contributed to the problem of nuclear proliferation.[10] By contrast, the Bush administration batted down any possibility of maintaining or renewing direct bilateral negotiations with the North Korean government in Pyongyang. In the absence of any direct channel of communications, paranoid fears in the most isolated nation in the world could only worsen.

The North Koreans were still years away from developing an intercontinental ballistic missile (ICBM) capability that could directly threaten the United States. Their attempt to test-fire a Taepodong-2, an ICBM with a range of between 4,000 and 10,000 kilometers, on July 4, 2006, failed, but they already had a reliable intermediate-range ballistic missile (IRBM) capable of striking any target in South Korea or Japan. Since then, North Korea has conducted additional tests, including in July 2009. But it appears unlikely that the country has yet mastered the technology of miniaturizing thermonuclear weapons sufficiently to enable them to fit in its IRBM warheads.

129

Nonetheless, the dangers of some disastrous miscalculation leading to a preemptive North Korean nuclear strike have grown over the last several years.[11]

As a result, in the years following the October 2002 diplomatic clash, Bush administration policymakers discovered that their aggressive face-off with North Korea had backfired. The confrontation boosted China's importance in the region, and it actually made the United States far more dependent on China's cooperation and goodwill in diplomacy in dealing with North Korea rather than the other way around.

Thus, China quickly came to benefit from North Korea's obduracy.[12] Pyongyang was dependent on Beijing, and grew even more dependent as a result of international pressure.[13] Even while China developed warm relations with democratic, free-market South Korea and enjoyed the benefits of attracting Seoul's high-tech industrial investment as well, it preferred to retain North Korea as a buffer between its own authoritarian society and the democratic, open South.[14] But since China was the only nation giving protection and any degree of support to North Korea, it therefore followed that China was also the only nation that could put any effective pressure on Kim Jong-il's regime.

The Bush administration saw very little evidence that China was exercising a moderating role on North Korea. But the fact that it was the only close neighbor of Pyongyang that even had the potential to bring constructive influence to bear on the "Hermit Kingdom" strengthened China's diplomatic negotiating position with Washington. Beijing quietly but surely became the locus of all Western and Japanese diplomacy aimed at dealing with the North. When Pyongyang reluctantly agreed in principle to participate in six-party talks on its nuclear program with China, Russia, Japan, South Korea, and the United States, meetings were invariably held in Beijing.[15]

The benefits for China were subtle and far-reaching. Beijing was able to present itself as a moderate, responsible force for regional stability. Its prestige throughout Asia rose because it was seen, correctly, as the nation that the United States needed to court rather than the other way around. And on the rare occasions when North Korean spokespeople and diplomats hinted at reviving the talks or making other concessions, the comments were almost always transmitted by Chinese intermediaries.

For example, on March 22, 2005, when North Korean Premier Pak Pong Ju hinted that North Korea was ready to rejoin the six-party talks, he did so in Beijing. "If conditions are right in the future, North Korea is willing at any time to participate in the six-party talks," Ju told Chinese Prime Minister Wen Jiabao.[16] His comments came only a day after U.S. Secretary of State Condoleezza Rice, also in Beijing, threatened sanctions or even tougher action against North Korea. If the six-party talks failed, she said, "We'll have to look at other options."[17] Rice's comments appear to have been a significant factor in provoking Ju's response.

There was no real sign that China was bothering to bring much, if any, pressure to bear on North Korea to curtail its nuclear program. But the fact that Beijing was willing to talk to the North Koreans, pass on U.S. messages, and host the six-party talks gave the Chinese a new credibility and reliable familiarity in the eyes of U.S. diplomats and policymakers.[18] The message for Bush administration policymakers appeared to be that one could do business with the Chinese after all.[19] Evidence suggests that after North Korea's apparently successful underground nuclear test in October 2006, a concerned Beijing began applying significantly more pressure on Pyongyang.

The fact that even the tough Bush administration found it necessary to deal with China on North Korea was a tough pill to swallow for American hawks thirsting for a 21st-century showdown with the Middle Kingdom.[20] But indeed, there are many reasons why the great transpacific clash of giants between the United States and China is hardly inevitable and ought to be avoided. As Susan Shirk warns, "A future crisis with the United States, especially one involving Taiwan or Japan, could arouse the [Chinese] public's ire to the degree that China's leaders might believe that the regime would fall unless they respond militarily to the insult to national honor."[21]

The two nations are on opposite sides of the world. China could spread its influence across continental Asia and not threaten vital U.S. national interests. U.S. policy realistically should aim at maintaining a balance of power in Asia to prevent any hegemonic power emerging there. Such a policy should not require resorting to direct military action. Russia, Japan, and South Korea will have their own interests in maintaining good relations with China but preventing her from unilaterally dominating the region.

The Taiwan Issue

The possibility of some future confrontation between China and Japan cannot be discounted, but it is by no means inevitable. Meanwhile, the potential for a Sino-U.S. clash over the eventual permanent status of Taiwan cannot be dismissed. The United States can and should seek to work with both Taipei and Beijing to avert such danger.

Here, the example of Margaret Thatcher, one of the great heroes of American conservatives, should provide an example to follow. Thatcher, who had risked most of the Royal Navy's surface fleet to regain control of the Falkland Islands from Argentina in the 1982 Falklands War, only two years later signed a deal with China that led to the reversion of vastly richer and more populous Hong Kong to the People's Republic of China in 1998.

Obviously, any final arrangement between China and Taiwan would be very different from that worked out between Hong Kong and Beijing. However, Thatcher recognized that Britain realistically could not, and indeed should not, attempt to continue to hold Hong Kong, or remain committed to its defense, when it clearly would not have the capabilities to do so indefinitely. The same logic applies to the United States, whose military is already dangerously over-strained. The last thing the United States needs is to be sucked into an open-ended commitment to defend Taiwan against China. What would make such a commitment dangerous is the determination of the current generation of leaders and policymakers in Beijing that Taiwan must not be allowed to establish full legal and de facto independence from the mainland. For many Chinese, and not just leaders in Beijing, the reabsorption of Taiwan into a unified China is essential to complete the work of national recovery after the traumatic Century of Humiliation from 1840 to 1948.

The period between President Bush's November 2004 reelection and his ringing second inaugural address in January was marked in Beijing by several ominous warnings about growing Sino-American tensions over Taiwan. In early December 2004, senior Chinese military officials warned of war if Taiwan's president Chen Shui-bian did not abandon his plan to hold a referendum on China's bellicose behavior. Beijing believed the plan might set a precedent for a referendum on full independence that Chen's ruling Democratic Progressive Party might win. "Taiwan independence means war," Maj. Gen.

Peng Guangquian told the official new China News Agency. "This is the word of 1.3 billion people, and we will keep our word."[22]

Prime Minister Wen Jiabao sounded a far more moderate and conciliatory tone in comments on December 5, 2004. But even he and his diplomats emphasized that Taiwan was the key issue, not China's gargantuan trade surpluses with the United States. "Taiwan is the most important and most sensitive issue in [Sino-American] relations," said China's ambassador to Washington, Yang Jiechi.[23] The danger remains that future Taiwanese leaders could miscalculate Beijing's response to their own rhetoric or actions, and that Washington could be taken by surprise by an unanticipated sudden crisis between the mainland and Taiwan.[24]

Defending Taiwan

In May and June 2006, new information surfaced concerning a top secret U.S. Department of Defense war plan to protect Taiwan against any Chinese attack. According to news reports, the plan, code-named OPLAN 5077 and updated in 2004 as OPLAN 5077-04, included provision for the use of nuclear weapons by U.S. forces and for U.S. anti-ballistic missile (ABM) defense systems to defend the island of 23 million people. *Washington Post* reporter William Arkin wrote that OPLAN 5077 dated back in its original form more than 20 years to the Reagan administration. But the plan, according to Arkin, was expanded and finalized in 2005, following 2004 guidance from Defense Secretary Donald Rumsfeld.[25] Elements of the *Post* story were later confirmed by the *Taiwan Times*. The paper said Adm. Dennis Blair, former commander in chief of U.S. Pacific Command, or PACCOM, had played a major role in the process of revising the OPLAN.[26]

In his report, Arkin noted that in recent years, the Bush administration had been putting greater importance on missile defense. He pointed out that, in the event of any Sino-American confrontation over Taiwan, "an improved naval missile defense capability . . . would allow the United States to interpose itself between Taiwan and China" to defend the island against ballistic missile attacks from the mainland.[27]

Such a missile defense deployment, in fact, could take different forms or be composed of different layers. The most obvious level would be the deployment of U.S. Aegis missile cruisers and destroyers armed with SM-3 missiles that could shoot down Chinese short-range ballistic missiles aimed at Taiwan. But the Aegis warships, like America's nuclear aircraft carriers, are vulnerable themselves. They would have to be defended by a phalanx of smaller ABM systems that could protect them against China's own Silkworm and Sunburn anti-ship missiles. The Sunburn, known by the Chinese as the Hai Ying or Sea Eagle HY2, is intended as a U.S. carrier killer. The missile, a version of the Russian N-SS-22 Moskit, can fly at Mach 2.5 (around 1,700 miles per hour) and carries a warhead weighing almost 500 pounds. It is also capable of delivering a tactical nuclear warhead.[28]

By 2006, the Chinese tactical anti-ship missile deployment facing the Taiwan Strait was already so formidable that it had the potential to force major U.S. naval assets like aircraft carriers and Aegis warships to operate from outside the strait itself. A 2006 report published by the Center for Strategic and International Studies warned that the U.S. Navy would not be free to operate within the Taiwan Strait, as OPLAN 5077 appears to require, in the event of a U.S. war with China over Taiwan.[29]

The report by Kurt Campbell, deputy assistant secretary of defense under President Bill Clinton, and center Senior Fellow Jeremiah Gertler, concluded, "Given the cost tradeoffs and a booming economy, China could easily continue to deploy six or seven offensive missiles for every Taiwanese defensive missile to overwhelm the island's defenses." Campbell and Gertler warned that new Chinese anti-ship cruise missiles, submarines, and fast-attack boats were poised to create "the capability to push U.S. ships out of even marginally-effective missile defense range. . . . Even if U.S. Aegis ships find a way to survive in an increasingly hostile anti-access environment, they face a real challenge to effectively defending Taiwan," the report stated. "That leaves the brunt of Taiwan's missile defense to (Patriot) PAC-3(s)" and other new U.S. ABM systems.[30]

The face-off between Chinese anti-ship missiles and American sea-based ballistic missile defense over Taiwan is compounded by another arms race between China and Taiwan involving cruise missiles. In January 2006, *Jane's Defense Weekly* reported that Taiwan had ambitious plans to produce at least 50 of its own Hsiung Feng, or Brave Wind, 2E cruise missiles by 2010, with long-range plans to deploy no fewer than 500. Taiwan's decision to produce missiles capable of threatening southern China dramatically escalates the arms race with the PRC and may tempt Beijing into taking preemptive military action.[31]

The Taiwanese Defense Ministry stayed silent on the *Jane's* report, a report that should have rung alarm bells in the Pentagon, not to mention elsewhere in the United States and throughout East Asia. It was a grim reminder that a possible military confrontation between the mainland and Taiwan could suck in the United States. Even with only conventional warheads, a massive cruise missile force deployed on Taiwan poses a very serious national security threat to China. The reported 360-mile range of the Hsiung Feng would put Hong Kong and Shanghai, the financial hub of China, within striking distance.

Although cruise missiles are far slower than ballistic missiles, they can be harder for state-of-the-art ABM interceptors to shoot down. Cruise missiles are programmed to hug the ground, regularly changing course by following the contours of the landscape, making it vastly more difficult, if not impossible, for ground-based missiles to intercept them. Also, cruise missiles are easily hidden and more road-mobile than larger ballistic missiles: Hsiung Fengs are reportedly designed with mobility in mind.

Furthermore, Taiwan's cruise missile force might not remain conventional for long. Taiwan's advanced industrial economy already has civilian nuclear reactors and, like Japan, South Korea, and other nations, Taiwan has the capability to develop its own nuclear weaponry relatively quickly.[32] If Taiwan ever builds and deploys a nuclear-capable cruise missile force, China could react by launching an overwhelming preemptive strike, with the enormous force of 825 ballistic missiles it had already assembled by mid-2006.[33] Consequently, the dangers of a full-scale missile war being set off by miscalculation will be great. There also remains the possibility that some future Chinese leader may deliberately initiate hostilities.

Taiwan's military-run Chungshan Institute of Science and Technology plans to extend the range of the Hsiung Feng to 600 miles. However, that would require the acquisition of specialized engine components from the United States. Washington has so far refused to allow the sale of such technology.[34]

The cruise missile program appears designed to become the centerpiece of Taiwan's "active defense" policy, which aims to counter any aggression before it reaches Taiwanese territory. That kind of "active defense" could instead provoke the kind of "active attack" it is meant to prevent. It is doubtful that China would sit back and allow Taiwan to guarantee its perpetual de facto independence.

The situation is reminiscent of 1961–62, when the Soviet Union placed its missiles in Cuba to deter the United States. During that tense period, President John F. Kennedy did not sit back and allow the Soviets and their communist Cuban allies to keep ballistic missiles to threaten the U.S. mainland. Instead, he risked a full-scale war to force the Soviet Union to withdraw the weapons.

Will China's President Hu Jintao or his successor go as far as JFK did in dealing with the missiles of Taiwan? Or might they go even further? During the cold war, every American knew the stakes of the game. Yet today, not one American in a thousand is probably aware of the extent of the U.S. commitment to protect Taiwan, or of the scale and cost of the conflict that might ensue, should it come to blows.

There is no overriding strategic reason why the United States should elevate the defense of de facto Taiwanese independence to the level of a core national security objective. Taiwan has vastly benefited from U.S. investment and protection for nearly 60 years. It has become an enormously prosperous nation in its own right. Its investments in the mainland are immense. Its long-term prosperity and security appear best guaranteed by some kind of "one nation, two systems" formula, similar to the arrangement Hong Kong enjoys. A Taiwanese commitment to de jure independence that led to its being bombarded by Chinese missiles from the mainland and forcefully occupied by the People's Liberation Army, with all the suffering such occupations invariably entail, would hardly be in the best interests of its people. Therefore, a U.S. commitment to defend Taiwan when the United States lacks the resources to offer a serious hope of deterring or preventing a Chinese invasion could in no way be described as moral.

By investing so heavily in short- and intermediate-range ballistic missile systems in its southeastern region, China has increased the level of risk the United States will have to take in any future confrontation over Taiwan. The massive investment China has made in its capacity to wage asymmetric cyberwarfare against the United States and its civilian and military information technology systems also adds to the deterrent capability Beijing has built up as leverage against the United States.

It certainly cannot be argued that a commitment to defend Taiwan against the PRC is essential for the United States to retain its leadership position in the region. Such a pledge may have already set it back. Japan and South Korea, America's two main allies in Northeast Asia over the past half century, fear that the United States could blunder into a confrontation with China, forcing them to either choose between the two or get caught in the crossfire.

The Roles of Japan and South Korea

Japanese and South Korean interests are not identical or well aligned. South Korean policy has been shaped by a widespread and deeply felt fear of Japan. These fears stem from Japan's colonial rule of the entire Korean Peninsula for the 40 years following the Russo-Japanese War of 1904–05. To this day, fear of Japan appears to be a far more prevalent popular emotion in South Korea than fear of China. Japanese Prime Minister Junichiro Koizumi's visits during his five years as premier to Yasukuni Shrine honoring those slain in World War II were widely criticized in South Korea. And Japan continued to claim sovereignty over Takeshima, or Dokdo, Island in the Sea of Japan, although it remained under South Korean control. The year 2005 was named "Korea-Japan Friendship Year" in a bid to improve relations. But the initiative backfired after Japan's Shimane Prefecture initiated its own "Takeshima Day" to push Japan's claim over the island. The move set off a wave of large anti-Japanese demonstrations in South Korea.

The pattern of trade points to ever-closer South Korean economic ties with China, whereas its trade ties with the United States have diminished in relative terms. For their part, the South Koreans are eager to court Beijing, recognizing it as the one state that has effective leverage over the still dangerous and unpredictable rulers in Pyongyang. Throughout history, the Koreans have identified themselves with the great fellow Confucian civilization of China, and they have feared their often-aggressive maritime and trading rivals on the home islands of Japan.[35]

South Koreans see the U.S. military presence as reassurance against Japanese revanchism, as well as protection against North Korea and China. Successive South Korean administrations were

137

disturbed by President George W. Bush's record of unexpected unilateral actions and statements toward North Korea. South Koreans want to see the United States come to an accommodation with North Korea, not provoke it into what almost all South Koreans see as an unnecessary and avoidable war in which they would pay a heavy price.[36]

For all the traditional distrust between Seoul and Tokyo, the Japanese assessment of Sino-American relations was very similar to that of the South Koreans in the late 20th century—both Seoul and Tokyo welcomed U.S. protection from China. But they both also wanted good relations between Washington and Beijing, not dangerously strained ones. However, Sino-Japanese relations became significantly more confrontational during Koizumi's premiership.

Koizumi did not try to distance Japan from the United States as Sino-American relations deteriorated. He worked hard to make the traditional U.S.-Japanese alliance stronger than ever. By the time he left office, he had committed Japan to buying and deploying four Aegis-class destroyers armed with SM-3 surface-to-air missiles adapted as ABM interceptors and 16 units of shorter-range Patriot Advanced Capability-3, or PAC-3, missiles as a second layer of defense. The Patriots were to be deployed between 2006 and 2010 and the SM-3-equipped Aegis ships between 2007 and 2010.[37]

Koizumi had such faith in U.S. ballistic missile defense technology that by the time he left office, Japan had spent more heavily on it than any other nation, apart from the United States. The main reason for this was fear, not of China but of North Korea. In 2006, Gen. Burwell Bell, commander of U.S. forces in South Korea, estimated that North Korea had deployed at least 200 Rodong missiles, putting most of Japan within their 780-mile range.[38]

Japan fears China but does not see conflict with her as inevitable. For most of the past decade, Japanese policymakers have quietly sought to foster a policy toward their neighbors inspired by what they regard as the highly successful détente policies of the late cold war. The Japanese want to create a web of communications channels and formal intergovernmental economic, security, and diplomatic structures that will defuse tensions and reduce the risks of war in the region. Koizumi departed from this long-established pattern. He made his priority throughout his five-year premiership the creation of an effective anti-missile defense shield for the cities of Japan. This entailed boosting the still-strong defense ties between Japan and the United States. At the same time, Japan sought to maintain stable relations with China. But Koizumi put much less trust in close diplomatic ties with Beijing than his Foreign Ministry. His successors, Shinzo Abe and Taro Aso, appear to be trying to warm relations with Beijing while pushing ahead with the development of ABM defenses in close partnership with the United States.

The potential flashpoint remains Taiwan. Yet if the Taiwan issue could be safely resolved by trilateral negotiations, then the chances of an amicable Sino-American relationship through the 21st century are excellent. China may well be entering a period of proud and somewhat aggressive nationalism. But it has wooed the countries of the Association of South East Asian Nations with compromise and low-key charm over the past decade, not with bullying or violence. From 2003 onward, as noted throughout this book, China has also actively sought to improve its relations with India. China's obvious extension of economic influence into Central Asia has proceeded so far peacefully and gradually.

Nor is China building a surface navy, as the Soviet Union did during the cold war, as a direct challenger and rival to the United States. As of late 2008, China did not possess even a single aircraft carrier, and plans for building or acquiring one are still in the early stages.[39] By way of comparison, India was building an ambitious 3-carrier fleet, and the United States has plans to maintain at least 10 operational flattops for the foreseeable future.

Stepping Back from the Precipice

Significant rivalry between the United States and China is possible in the coming decades, especially in competition over increasingly scarce energy resources. But there is no reason why this competition should spiral out of Beijing and Washington's control. After all, in the century from 1870 to 1973, the two greatest global rivals in the race to control oil reserves, especially in the Middle East, were the United States and Britain. Yet at the same time, the two nations were allies in both world wars and in the long confrontation of the cold war.

It has been argued that the common culture and similar political and economic systems were the secret of this success. But the United States had fought two wars with Britain in the first 40 years of its existence, and anti-British sentiment remained strong through the 19th century. For that matter, the United States and the Soviet Union, while ideological rivals of the most intense kind, managed to avoid any direct military confrontation during the cold war.

Aside from the issue of Taiwan, many lesser issues have contributed to the steady deterioration of relations between the United States and China since 1989. Yet none of them individually, nor all of them together, should outweigh the very real interests that China and the United States have in maintaining mutually beneficial trade ties and avoiding military confrontation.

A policy of confrontation toward China carries enormously high economic risks for the United States, even if a shooting war never breaks out. In 2003, for the first time in history, China passed the United States as a magnet for foreign direct investment. The Chinese, meanwhile, continued to invest heavily in the United States. By the end of 2007, some 20 percent of foreign-owned U.S. Treasury securities were held by the Chinese State Bank or by Chinese financial institutions beholden to it.[40] China's annual balance-of-payments surplus with the United States has run well in excess of $200 billion for years. This is the largest current trade imbalance between any two nations in the world.

Therefore, confrontation with China now carries the risk of a dangerous run on the U.S. dollar that could destabilize the American economy. In April 2007, Oxford Analytica, an international strategic analysis firm, ranked "United States: Deep Recession" and "China/ Taiwan: Armed Hostilities" as numbers two and three, respectively, on its list of extreme global stress points. (Number one was "United States/Iran: Strike on Iran.") It should further be noted that if hostilities broke out between the PRC and Taiwan (stress point number three), it could easily trigger a deep recession in the United States (number two), and an economic crisis in China.

It has never been wise for debtor nations to turn on their creditors. More often than not, it is the creditor nations that pull the strings. U.S. global dominance throughout the 20th century was based first and foremost on its industrial and financial supremacy. The same was true of Britain throughout the 19th century.

The policymakers in the Bush administration who at first appeared so anxious for confrontations with China soon had other problems to deal with. Within 48 hours of the September 11 attacks, the same

Paul Wolfowitz who only a few years earlier had envisaged a long-term global confrontation with China was urging President Bush instead to invade Iraq, because, he argued at the time, it would be far easier to do than to hunt down the perpetrators of the September 11 atrocities.[41] Bush initially ignored this advice, but within 18 months Wolfowitz got his war.

In the three years that followed, sure enough, the Bush administration careened off on an ill-defined global crusade against "terror," launching two successive invasions followed by difficult, costly, and counterproductive occupations: first in Afghanistan, then in Iraq.

The avoidance of conflict with China may have been the silver lining to the dark cloud of America's struggles elsewhere. Even in the U.S. media, a new obsession with remaking the Middle East sucked the air out of efforts to elevate peripheral issues, such as Chinese environmental and human rights policies, or Chinese policies in Tibet or toward Taiwan, to the forefront of Sino-American relations.

The history of China's occupation of Tibet, as noted earlier, has certainly been an ugly and distressing one. But it is difficult to see what U.S. policymakers could do about it. It is noteworthy that neighboring India has not even tried. The Indians have had an excellent humanitarian record in welcoming Tibetan refugees. They have allowed them to stay in India and have sought to preserve their religious and cultural heritage there. But starting with Nehru's tacit support of China's occupation of Tibet in 1950, the Indians have run no risks and taken no initiatives of their own in seeking to affect the situation in Tibet.[42]

Nor has India given any support to efforts within the U.S. Congress to take any such action. Indeed, Indian policymakers and security strategists alike seem to believe that supporting U.S. efforts to influence China's Tibet policy might establish worrisome precedents that U.S. administrations might then use against continued Indian control of Muslim-majority Kashmir.[43] Even after the Bush administration launched its policy of strategic engagement and high-tech cooperation with India, the Indian media continued to express concern about possible U.S. efforts to meddle in the Kashmir issue.

India's continued caution on Tibet and its warming relations with China under both Hindu nationalist–led and Congress Party–led governments in the early 21st century made clear that Indian-U.S.

engagement would not lead to any coordinated action to weaken China's hold on Tibet. India's rejection of such a policy, coupled with Delhi's growing clout in Washington, made it far less likely that any U.S. administration would be tempted to give effective support to Tibetan nationalist groups. Pro-Tibetan pressure groups have enjoyed a relatively high public profile in the United States, but that has never translated into significant influence.

The same considerations apply to the many criticisms that American environmentalists have leveled against China's ambitious industrialization projects. It is certainly true that air pollution over China's cities is awful and that, from a purely environmental perspective, there are many reasons to be concerned about the consequences of the colossal Three Gorges Dam project to tame the Yangtze River. But such considerations were never allowed to get in the way of America's own drive to industrialization in the mid- to late 19th century, and it is indeed a smug and hypocritical application of double standards, as the Chinese argue, for Americans to lecture them on such matters.

What, then, of the much-hyped and feared Chinese military buildup? China is certainly building a formidable force designed to win a limited conventional conflict with the United States over Taiwan. But as noted above, it is not building forces capable of projecting Chinese power across the Pacific and Indian oceans. It shows no interest in facing down U.S., Indian, or Japanese naval forces deployed beyond the Taiwan Strait. Unlike India, China is not yet building or planning to build a fleet of aircraft carriers. Unlike India, China is not investing significant sums in the necessary infrastructure of maritime and airborne power projection. It is quite feasible that 10 or 20 years down the line, China may make such a strategic investment. But it has not yet done so.

The main purpose of China's diesel submarine buildup appears defensive in nature: to harass the U.S. surface fleet in the western Pacific and to prevent the U.S. Navy from operating too close to the Chinese mainland. The overwhelming thrust of Chinese military procurement and deployment programs has been focused on Taiwan. Of China's 2,250 operational combat aircraft, 490 were deployed within range of Taiwan. Of its 74 destroyers and frigates, 53 were deployed in its East and South Sea Fleets. The People's Liberation Army Navy also had 54 medium and heavy amphibious landing ships, all but 7 of which were deployed in the East and South Sea Fleets.[44] This is still a far cry from building any balanced naval fleet capable of achieving global or even hemispheric domination.

The 2008 U.S. Department of Defense assessment of China's military power predicted that by 2010, China's strategic forces would probably comprise a combination of enhanced, silo-based ICBMs (CSS-3 and CSS-4), medium-range ballistic missiles (CSS-5), solid-fueled, road-mobile ICBMs (DF31 and DF-31A), and sea-based submarine-launched ballistic missiles (JL-1 and JL-2). The report says that by late 2007, China had deployed between 990 and 1,070 CSS-6 and CSS-7 short- and medium-range ballistic missiles opposite Taiwan. Also, China is acquiring a large arsenal of highly accurate cruise missiles, many of them produced in Russia.[45]

These developments are extremely significant. Liquid-fueled ICBMs are far slower to prepare and launch than solid-fuel ones. Liquid fuel, unlike solid fuel, cannot be kept indefinitely in the missiles. It must be pumped in before launch, and such launch preparations are routinely monitored by surveillance satellites. It would be extremely difficult to launch a preemptive strike with such weapons without detection. By way of comparison, the United States possesses approximately 500 land-based ICBMs, plus several thousand more submarine-launched ballistic missiles and bombs that can be targeted against strategic installations in Russia and China.

No U.S. strategist or political leader should doubt the seriousness of China's determination to reabsorb Taiwan. The Defense Department report concluded that "although Beijing professes a desire for peaceful resolution as its preferred outcome," China's force deployment within range of Taiwan provided "reminders of Beijing's unwillingness to renounce the use of force."[46]

The old dictum that the enemy of my enemy is my friend still holds true in international diplomacy and strategy. So long as Chinese leaders have good reason to believe that an eventual military showdown with America over Taiwan is unavoidable, they will continue to be motivated to quietly support nations around the world from North Korea to Iran that may eventually challenge or threaten the United States and its allies.

China continued to maintain, and even increase, its trade volume with North Korea as the nuclear standoff between Pyongyang and Washington continued through 2005 and 2006. In the first half of

2006, China's trade volume with North Korea rose to $774 million, an increase of 4.7 percent over the same six-month period in 2005. This pattern appeared to change after the North Korean missile tests of July 4, 2006, and the apparently successful nuclear test on October 9, 2006, with China exerting pressure on officials in Pyongyang for such provocations. Still, the overall pattern of growing trade and free food aid was an indication of Beijing's determination to keep North Korea functioning as an effective buffer between the PRC and democratic, free-market South Korea and Japan.

China supported another "axis of evil" state. Beijing's rapidly growing appetite for Iranian energy resources has been documented in an earlier chapter. In April 2004, the Bush administration sanctioned Chinese companies, including several Chinese army–owned firms that manufactured chemical and biological systems critical for the development of weapons of mass destruction and for supplying advanced military technology to Iran.[47]

While China strengthened its ties to Iran, the United States plunged into a major military commitment in Iraq. With U.S. military power bogged down in Iraq since March 2003, China has enjoyed unprecedented clout and freedom of action relative to the United States. Policymakers in President Bush's second term faced the challenge of trying to deter China over Taiwan while at least 140,000 U.S. troops were committed in Iraq. At the same time, Washington was dependent on China's goodwill in their diplomatic efforts to get North Korea to abandon its unilateral drive to produce nuclear weapons and the long-range missiles to carry them.

These various trends help explain why, in December 2004, President Bush announced that the United States would not support any Taiwanese referendum that moved the island toward full independence. The move was a significant departure from hawkish conservative rhetoric in Washington. Unforeseen problems in the Middle East were inducing realism and caution in U.S. policymaking, particularly in dealings with other parts of the world.[48]

It was clear, however, that Bush's statement on Taiwan would not be enough for Beijing. Chinese leaders wanted Bush to use U.S. influence to actively restrain President Chen and convince him not to hold the referendum. In March 2005, China's National People's Congress passed an anti-secession law. The People's Republic of China thereby locked itself into confrontation with Taiwan—and

144

implicitly the United States—if Chen or any of his successors tried to declare full, legal independence.

"Taiwan," writes the Cato Institute's Ted Galen Carpenter, "is unlikely to declare independence formally." But its leaders, he continues, "are taking a variety of actions that stop just short of that ultimate provocation." The danger was therefore real, he concludes, that "at some point a Taiwanese government may miscalculate and provoke Beijing beyond endurance."[49]

Carpenter's concern about the explosive potential in the Taiwan-China conflict was not at first widely shared in Washington. But Bush's unprecedented tough talk to the Taiwanese in December 2004 suggested that the White House was beginning to appreciate some of the dangers. Those dangers have only grown more acute in the intervening five years.

At first glance, the 2008 elections of President Ma Ying-jeou in Taiwan and President Barack Obama in the United States would appear to greatly reduce the risk of Sino-American conflict over Taiwan. However, there was no indication in 2008 that the People's Liberation Army was reducing the rate of its military deployments against Taiwan. And the longer-term danger remains of a major, unexpected swing to aggressive nationalism by new leaders in China in the future. This book has documented many such swings that were unanticipated by the West over the past century and more. And it certainly remains the case that the reintegration of Taiwan into united China is a cherished goal of the Chinese leadership and people.

However, for the Chinese to succeed in convincing Obama administration policymakers and congressional figures that they were serious about Taiwan, they would have to overcome the engrained habits of thought and all the experience of U.S. policymakers in dealing with Beijing over Taiwan built up over the previous three plus decades since President Richard Nixon and Chairman Mao Zedong signed the first Shanghai Communiqué on the status of Taiwan in 1972. China in the 21st century is a very different country from the nation that Mao Zedong and Deng Xiaopeng had led.

The Sino-Russian Axis

U.S. policymakers, both Republicans and Democrats, have been slow to recognize the importance of China's joint leadership role with Russia in the Shanghai Cooperation Organization. This book has discussed the formation and early activities of the SCO at some length precisely because of its importance to Chinese grand strategy and policymaking, and also because the SCO is so often ignored.

For years, U.S. policymakers dismissed the SCO as sentiment without substance. They noted that, unlike the North Atlantic Treaty Organization and the Warsaw Pact, the SCO did not have a permanent planning and coordinating military staff of its own. Far from driving back U.S. influence in Central Asia, at first the SCO was forced to accept an unprecedented expansion of U.S. military power in the region after the terrorist attacks of September 11, 2001. Putin, China's SCO partner, worked with the United States when it negotiated the use of the Karshi-Khanabad air base in Uzbekistan as a forward center to supply U.S. and allied forces in Afghanistan. From this base, U.S. forces toppled the Taliban regime that had protected Osama bin Laden and his al Qaeda terrorist organization when they plotted the 9/11 outrages.

But by August 2005, Russian-Chinese military cooperation had quietly advanced to the point where the two countries conducted the most ambitious joint military exercises in their history. Held on the Shandong Peninsula of northeastern China, the maneuvers were announced as anti-terrorist exercises. If so, they were a preparation to fight terrorists on steroids. More than 10,000 troops, including amphibious assault forces, were involved. So were major naval and air units from both nations. The exercises tested the interoperability of the Chinese and Russian armed forces, involving naval, air, and ground units. Even when China and the Soviet Union were allies against the United States at the height of the cold war from 1949 to 1958, they never carried out such joint maneuvers.

The joint exercises practiced landing large numbers of forces from the sea against a hostile, defended shore. Some of the paratroops practiced reaching an "assault position and the launching of an attack on enemy positions."[50] China and Russia insisted that the exercises were not directed against any specific third country. But aside from the Taiwan case already noted, the United States and its closest Asian ally, Japan, feared that other nations were in the planners' minds. After all, the exercises also involved practicing the deployment of submarines and long-range bombers to strike back against the fleet of any other power, and only the United States

146

and Japan have forces that could qualify as comparable targets or potential foes.

The exercises were also "a good opportunity for Russia, the largest arms supplier to the People's Republic, to showcase new weapon systems," according to Sergei Blagov of the Washington-based Jamestown Foundation. Blagov noted that the exercises were full-scale war games. Ships from the Russian Pacific Fleet sailed to China's coasts, and forces from the Pskov 76th Airborne Division were also deployed.[51] In short, the exercises involved maneuvers that would be unprecedented against ordinary terrorists.

China's official Xinhua News Agency defended the reassuring counterterrorism cover story by saying the exercises were meant to practice "dealing with crises and organizing coordinated actions in the backdrop of the fight against terrorism, separatism, and extremism."[52] But the use of the term "separatism" suggested another possible purpose, at least for the Chinese. For if China were ever to consider projecting its overwhelming military power against the offshore island of Taiwan, then it would have to employ exactly the kind of maneuvers undertaken in the exercise. And if Russian forces at some point in the future were ever to be deployed in support of any Chinese military operation to deter U.S. intervention in defense of Taiwan, then the two armed forces would require joint experience in full-scale operational cooperation, just as they had done in the Shandong exercises.

The idea that Russia would actively participate in any Chinese military operation against Taiwan remains very unlikely. However, the fact remains that the Russians have continued to participate with the Chinese in these exercises. Also, while Moscow has shown a marked reluctance over the past decade to sell China advanced land warfare weapon systems that could eventually challenge Russian military superiority in Eurasia, the Kremlin has shown no such restraint in selling China warships, submarines, and, most of all, anti-ship cruise missiles, that could be used against U.S. naval vessels in a conventional war.

Some American observers were critical of the Shandong exercises. "The anti-American axis is beginning to work," commented analyst Ariel Cohen of the conservative Heritage Foundation.[53]

Some Russian analysts came to similar conclusions: "The exercises are the logical continuation of the first signs of cooperation between

Russia and China in the struggle against 'orange revolutions,' separatism, and the dominant influence of the United States in the Euro-Asiatic sphere," said an article on the Russian newspaper website *Gazeta.ru.*[54]

For the most part, however, U.S. leaders and analysts were complacent, just as they had been in July 2005, when the SCO issued a call to roll back U.S. influence in Central Asia.[55] These warnings elicited no significant response from the U.S. government.

But the Shandong exercises provided the military substance behind those earlier diplomatic statements. As the Bush administration pushed energetically toward ever-deeper technical cooperation with India, Russia and China were reacting by integrating their practical war-making capabilities on a hitherto unprecedented scale.

For all the novelty of the war games, they were in many respects the inevitable outcome of a slow process going back well over a decade. Russian Foreign Minister Sergei Lavrov told a press conference in Beijing on March 22, 2006, that the strategic partnership between the two giant nations was "irreversible." The creation of the SCO provided a natural environment to foster the growth of these ties. The Sino-Russian hothouse is now bearing fruit.

Russian President Putin signed 22 cooperation agreements with China during his two-day state visit in March 2006. Moscow and Beijing both emphasized that the success of Putin's visit and the far-reaching agreements concluded during it would propel their global strategic partnership to higher levels than ever before. Yet the state visit did not make the front page of the *New York Times* or the *Washington Post.*[56]

Among the agreements, Russia's gigantic utilities corporation, Unified Energy Systems, signed a contract to export electrical power to China's State Grid Corporation. Rosneft and Gazprom, the Kremlin's favored main oil- and natural gas–producing corporations, signed agreements to supply energy and carry out joint ventures with the Chinese National Petroleum Corporation, providing favorable access to China's energy-hungry economy.[57] The Shanghai Industrial Investment Corporation signed off on a giant development project in St. Petersburg, Russia's second-largest city.[58] Other agreements covered cooperation in outer space, civil aviation, agriculture, labor services, and anti-terrorism. Even the telecom giants Kosmicheskaya Svyaz and China Netcom Group closed a deal on providing international satellite television coverage from the 2008 Olympic Games in Beijing.

"Strategic cooperation between the two countries globally, region-ally and bilaterally enjoys still wider prospects," explained the official English-language *China Daily*, which characterized the growing "exchanges in defense technology and coordination of military acts" as matters of "great significance."[59]

The growth in strategic ties was not a smooth process. In the period 2005–8, tensions grew over Russia's continued refusal to sell its most advanced weapons to China. The weapons that Beijing wanted to buy, and Moscow refused to sell, included sophisticated systems such as the Shmei—or Bumblebee—rocket infantry flame-thrower, 120mm Nona-SVK and Vena self-propelled guns, 152mm Msta-S self-propelled artillery systems, and 300mm Smerch (Tor-nado) multiple-launch rocket systems. Nor would Russia sell China its T-90S main battle tanks, BMP-3 infantry fighting vehicles, BTR-80 armored personnel carriers, Mi-28 Havoc attack helicopters, or Kamov Ka-50 Hokum "Black Shark" attack helicopters.[60]

Nevertheless, there were other aspects to China's enthusiasm for the SCO and its new partnership with Russia. Through the 1990s, China did not appear to have taken the growth of U.S. military power in Central Asia and the spread of democratic sentiments in the region too seriously. But that changed in the early 21st century.

First came the U.S. agreement with Uzbekistan to operate the Karshi-Khanabad (K-2) air base in order to prosecute the 2001 war against the Taliban in Afghanistan. Then in 2005, the wave of demo-cratic revolutions that had already swept Ukraine and Georgia among the former Soviet republics in Europe spread to Central Asia. What became known as the Tulip Revolution toppled President Askar Akayev of Kyrgyzstan in 2005. Then major demonstrations against Uzbekistan's President Islam Karimov rocked the provincial city of Andijan. Government forces crushed the demonstrations at the cost of several hundred dead. An alarmed Karimov blamed the United States for encouraging grass-roots democratic movements in his country and expelled the U.S. Air Force from K-2.

For China, the Tulip Revolution and the unrest in Uzbekistan carried an equally alarming message. Beijing found that the conta-gion of popular democratic revolution—a phenomenon that in Chi-nese history had repeatedly led to appalling chaos and dangerous national weakness—could leapfrog eastward from Ukraine and Georgia to the Central Asian republics. What was to stop it spreading from Central Asia into China?

China has never had reason to seriously fear Islam. But in the modern period, its leaders have had plenty of reasons to fear the uncontrolled spread of democracy within their own country. The SCO provided a framework to work with the existing governments of Central Asia to prevent that eventuality. Just as China needed North Korea as a buffer against democratic contamination from South Korea and Japan to its northeast, it was using the former Soviet republics of Central Asia, through the SCO, as a buffer to its west. The SCO also allowed China to quietly increase its influence in those regions without risking tension with Moscow.

In fact, Chinese expansion into Central Asia and Southeast Asia may be a historical inevitability. China has economic momentum on her side. By spring 2005, her population had plateaued at 1.3 billion, with further growth stifled by the one-child policy. Meanwhile, economic growth rates were again exceptionally high. These figures were not based on some Ponzi scheme or a phantom financial bubble: they reflected an awesome industrial reality. China's insatiable hunger for oil and natural gas was propelling it to seek a dominant role in Central Asia's Caspian basin, and it willingly exerted influence over the affairs of nations like Kazakhstan and Azerbaijan because of the importance of their energy resources.

In the face of these inexorable economic and strategic realities, the long-term prospects for the United States to maintain its influence in Central Asia and propagate democracy there was akin to King Canute ordering the tide to stand still.

Even worse from the viewpoint of vital U.S. national interests, an obsession with propagating democracy throughout Central Asia not only looks sure to drive Russia and China ever closer together against the United States but also is bound to distract U.S. strategic planners from the very real inroads the Chinese are making in the Western Hemisphere, from Brazil and Venezuela to Canada's oil shale fields.

Such a clash of civilizations between the continental superpowers is far from inevitable. China in the coming decades may be more likely to come into fundamental conflict with Russia. There are only around 30 million ethnic Russians living in the area east of the Ural Mountains all the way across to the Pacific Ocean and only 7 million inhabitants of Russia's Far East province. There are 138 million Chinese in the three PRC provinces next to the Far East province. Russia's total population is only around 145 million, and the Russian government itself acknowledges that the figure may fall by more than 25 million over the next three decades. Russia's population today is therefore less than the estimated population of Pakistan or the single Indian state of Uttar Pradesh. Given these demographic trends, the task of maintaining control over the vast territory and resources of Siberia and the Far East region will become ever more difficult for Moscow.

However, foreign ministry officials, senior military officers, and strategists in Russia today overwhelmingly believe that it is the United States and the North Atlantic Treaty Organization that pose the greatest long-term strategic threat to Russia, and that Russia needs to retain the strategic depth and strength afforded by its continuing close relationships with China and India to repel this challenge from the West.

Meanwhile, the problems posed by China's burgeoning population and the hunger for energy resources driven by her rapid industrial expansion are bound to become ever more acute. This policy also impels China to greater involvement in Central Asia and underscores its need to manage its relations with Russia in the region harmoniously and carefully. China's massive investment in Kazakhstan, especially in Kazakh oil fields, is a practical expression of these concerns Therefore, U.S. policies that alienate and alarm both Russia and China may be strategically shortsighted.

The Case for Improved Sino-American Relations

Chinese statesmanship, even under the mercurial Mao, has consistently been adaptive, flexible, and pragmatic. In 1972, the hostile China of the previous 23 years changed in a second, or so it seemed, to the warm and welcoming China that greeted President Nixon, and Mao was still its Great Helmsman at the time. This teaches that it may be unwise to assume China will remain locked into an attitude of increasing hostility toward the United States for years or decades to come. If the dangers of collision over the Taiwan issue can be defused, then even the current leadership in Beijing may prove surprisingly open to improved relations. That could be the case whether the government of China at the time is democratic or repressively authoritarian, as Mao's certainly was at the time of the 1972 Nixon visit. But the corollary of this argument also applies. An increasingly democratic China may experience an intensification of nationalist passions, rather than a reduction of them. If the political process in China were to allow for greater popular representation, or if the Beijing leadership grew more sensitive to popular impulses, this evolution could make China more hostile and dangerous to the United States rather than less so.

U.S. policymakers in the Clinton and the second Bush administrations assumed that China would prefer not to have to risk a potentially ruinous war with the United States over Taiwan. Up to now, that has been the case. It may also be the case that, should the Taiwan issue be defused, the United States might rapidly regain its old attraction in Beijing's eyes as a stabilizing buffer against Japan.

Despite the growing strains between Washington and Beijing over Taiwan, the Sino-U.S. relationship remains a classic case of codependency. China has benefited enormously from its vast exports and hugely favorable annual trade surplus with the United States, while the United States has grown increasingly dependent on the willingness of the Chinese State Bank to hold U.S. Treasury bonds. Until the U.S. government's soaring annual budget deficits can be eliminated or significantly reduced, the United States will need to cultivate China, not to mention many other foreign investors. Nor does China present the United States with some kind of global ideological challenge comparable to those posed in the past by Nazism, Communism, or, as has been so widely argued, extreme Islamist fundamentalism. Mao's communism is no longer a living ideology in China.

Provided the United States does not stumble into a war with China, the PRC may mature and gradually evolve though a period of free-market consolidation economically, and "benign" authoritarianism politically, so that it could expand its middle class sufficiently to make the eventual transition into real democracy, much as its neighbors Taiwan and South Korea successfully did. But this transition could take decades or even generations. After entertaining such high hopes for China for so long, it will be very difficult for American policymakers to avoid going to the other extreme and turning China into an object of fear and hatred. They made that mistake after the communist takeover at the end of 1948. It will be difficult for U.S.

opinion shapers and policymakers to resist the temptation to demon-
ize a China that is suddenly confident and self-assertive, and America's creditor rather than her debtor. But the effort must be made.

It is as premature to assume China's undying enmity in the future
as it will be to assume India's undying friendship and loyalty. Both
of these great nations need to be respected and understood on their
own vast and complex terms.

6. India and China Today

Part I: India

On May 13, 2004, Indian politics turned upside down and, though they did not seem to realize it at the time, the geopolitical calculations of the Bush administration turned with them. That was the day it became clear that enormous rural voting had swept Prime Minister Atal Behari Vajpayee and his Bharatiya Janata Party from power. The opposition Congress Party, led by Sonia Gandhi and Manmohan Singh, was the chief beneficiary of the democratic wave. The Congress Party and its allies won 219 seats in a house of 543 members. With the assured support of an additional 63 members from the communist parties, Congress was guaranteed the right to form the next government.

The BJP's stunning electoral loss also dealt a body blow to the neoconservatives in the Bush administration who saw Vajpayee's BJP as a natural ally in creating a strategic relationship to contain China and even project joint power into the Middle East.[1] The 2004 election proved that India was, indeed, a real democracy; real democracies decide elections for themselves, and the outcome is not invariably the one that outside allies want or expect.

This was the central flaw behind the belief that holding free and fair elections would bring friendly leaders and policies to power: there was absolutely no empirical evidence to support it and a very great deal to disprove it. The two years following neoconservatism's emergence as a political force saw elections in Iran, Iraq, Egypt, Kuwait, and the Palestinian Authority either reelect strongly anti-American parties to parliamentary majorities or significantly strengthen their standing. The results in India were milder than that in their effect on U.S.-Indian relations. But they certainly demonstrated the limited capacity of U.S. policymakers to predict political developments, even in friendly, English-speaking democracies.

Continuity and Balance

The new government led by Prime Minister Manmohan Singh started out with continuity. He continued Vajpayee's free-market policies. This should have come as no surprise, as Singh had initiated many of them as a highly successful finance minister in previous Congress-led governments. Strategic engagement with the United States also continued smoothly.

Indeed, in July 2005, Bush and Singh signed a potentially far-reaching agreement on nuclear cooperation, which was overwhelmingly approved by the U.S. Congress the next year. Bush and Singh also reached an agreement on joint ballistic missile defense development. This was the highest priority for India because of the intermediate-range missile threat it faced from neighboring Pakistan. However, as of May 2009, this agreement still had not been approved in India, and there also remained considerable opposition to the deal within the United States and international nuclear nonproliferation community, even though the U.S. Congress did pass the agreement by a wide margin.

Significantly, India sought to develop its own intermediate-range ballistic missile capability—independent of U.S. aid—even while these agreements were being negotiated and pushed through the U.S. Congress. But Delhi's efforts were unsuccessful in the short term. In July 2006, after years of delays attributable to both technical snags and a desire to avoid the danger of stirring up more U.S. congressional opposition to the nuclear cooperation agreement, India finally test-launched its Agni III intermediate-range ballistic missile with a projected range of 2,100 miles—far enough to reach almost all of China. But that test failed when the missile malfunctioned in flight. It was not until April and May 2007 that India finally succeeded in carrying out two successful test firings of the Agni III.[2]

The implication of the early troubles of the Agni III following earlier development failures was that India would urgently require as much advanced military technology as it could get from the United States, Russia, and other sources for the foreseeable future. This augured well for the future of the Indian-U.S. relationship but, again, only on the cautious, compartmentalized terms that the Singh government was already following. In 2007 and 2008, the Indian government continued to buy much more of the advanced technology it needed from Russia than from the United States.

Singh's policy of compartmentalization in foreign affairs allowed his government to have the best of both worlds. The Singh government reaped the benefits of the relationship with the United States that Vajpayee had pioneered, while taking steps to revive the good relations previous Congress-led governments had enjoyed with China, Russia, and the Muslim world.

Congress was the party of India's founding and, historically, the party of religious reconciliation and secular values. Its sympathetic foreign policy toward the Muslim world had been the natural complement to a strategy of defusing national tensions between the Hindu majority and the Muslim minority.

Congress Party leaders feared that the Bush administration's efforts to reshape Central Asia and the Middle East might backfire, unleashing an Islamist backlash that could topple or destabilize India's major Muslim neighbors—from Pakistan and Bangladesh to oil-supplying Iran. Finally, as the party steeped in an anti-colonialist tradition, many of the Congress Party's prominent figures found the quasi-imperial implications of U.S. policies in Iraq and elsewhere both repugnant and alarming.

This was not evident to Bush administration policymakers at the time. Singh—a very reassuring figure to American conservatives—became prime minister. Sonia Gandhi remained party leader, and although she declined the opportunity to formally lead the new government, she continued to wield significant influence on policy-making behind the scenes.

Like her late husband, Rajiv, Sonia Gandhi had not looked for a prominent political career. Rajiv Gandhi had been propelled to the leadership of his nation by the assassination of his mother, Indira. Similarly, Rajiv's assassination had propelled the Italian-born Sonia to the leadership of Congress. The couple had been close, and she remained loyal to his memory as well as to his policies. Prominent party figures who had been loyal to Indira and Rajiv extended their loyalty to Sonia as well. She exerted her influence quietly, emphasizing that Congress should keep faith with its traditional values in domestic and foreign policy, and did not publicly criticize Singh.[3]

In foreign policy, the Sonia wing of the party promoted maintaining close ties with Russia and improving ties with China. This wing did not dominate the Singh government, however. Indeed, Mani Shankar Aiyar was removed from the sensitive post of petroleum minister in part because his efforts to woo Iran angered U.S. diplomats. On the whole, however, the anti-American Sonia Gandhi loyalists offset the

157

ardent champions of Indian-American partnership within the Congress–United Progressive Alliance ruling coalition.

The military procurement policies of the new government reflected this tension between engagement with the United States and developing closer ties with Russia and China. Russia remained India's main supplier of warships. When India needed to buy new frigates, it did not look to the United States or to any major European nation to build them. In 2006, India signed a $1.6 billion agreement with Russia to build three new frigates in Russian shipyards. And India's ambitious plans to develop a three-aircraft carrier fleet were also based on Russian construction and upgrading of existing ships.

The traditional alliance with Russia remained popular in India. Even Vajpayee had taken care to maintain and strengthen it. The Manmohan Singh government did so as well. Improving relations with China likewise enjoyed broad public support. In 2005, India applied for, and was granted, observer status in the Shanghai Cooperation Organization. Iran, Mongolia, and Pakistan now also enjoy SCO observer status. As discussed in chapter 2, the SCO consists of four of the five former Soviet republics of Central Asia: Tajikistan, Uzbekistan, Kyrgyzstan, and oil-rich Kazakhstan, along with Russia and China. Engagement with the SCO was an important area where the Manmohan Singh government deviated from the more cautious behavior of the Vajpayee government. Building ties to the SCO was an assertion of the traditional orientation of Congress governments led by the Nehru-Gandhi family. It reflected the quiet influence of Sonia Gandhi and her loyalists in the Manmohan Singh government. Obama administration policymakers engaging India will need to keep in mind that Gandhi loyalists still hold many levers of power in the Congress Party. Washington will also need to remember that a strong association with the SCO continues to enjoy broad support across the Indian political spectrum.

Indian policymakers were also concerned about the volatility of domestic U.S. politics. As the Bush administration's economic and strategic problems grew in 2005–6, the U.S. president's popularity fell sharply. There was no guarantee that Bush would be succeeded by a like-minded Republican in the 2008 U.S. presidential election. And even with Republican majorities in both houses of Congress, the Bush administration found Republican as well as Democratic senators attaching amendments to its legislation that sought to launch a new era of U.S.-Indian nuclear cooperation.

By mid-2006, Indian policymakers therefore had ample reason to worry that domestic U.S. politics might upend their hopes for closer strategic ties with the United States. This uncertainty motivated New Delhi to avoid becoming too dependent on Washington; Singh's India was not prepared to risk conflict with Iran, China, or Russia if that was the price for partnership with the United States. Indian leaders were sincere in their desire for closer strategic relations with the United States, and it was certainly in Washington's interest to cultivate closer strategic and economic ties with India. But such sentiments could only carry so far.

The drive to create and maintain a strategic relationship with the United States has real support among major strategic thinkers in Delhi. For example, retired Rear Admiral Raja Menon argues that India needs to maintain "a strategic partnership with the strongest power on earth." Menon disputes the prophets of decline both in the United States and around the world who believe U.S. economic and consequent global power decline is inevitable. He forecasts a new wave of U.S. global technological leadership that is about to burst out based on "knowledge in IT [information technology], in nano-technology, biotechnology, space and new electronics. With the outstanding performance of Indians in all these knowledge industries in the USA, the blow-back effect for India will be huge."[4]

Kanakasabapathi Subrahmanyam, widely described as the dean of India's strategic thinkers and a prominent proponent of realpolitik, also threw his formidable influence behind the U.S.-Indian nuclear deal. Like Menon, he visualized it as a springboard to a far more comprehensive and long-term strategic association between Delhi and Washington. Indeed, Subrahmanyam, for all his realist credentials, clearly visualized the relationship in ways very similar to those expressed by neoconservatives and pro-democracy advocates in the United States. He envisaged a world of six major global powers: the United States, Russia, China, India, Japan, and the European Union. In such a world, the United States would recognize the need for major partners, and it would especially value India's role in helping to counterbalance China. However, despite his prestige, Subrahmanyam could not carry a consensus of major Indian strategic thinkers with him on the nuclear deal or the wider issue of close strategic association with the United States.

Indian strategists are perfectly clear and open in seeing India's future relationship with the United States as being one of equals and independent actors, but they differ on how to put this into practice. For example, Brahma Chellaney, professor of strategic studies at the Center for Policy Research in Delhi, defines the desired relationship between India and the United States (from the Indian point of view) as one of "strategic partners."[5] But Bharat Karnad, a colleague of Chellaney at the Center for Policy Analysis, has been fiercely critical of the U.S.-Indian nuclear deal and of Subrahmanyam's support for it. Karnad blasted the agreement for, he alleged, "negotiating away (India's) military-cum-political independence and leverage—its nuclear force frozen in its present small size and featuring weapons that are untested, unproven, unsafe and unreliable."

"If the Manmohan Singh government were serious about making India a great power," Karnad explains, "it would articulate an Asia-girdling vision, an 'Indian Monroe Doctrine' . . . to encompass the entire Indian Ocean basin on the seaward side and the landmass stretching from the Caspian, Central Asia to the Vietnamese littoral on the South China Sea and to provide the geopolitical justification for sizable Indian nuclear and conventional military forces."[6]

India is not dependent on the United States, as Japan and Germany were after their defeat in World War II, Chellaney points out. "In the 21st century . . . any new friend America makes . . . is going to seek a semblance of equality in the relationship. It is important for U.S. policymakers to understand a different mindset in a country like India and respect it."[7]

The lesson for U.S. policymakers is clear: India is a valuable friend and trading partner. There are clear areas where India would welcome long-term strategic partnership with the United States, such as intelligence sharing against Islamist extremists and attempts to acquire nuclear weapons, or in developing ballistic missile defense systems. But India is not going to risk getting caught up in any armed conflict with China or with significant parts of the Muslim world on behalf of the United States. There is only one thing that U.S. policymakers can do about this: they have to accept it as the way the world is.

The Asian Dimension

Shortly after taking power, the new Indian Congress-UPA government signaled to both China and Pakistan its very real desire to improve relations. On January 24, 2005, Chinese Vice Foreign Minister Wu Dawei visited New Delhi for two days of strategic talks with Indian Foreign Secretary Shyam Saran. The agenda was ambitious and wide-ranging. China's official *People's Daily* reported, "Among the topics discussed were the issues of globalization, energy security, democratization of international relations, reform of the United Nations, non-proliferation and anti-terrorism and the situation in Iraq and on the Korean peninsula."[8]

The two sides also briefed each other on their respective foreign and security policies and reached common ground on a wide range of issues. China's statement even hinted at a mutual desire to work at further improving the relationship "to look beyond bilateral disputes and develop and upgrade ties in a global perspective."[9]

Most significantly, from a U.S. perspective, India and China repeated "their unequivocal stance that they advocate democratization of international relations and multi-polarity."[10] "Multi-polarity" is a favorite Russian and Chinese diplomatic code word for a world with several independent centers of power; in other words, a world that is not dominated by the United States.

Given the Congress Party's traditional suspicion of Anglo-American military operations in the Middle East and Southeast Asia, its compartmentalization policy—maintaining good relations with Russia and China even as it reached out to the United States—should have come as no surprise in Washington.

Manmohan Singh's government was equally consistent when it carried compartmentalization into its energy policy as well. Here too, developing closer ties with Washington was not a significant impediment to improving relations with Central Asian, Middle Eastern, and other nations at the same time. However, there was one exception to this rule: Iran under President Mahmoud Ahmadinejad proved to be a dubious and difficult energy partner. Singh's government moved energetically to obtain equal access to blocks of Iranian oil and gas and to build a series of oil and gas pipelines.[11] This strategy was driven by necessity. But it also reflected the experience and vision of Singh's first petroleum minister, Mani Shankar Aiyar, a prominent figure in the Sonia Gandhi wing of the Congress Party and a former adviser to her late husband Rajiv.

Aiyar's strategy foundered at first. The problems of negotiating a secure pipeline route to India from Iran across increasingly unstable parts of southwestern Pakistan proved to be difficult. The proposed pipeline would have to be more than 1,600 miles long, crossing rugged terrain through the heavily militarized Iran-Pakistan and Pakistan-India frontiers. It would be exposed to security threats from forces hostile to the Iranian, Pakistani, and Indian governments. Guarding the pipeline posed a daunting security challenge.

The pipeline initiative with Iran infuriated the Bush administration. Secretary of State Condoleezza Rice expressed U.S. concern over the deal when she visited New Delhi and gave a press conference on March 16, 2005, at which she communicated her displeasure directly to Indian Foreign Minister Natwar Singh.[12] Aiyar was eased out as petroleum minister and by mid-2006 had been demoted to youth and sports minister.

It was revealing that the main disagreement between Iran and India in the 2006 negotiations over the project revolved around the pricing of the gas. Iran wanted the price linked to the international market. It offered gas to India at $7.2 per million British thermal units, with a 3 percent annual increase. However, India said it was ready to pay only up to $4.25 per million BTUs for the desperately needed gas.[13]

The $8 billion project, which would supply around 60 million cubic meters of gas a day to India and up to 30 million cubic meters a day to Pakistan, would help meet New Delhi's growing energy needs, provide Islamabad with hundreds of millions of dollars (euros) in transit fees, and give Iran a larger slice of an important market. In 2006, Indian and Iranian officials hoped the pipeline could be operating within five years.

Those hopes have not been matched by reality. The Iran-Pakistan-India pipeline still remains a pipe dream. Deadlines for agreements have come and gone. As of early 2009, the project looked increasingly unlikely because of the deepening instability in Pakistan and because of the increasingly strained relations between India and Pakistan following the Mumbai terrorist attacks in November 2008. If the pipeline were ever to be built, it could only operate successfully if India and Pakistan reduced tensions and resolved their ongoing conflicts. President Barack Obama and U.S. policymakers made clear that reducing such tensions would be one of their diplomatic goals, but that seems increasingly unlikely.

Beyond the obvious economic benefits, India and Iran both have reasons to want to see the pipeline built. India also has the potential to be a valuable long-term customer for Iranian natural gas. Iran wants good relations with India and certainly does not want India to make common cause with the United States in trying to halt the Iranian nuclear project. Tehran also has a clear strategic interest in maintaining warm ties with Russia and China.

From a U.S. perspective, the building of the pipeline would give India a serious strategic stake in maintaining the independence and stability of the Islamic Republic. Therefore India's interest in building the pipeline demonstrates its continuing commitment to achieving its own strategic goals, even when they are clearly very different from those of the United States.

The strategic implications of the pipeline project go far beyond the three countries directly involved. Iran also signed an enormous $70 billion oil and natural gas deal with China in October 2004 that locked both countries into a 30-year relationship. Under that deal, Iran was committed to supplying 150,000 barrels of crude oil a day to China at market prices for the next 25 years from its giant Yadavaran field.[14]

Following the China gas deal, Iran's deal with India served notice that Iran was eager to seek lucrative energy arrangements with both of the emerging superpowers of mainland Asia. And having the friendship of China and India was clearly an attractive prospect to an Iran still facing the threat of U.S. military action.

The Indian deal with Iran was not concluded behind China's back. New Delhi and Beijing made some effort to harmonize their thirst for oil and gas from the Middle East (and other regions) to avoid a potentially dangerous energy rivalry getting out of control. The indefatigable Aiyar was at the center of this too. On January 6, 2005, he played host to an "energy summit" of petroleum ministers from China, South Korea, and Japan, as well as from eight nations in the Organization of Petroleum Exporting Countries to try to create a new "Organization for Oil Importing Countries."[15]

It remained to be seen if such an organization could be created, and if it could, whether it would be able to defuse and harmonize the insatiable energy needs of India and China, let alone Japan. Aiyar was seriously committed to the idea. He had long been a proponent of reviving and transforming the ideals of the old Non-Aligned Movement to bring together India and China in a new partnership to lead Asia in the 21st century. Despite the efforts of the Bush administration to separate the two giants of Asia, despite the White House's determination to pursue strategic engagement with India, and despite the collapse of communism, those NAM dreams stubbornly refused to die. In the end, however, the Chinese did not respond to Aiyar's overtures. India lost lucrative energy contracts in Kazakhstan and Nigeria to state-owned Chinese oil companies. According to one Indian commentator, Aiyar "cried foul when Beijing won the Kazak deal."[16]

However mind numbing the details of this internal Indian policy debate appeared to nonspecialists, understanding them is essential to appreciating how and why Indian policymakers will make decisions on key energy and other strategic issues. U.S. policymakers have consistently been ignorant of this important dimension. They cannot afford to be as they move forward.

Relying on Russia

Obama administration policymakers need to understand that the pattern of New Delhi's dealings with Russia, China, and Iran in the first years of the Singh government clearly showed India's crucial energy needs. And it demonstrated the constraints that these energy issues imposed on Indian-U.S. strategic relations.

The Singh government's energy negotiations with Russia proceeded more smoothly than those with China. Boosting oil and gas imports from Russia fitted well into Manmohan Singh's grand strategy. Russia, India's most important strategic ally for some four decades, had proved to be far more stable under President Vladimir Putin than it had been under his predecessor Boris Yeltsin. Even while the pro-American Vajpayee government eagerly sought to develop closer strategic ties with the Bush administration, it took care never to endanger its ties with Moscow. The only constraint on India's imports of natural gas from Russia would be building and securing the necessary infrastructure.

Putin's state visit to India in early December 2004 seemed to validate Aiyar's vision of putting India at the center of a web of energy relationships uniting Asia. India pursued new energy deals with Moscow that could amount to as much as $20 billion in value. Putin gratefully accepted an Indian investment of $3 billion in the Sakhalin-3 oil field in the Russian Far East and in the joint Russian–Kazakh Kurmangazy oil field in the Caspian Sea that held up to 1 billion tons of oil. India already owned a 20 percent stake in Russia's energy-rich Sakhalin-1 block. Sakhalin-3 consists of three blocks—Ayashsky, Kirinsky, and Odoptinsky—with combined estimated reserves of 4.6 billion barrels of oil and 770 billion cubic meters of gas.

Russia has been pushing vigorously to prevent Western oil companies from maintaining too much of a share in the Sakhalin fields.[17] By contrast, Russia expressed interest in getting India's national Oil and Natural Gas Company to invest in gas fields in the Far East, eastern Siberia, the Barents Sea, and the Timan-Pechora regions.[18] The plan, which included pipeline projects of gas supply as well, would also involve Gazprom, Russia's state-owned gas-producing giant; Rosneft, the Russian state oil company; and Transneft, the Russian oil transportation corporation.[19]

Following the December 2004 meeting, Indian Prime Minister Singh explained that he and Putin had "laid out several new milestones" that included a strategic agreement for cooperation in the oil sector. They reached a formal agreement to boost joint efforts to deliver crude oil from Russia and Central Asian countries to India besides picking up equity in oil and natural gas fields in Russia.[20]

Over the next two years, the Russian-Indian natural gas relationship prospered. In July 2006, Gazprom signed an agreement with the Gujarat State Petroleum Corporation for joint exploration and development of onshore and offshore hydrocarbons. The agreement called for establishing a joint working group to study opportunities for Gazprom's involvement in the growing oil and gas industry in India's Gujarat State.[21]

In courting Russia, India had its own powerful cards to play. The growing dynamism of the Indian high-tech economy gave Indian companies the financial clout to provide the investment Russia desperately needed to develop and recapitalize its own oil industry infrastructure. And Russia still trailed in exactly the IT areas that had so boosted India's fortunes.

Indeed, during his December 2004 state visit to India, Putin sought to cash in on India's success in creating a rival to Silicon Valley. The Russian leader called for a bilateral effort to develop information technology and tap new markets, telling business leaders and government officials during a tour of India's high-tech hub of Bangalore, "I see the foundations of a strategic partnership in high-technology projects."[22] By 2005, India was the world's leading IT outsourcer, commanding more than 20 percent of the global market, compared with less than 1 percent for Russia. At the time of Putin's visit, the *Moscow Times* quoted market watchers as saying that Russia's share of the market would shrink even more unless the government subsidized the industry soon.[23]

There were limits to how far the strategic ties between Russia and India would go. For example, although Russia offered India a strategic defense partnership to jointly develop high-tech weapon systems, there were strings attached. In late 2004, Russian Defense Minister Sergei Ivanov confirmed that Russia was ready to sell India submarines—essential weapons to control the oil sea-lanes into the Indian Ocean coming from the Persian Gulf—but he drew the line at the Indians' request to buy outright or lease a Project 941 (Typhoon) ballistic missile submarine.[24]

On the whole, however, Ivanov and Putin's visits to New Delhi confirmed that the growing military ties between Russia and India were more substantive than those between India and the United States.[25] In October 2008, a report by the South Asia Analysis Group concluded that 70 percent of India's armed forces were outfitted with Russian equipment. India in 2008 accounted for 40 percent of all Russian arms exports.[26] India remained dependent on Russia for its main air superiority interceptors, the Sukhoi-30MKI fighters; its main battle tanks, the T-90s; and its main naval surface superiority vessels, the Talwar-class stealth frigates. However, delivery of all three systems was dogged by serious delays. In response, Indian officials were still pressuring Russia in late 2004 and early 2005 to include stiff penalty clauses in all such weapon procurement contracts in the future. However, India continued to look to Russia and not to other major suppliers. In late 2007, India ordered additional T-90S main battle tanks from Russia to augment the 347 it had bought several years before.

In 2007, Putin authorized the biggest restructuring of the Russian defense industry since the collapse of communism with its primary purpose being the ending of bottlenecks in supplying spare parts and maintenance service for export orders.[27] Meanwhile, Ivanov dangled new carrots in front of the Indians. He suggested that the time had come to move defense cooperation beyond that of a buyer-seller relationship.[28]

Ivanov's suggestion materialized in a series of joint military exercises in October 2005. Russian and Indian warships, five from each country, carried out maneuvers off India's Visakhapatnam port on its eastern coast. Over a seven-day period, the Indian contingent from Eastern Naval Command operated with the Russian vessels from Moscow's Pacific Fleet. The naval ministries of both countries called the exercises the most productive operation since they began joint training on the high seas in 2003.[29]

The pace of joint military cooperation between Russia and India continued in 2006. The two countries invested $300 million in BrahMos Aerospace, established to design, develop, produce, and market the missile. In July, the two countries publicly announced plans make 1,000 BrahMos supersonic cruise missiles over the next 10 years through their joint-venture company, and they have set their sights on much more. "We already have a capacity to produce 100 missiles a year," one Indian official told the Press Trust of India. "One thousand missiles in ten years is a reasonable target. Nearly 50 percent will go to exports." According to Sivathanu Pillai, a chief controller of research and development in the Defence Research and Development Organization, Indian policymakers hoped to start supplying the new home-produced cruise missiles to the Indian Army before the end of 2007. They also planned to install them on the Russian-supplied Sukhoi-30MKI combat jets of the Indian Air Force.[30]

But cooperation did not stop there. In April 2007, similar joint Russian-Indian naval exercises called INDRA-2007 were held in the Sea of Japan. The Russians described it as a "live fire exercise" that also involved "air defense and anti-submarine maneuvers" to test the interoperability of warships from both navies.[31]

These exercises underscored the crucial fact that despite the Bush administration's determined effort to forge a far-reaching strategic alliance with India, Russia remained the dominant arms supplier to New Delhi, far outstripping both the United States and Israel.

The same pattern can be seen in India's aircraft carrier development program. India looked to Russia, not the United States, to provide the ships for its ambitious program. As of 2005, the Indian Navy had only one carrier, the aging *Viraat*, scheduled to leave service in 2010. But the former Soviet/Russian aircraft carrier, the

44,570-metric-ton *Admiral Gorshkov*, was being slowly refitted in Russia to reemerge in 2008 as the INS *Vikramaditya*, complete with a complement of 16 Russian-built MiG-29K jet fighters.[32]

Meanwhile, India's own domestic shipbuilding industry received a boost on April 11, 2005, when the Cochin Shipyard started steel cutting on a second 37,500-ton air defense ship. This vessel is designed to carry 12 MiG-29Ks, 8 light combat aircraft (Tejas), and 10 helicopters and is capable of a maximum speed of 28 knots. It is expected to be deployed in 2012 and will be operationally deployed for 45 days at a stretch.[33]

The fact that, for the first time, India was attempting to build an aircraft carrier of its own carried enormous implications for the future. As Vice Admiral Yahswant Prasad explained to the *Times of India*, the manufacture of the air defense ship enabled India to "join a very elite group of nations (the United States, the United Kingdom, Russia, and France) capable of designing and building an aircraft carrier." Pointedly, neither the admiral nor the newspaper included either Japan or China in that "elite group."[34]

And Prasad made clear that further expansion was planned. "After 2012, with both Vikramaditya and ADS [air defense ships] operating on the high seas," he said, the Indian Navy "will explore the option for a 'follow-on' carrier to be built indigenously."[35]

In other words, Indian naval and strategic planners were planning to operate a permanent fleet of at least two and possibly three of their own aircraft carriers in the Indian Ocean by the second decade of the 21st century. Such a fleet would be capable of patrolling the major oil export routes out of the Persian Gulf. Only the U.S. Navy boasts a similar capacity. Since Japan, South Korea, and China were all expected to remain to a significant degree dependent on Middle Eastern crude imports for the foreseeable future, this carrier fleet will give India strategic leverage that may induce Japan and other nations to eventually enter into a closer strategic relationship.

China's strategy for projecting power in the Indian Ocean has been labeled the "chain of pearls" by some strategists.[36] China has been energetically investing and buying influence in Pakistan, Myanmar, and Sri Lanka. One of the most striking examples is the massive Chinese investment in constructing a new port on Pakistan's Indian Ocean coast at Gwadar. Indian analysts fear that China will convert that influence into naval and air bases in the coming decade.

The Indians fear that China will eventually surround them with bases that will contest control of the Indian Ocean. India's carrier fleet may give it the capability to threaten those bases in the event of a conflict. Alternatively, India might offer to cooperate with China in maintaining security in the sea-lanes to and from the oil-producing regions. In other words, India's new carrier fleet will give it important new options in the event that relations with China either deteriorate or improve.

Furthermore, the fact that the two new carriers were to be equipped with Russian rather than American aircraft suggested that India's planners remained more comfortable depending on Russia rather than the United States for their essential hardware.

India's continued dependence on Russian military hardware has a downside. The Russians have been unable to provide India with sufficient spare parts for these weapon systems. In particular, India's aging fleet of MiG fighter jets has been dogged by a series of fatal accidents, often attributed to the poor quality of the spare parts provided for the planes.[37] Nevertheless, the growing warmth between Putin and his Indian counterparts contrasted strikingly with the growing unease in both Moscow and New Delhi toward U.S. policies. At a time of growing tensions and even distrust between the United States and Russia, the Congress-UPA government's strategy of wooing both Russia and Iran demonstrates the limits of how far it would go to satisfy Washington.

Tensions with Washington

And yet the Bush administration at times seemed wholly ignorant of the degree to which its policies were distrusted and resented in New Delhi. On March 25, 2005, State Department officials announced that the United States would sell state-of-the-art F-16 jet fighters to Pakistan. India, despite its supposed strategic honeymoon with Washington, and its warming relations with Pakistan itself, was livid.[38]

Washington contended that the sale of the planes was essential to shore up Pakistani President Pervez Musharraf and was a reward for his cooperation in hunting al Qaeda and shutting down the huge, extended web of nuclear proliferation sales run for decades by Pakistan's top nuclear scientist, Prof. Abdul Qadeer Khan.

169

But New Delhi worried that the sale would tilt the Indian-Pakistani power balance in Pakistan's favor. The F-16 could be used as an attack bomber and was even capable of carrying nuclear weapons. It has a range of more than 2,000 miles. Small, fast, and agile, it had been designed as a pilot's plane and its electronic equipment gave it a decisive edge over the Russian-built fighter bombers that still made up India's frontline air arsenal.

Supporters of the Bush administration argued that the sale would not affect the balance of power between India and Pakistan. "The argument that Pakistan wants the F-16 to deliver nuclear weapons to India, ignores the fact that it can already do that in other ways," the *Wall Street Journal* editorialized.[39]

But this argument was disingenuous. So long as Pakistan could only launch nuclear weapons against India from a handful of launching sites with conventional missiles—and it clearly lacked the resources to build many more of them—Indian satellites could monitor those few sites and give at least some warning of a preemptive nuclear strike. But it would be nearly impossible to keep track of 70 F-16s capable of delivering nuclear attacks on any of the teeming cities of northern and central India. The plane was just too small, too maneuverable, and too fast. Further, there would be no way to differentiate between routine training and defensive flights over Pakistan's own airspace and strategic nuclear attack missions that could cross into Indian airspace on a moment's notice. The Pakistanis would simply have too many F-16s in the air at any one time.

Although U.S. leaders correctly surmised that India would be unhappy about the sale, they seemed completely befuddled as to the extent of the damage. White House officials told the *New York Times* that on the morning of March 25, President Bush personally phoned Prime Minister Manmohan Singh to inform him of the decision to sell the planes.[40] Singh responded, predictably, by expressing his "great disappointment" at the arms sale and warned that it would undermine regional security.[41]

The F-16 arms deal elicited concern from Americans as well. Critics noted that the F-16s are almost completely irrelevant for any operations against al Qaeda. "I know we want to be friends with Pakistan because of the terrorism thing, but you don't fight terrorists with F-16s," Larry Pressler, the former Republican senator from South Dakota, told the *New York Times*. Pressler, who had given his name to the amendment that halted F-16 sales to Pakistan in the 1990s, was convinced that the F-16s would decisively change the nuclear balance between India and Pakistan, a consideration that, if true, was bound to make a mockery of whatever remained of strategic partnership between Washington and New Delhi.[42]

"F-16s are capable of nuclear delivery. That's about the only reason Pakistan wants them," Pressler said. "The only people they are in a fight with are in India. India will now have to get the same thing somehow. So it raises tensions and stakes without meeting any of our objectives."[43]

As it happened, the F-16 controversy did not impede negotiations and eventual agreement on U.S.-Indian civilian nuclear cooperation. The U.S. media quickly forgot about it. But when the first 36 F-16s were due to be provided to Pakistan under the deal in mid-2006, Indian officials privately restated their displeasure to American colleagues.[44]

It did not help that the F-16 row followed quickly after another highly publicized controversy over the dramatic escape of an alleged U.S. spy who had been operating inside India's own intelligence agency in 2004. In early May 2004, Rabinder Singh, an agent of India's external security agency, fled to the United States, just two weeks before Congress's election victory. In the ensuing investigation, the chief of India's Research and Analysis agency and the head of its counterintelligence wing were both forced to retire after being blamed for allowing Singh to escape.[45] Protestations to the contrary, friends do spy on friends in the real world, but the timing of Rabinder Singh's flight to the United States right before the Indian elections and the publicizing of his defection so soon before the F-16 sale to Pakistan, were particularly unfortunate.

By the middle of President George W. Bush's second term of office, his administration could look back on a mixed record of achievement in cultivating close strategic ties with India. On the positive side, it had established close cooperation on a wide range of issues, including ballistic missile defense. The solid bipartisan support within India for strategic engagement with the United States had been demonstrated after the surprise Congress-UPA victory of 2004. Despite the domestic political upheaval, New Delhi's relationship with Washington did not skip a beat.

But India had not abandoned its old friends for new ones. Relations with Russia and Iran improved significantly at the very same time ties were growing with the United States. And far from making any common cause with Washington to contain China, successive Indian governments worked hard to reduce tensions, resolve border disputes, boost trade, and initiate strategic negotiations with Beijing.

The lessons for U.S. policymakers were clear: close ties with India were valuable, and India was eager to have them. But sweeping dreams about long-lasting and exclusive intimate alliances based on shared values and democratic institutions were no match for the imperatives of realpolitik.

In the Bush administration, policymakers focused on South Asia were inclined to greatly exaggerate the degree to which India was prepared to become a close U.S. strategic ally. In the Obama administration, however, there is the danger that policymakers will go too far to the other extreme and underestimate the degree to which they are angering and alienating India.

Obama administration officials need to understand that India is not diplomatically and strategically isolated in Asia: it retains its historic alliance with Russia, it has moved greatly in recent years to improve relations with China, and it retains very good relations with Iran. U.S. officials, therefore, should avoid lecturing India on a wide range of issues, such as civilian nuclear policies, compliance with the Kyoto Protocol, and human rights. Above all, they need to avoid becoming involved in any negotiations that might alter the status of Kashmir.

India will remain eager to gain access to U.S. advanced military technology. It should be made clear to India that the U.S. government is ready to consider such concessions, but only in return for more open access to the Indian market for advanced weapon systems than it has yet received.

The Mumbai terrorist attacks of November 2008 demonstrated that India's elite special forces are still in a woeful state to carry out complex counterterror operations, such as the rescue of hostages. The Obama administration should offer the Indian government a program to bring India's special forces up to world-class caliber. This would be especially valuable, because Russian special forces have shown themselves tragically inept in these areas in recent years, as the September 2004 massacre of civilians and schoolchildren by Chechen terrorists in Beslan showed.

Also, the Indian immigrant community in the United States is highly integrated, wealthy, and successful, and this provides a very strong connection that successive U.S. governments can use to build up their influence in Delhi. Russia and China do not have expatriate Indian communities in their countries that can exercise influence in any comparable way.

Part II: China

When President Hu Jintao came to power in September 2004, he was widely expected to be a reforming, liberalizing leader. Some reforms did come. Democracy did not.

Hu quickly signaled that democracy would have to wait in China. He made clear he was determined to crack down on critics of the government.[46] Fearing that the funeral of a prominent former Communist Party leader would trigger widespread popular demonstrations against the government, Hu warned Chinese dissidents to stay home. The party leader in question was Zhao Ziyang, who fell from power on June 24, 1989, after expressing his sympathies with the pro-democracy protests in Beijing's Tiananmen Square. He died on January 17, 2005, at the age of 85, after spending the last 15 years of his life under house arrest.

The massive precautions that Hu authorized to prevent any rekindling of the popular democratic flame on the occasion of Zhao's death were a sign of the times. Far from liberalizing China's politics, Hu at first even experimented with reviving doctrinaire Marxist-Leninism in line with Mao's thought. For example, a year before, he had approved a lavish celebration of the 110th anniversary of Mao's birth.[47]

Chinese leaders had been alarmed by the "Orange Revolution" in Ukraine, when pro-Western President Viktor Yushchenko eventually prevailed over a pro-Russian candidate, Viktor Yanukovych, by riding a wave of widespread popular protests. According to veteran China watcher Willy Wo-Lap Lam, "The Hu leadership agreed with Moscow's assessment that Yushchenko's victory the second time around was due to heavy support from the Western alliance led by Washington."[48]

As a result, Lam continued, Hu's advisers feared a domino effect could develop across Eurasia, starting in the former Soviet Central Asian republics. Similar popular uprisings in Uzbekistan, Tajikistan, and Kyrgyzstan could threaten the cohesion of the Russian- and Chinese-led Shanghai Cooperation Organization. Eventually, the destabilizing contagion of democracy, as Beijing leaders saw it, could reinfect China itself. The rapid toppling of the 15-year regime of President Askar Akayev in Kyrgyzstan in late March 2005 appeared to confirm the Chinese leadership's darkest fears.

Lam also cited a widely quoted editorial in the official *People's Daily* in early January 2005 that had warned, "Hostile forces have not abandoned their conspiracy and tactics to Westernize China and to divide up the country." Now, Lam continued, the Chinese Communist Party's "fears about 'subversion' allegedly spearheaded by the U.S. have been translated into tough tactics against the nation's liberal academics, writers and journalists."[49]

During Hu's first years in office, the People's Republic moved further down the path of assertive nationalism that it had embarked on under Jiang Zemin. The Jiang era displayed parallels to Germany's later Weimar era from 1924 to 1931, when the dark memories of World War I were partially buried in a brief period of economic growth and good times. But in Germany and Japan, the succeeding decade of the 1930s saw the rise of fascism. China's evolution toward nationalist authoritarianism in the first decade of the 21st century, and its steadily worsening relations with the United States, suggested China might follow a similar course.

It appears quite feasible that Hu or his successor could eventually use extreme, aggressive nationalism to discredit their domestic enemies, just as Mao used the Cultural Revolution to regain his full power. By early 2009, China still appeared a considerable distance from a wave of intensely violent reaction like Mao's Cultural Revolution, but the danger of a reversion to a period of rigid, doctrinaire intellectual repression could not be ruled out.

In 2007, James Mann, one of the foremost experts on China in American journalism, tackled the conventional wisdom that continued economic growth would inevitably bring democracy to China. Mann argued that China was not mellowing toward democracy. He maintained that its authoritarian system could survive for decades to come and would only grow more powerful as its economy grew.

In his popular book, *The China Fantasy*, Mann suggested that China did not face a stark choice between democracy, the so-called Soothing Scenario, or a dramatic collapse of Beijing's political system, the Upheaval Scenario, which would also destroy the authoritarian state. Instead, he predicted a third, more likely way: the survival of the authoritarian state and its growth in power. Mann also predicted that the Beijing government would increasingly turn to nationalist propaganda and policies to distract its population from the growing divisions between rich and poor.[50]

Optimists in the United States tended to assume that this kind of thing was inconceivable a quarter of a century after Deng Xiaoping had unleashed the energies of free-market capitalism in the world's oldest and most populous nation. Since Deng's reforms, it had been widely assumed by many U.S. policymakers, both Democratic and Republican, that the application of liberal economic free-market principles in China had made any revival of Marxist-Leninist and Maoist thought impossible.

But Hu and his colleagues did not believe that political liberalism was either inevitable or irresistible. The long view of history, including the wildly unstable oscillations of Chinese politics over the past 160 years documented in chapter 2, suggests that a reversion to repression, or a strengthening of the current authoritarian system, remains a serious possibility.

Problems of Interdependence

A possible dramatic tilt toward repression was not the only storm cloud hanging over China's future. As U.S.-Chinese relations have slowly but steadily deteriorated over the last decade, questions have arisen over foreign direct investment in the People's Republic.[51] Given its dependence on foreign capital, there are two possible scenarios that could send the Shanghai banking network into shock: The first would be a catastrophic fall in the value of the U.S. dollar, triggering the collapse of China's main export market—the United States. The deep and persistent U.S. federal budget deficits incurred every year by the Bush administration made this a very real possibility.

In September 2008, this foreboding scenario came true. The U.S. housing bubble burst, and the two U.S. mortgage giants Fannie Mae and Freddie Mac collapsed. Venerable Wall Street institutions melted down. This in turn led to a collapse of U.S. consumer spending, which had an almost immediate negative effect on China's export-driven economy. It remains to be seen how far the U.S. and Chinese economies will fall. As of September 2008, the month the Wall Street crisis erupted, the Chinese government held $585 billion in U.S.

Treasury bonds, a larger sum than any other nation.[52] To preserve the value of these assets, the Chinese government hopes that the Obama administration will be more responsible and successful than its predecessor in restoring confidence in Wall Street, the U.S. economy, and the U.S. government.

The ongoing financial crisis is the most profound event to challenge Sino-American relations since the Taiwan Strait confrontations of the mid-1990s. U.S. and Chinese leaders both recognize the dangers, but that does not mean that they will be able to avert them. The Obama administration needs to resist excessive protectionist tendencies from the Democratic Party and Congress, and it also needs to be prepared, as the Bush administration was not, to take whatever measures are necessary to retain international investor confidence in the dollar and in the value of U.S. Treasury bonds. At the same time, Chinese leaders will need to recognize that the recent dramatic fall in U.S. consumer spending is unlikely to be fully reversed for several years to come, even assuming that Obama's economic policies are successful.

An even more ominous scenario would be if the current economic crisis leads to a xenophobic anti-Western and specifically anti-American reaction in China that could cause a serious confrontation between the United States and China. Such a clash could certainly induce the State Bank of China to dump its enormous dollar holdings, triggering a precipitous fall in the dollar. That would very likely set off rampant inflation in the United States and a greater economic crisis than any America had experienced since the Great Depression.

But such a crisis would have grave consequences for China, too. It would, as in scenario one, destroy the U.S. export market for Chinese goods. Bereft of its $200 billion annual balance-of-trade surplus with the United States, all the systemic problems piled up in China's own financial system would explode. Any war with the United States would ignite the passions of popular nationalism, perhaps even violently anti-American demonstrations throughout China on a scale comparable to those of May 4, 1919, or the mass meetings of 1965 that launched Mao's Cultural Revolution. It would be Tiananmen Square in reverse, the opposite of the great pro-democracy demonstrations in Beijing in June 1989.

At the time of this writing, such scenarios still appear alarmist and far-fetched to almost everyone in the United States and China.

The long-term fall in the value of the dollar was clearly under way, and the U.S. budget deficit, far from lessening, was getting worse. The Shanghai banking network, meanwhile, appeared to be weathering these changes well, and the election of President Ma Ying-jeou in Taiwan offered better hopes of averting a collision between China and the United States over the island's future status.

Even if the leaders in both Beijing and Washington recognize the need to reduce tensions and manage their bilateral relations carefully, however, the wild shifts in Chinese history, and especially in its interaction with the West documented in this book, should give one cause for concern. If the United States fails to resolve its differences with China over the Taiwan issue, an extreme nationalist reaction could push future leaders in Beijing to throw caution to the wind and nationalize American investments in their country. This phenomenon has occurred in other nations over the past century. Such nationalization waves occurred in Mexico in the 1930s and in Venezuela in the 1970s.[53] China is hardly immune to such events.

American Parallels

In certain respects, the China that has emerged in the first decade of the 21st century bears some resemblance to 20th-century America. This comparison can be taken too far and is not meant to imply any political, ideological, or moral equivalence. The differences are obvious. Notwithstanding the stain of racial segregation across the South, the United States of the late 19th and early 20th centuries, was an established, stable democracy. It was on excellent terms with its northern neighbor Canada and, until the Mexican Revolution of 1910–17, the United States enjoyed good and stable relations with its southern one as well. Freedom of speech, sanctity of private property, and the rule of law were all deeply engrained, and multiparty national elections had been securely established since 1828. In 1900, the United States' financial and economic stability, in fact, was far stronger than China's in the early 21st century. Far from being a nation dominated by only one ethnic group, it was absorbing the largest peaceful migration in the world.

Nevertheless, in geopolitical terms, and in terms of the popular nationalism rising in it, China is emerging as the world's next industrial colossus in the early 21st century. The America of William McKinley and Theodore Roosevelt emerged from an exceptionally peaceful period of unparalleled industrial and free-market economic growth in the three decades following the Civil War. China has just had a similar period of peaceful, inward-focused industrial expansion and wealth creation.

Gilded Age America took care to avoid foreign entanglements, traumatized as it was by the massive slaughter of its own Civil War. The China of Deng Xiaoping and Jiang Zemin was equally cautious as the country slowly recovered from 28 years of Mao Zedong's bloodstained rule. Postbellum America was happy to shelter behind the Pax Britannica of the British Royal Navy. Post-Mao China was eager to have the United States to restrain and deter the Soviet Union, not to mention neighboring Japan.

But eventually, both giant nations outgrew their protectors. The expansionist, nationalist fervor of a new generation of Americans focused on Spain and its continued occupation of Cuba. In 1898, the United States astonished the world, not merely by invading Cuba but also by projecting power halfway around the world, sending a naval squadron to the Philippines where it easily bested Spain's aging Far Eastern fleet.

It would be much easier for Chinese public opinion in the first decades of the 21st century to support a limited war with the United States to reintegrate Taiwan with the mainland than it was for the American public to rally behind a war to liberate Cuba and eventually take control of the Philippines half a world away in 1898. Susan Shirk, former deputy assistant secretary of state in charge of U.S. relations with China in the Clinton administration, warned: "In China, leaders are under increasing domestic pressure to use force as the military becomes stronger and the Party's control over information reaching the public becomes weaker. Growing economic interdependence does not make war unthinkable."[54]

The weak and ailing Spain of 1898, a troubled, impoverished country that hadn't been a major European power since the 18th century, is in no way comparable to the United States of the early 21st century, still the world's superpower nearly 20 years after the collapse of the Soviet Union. Nevertheless, precisely because the United States is so dominant, it runs the risk of strategic overextension. The United States' continued difficulties in Iraq and Afghanistan reveal the limits of American power.

Should the United States at some point become preoccupied with a widening conflict in the Middle East, one that could draw in Iran and other nations, China might use the opportunity to pressure Taiwan into surrender, in defiance of U.S. pledges to defend the island. Alternately, nationalist forces in a China suffering an economic/financial crisis and looking for scapegoats, might stumble into a risky and costly war with the United States.[55]

Miscalculations happen in history. Popular emotions convulse nations, be they democracies like the United States in 1898 or authoritarian, centralized systems like imperial Germany and czarist Russia in 1914. Since the end of the cold war, the United States has allowed relations with China to deteriorate so far that many in China's ruling circles, and even among her general population, now regard the United States as their enemy, a barrier to their greatness in the new century. This is an extremely dangerous state of affairs for U.S. national interests, and it is one that could have been easily avoided; it still can and should be reversed.

In the first decade of the 21st century, U.S. policies toward the rising superpowers of Asia remain distorted by overly simplistic assumptions and wishful thinking. Policymakers demonized China despite the fact that the United States should have no permanent conflict of interest with China. Washington believed that it could create an alliance with India to confront and contain China, even as New Delhi was clearly expanding its ties to Beijing and Moscow. The idea that India will accept a subordinate role to the United States in confronting China is an idle fancy.

These myths continue to seriously distort U.S. perceptions of Asia. The principles that should guide U.S. policies toward both India and China in the coming years will be discussed in the next and final chapter.

7. Conclusion: The Unknowable Future

By 2009, the combined population of India and China was more than 2.5 billion—more than one-third of the entire human race. The rise of both nations to great-power status was assured. The United States retained a dominant position in the world, but the rise of new centers of power, especially at New Delhi and Beijing, guaranteed that the 21st century would be multipolar. The best prospects for maintaining U.S. global leadership and general prosperity lie in recognizing the reality that America's unipolar moment has already passed.

It is also essential for U.S. policymakers to acquaint themselves with the long and complex histories of China and India. As this book has documented, ignorance of the long-term influences and (often traumatic) experiences of civil war and Western colonialism that shaped the creation of modern India and China have repeatedly led Washington policymakers of both parties into serious miscalculations and errors of judgment in dealing with both the Asian giants.

That is why this book begins with surveys of Indian and Chinese history, with particular emphasis on the past century and a half. Those surveys were not made for specialists in these areas but for 21st-century American policymakers who do not read detailed historical studies. Presidents hailing from the Democratic Party, and the human rights, religious, and environmental activists seeking to influence them, have not noted the traumatic results that anarchy, civil war, foreign invasion, and the era of the warlords from 1915 to 1949 have had on shaping 21st-century Chinese nationalism and the broad national consensus on national security policy. Republicans and the pundits who urge a close strategic partnership between the United States and India do not realize how deeply the experience of 190 years of British domination over all or most of the subcontinent has etched suspicion of Western (and especially English-speaking) imperialism and influence into Indian leaders, parliamentarians, and policymakers.

The loss of Hong Kong to Britain in 1842 started the most humiliating and horrific century in China's modern history. In terms of human suffering and degradation, not to mention the number of violent deaths recorded during it, nothing comparable had been seen in the 600 years since the Mongol conquest by Genghis Khan and his successors. That is why the total reunification of China, a process that is universally agreed in the People's Republic to include the reintegration of Taiwan, is of such central concern to Chinese policymakers.

As the first chapters of this book documented, coastal China and northern India, especially Bengal, were among the most prosperous economic zones on the planet for most of the past 2,000 years. In both countries, the poverty and degradation that they collapsed into over the last 150 years were blamed on, and were indeed largely attributable to, the rapacious effects of extremely unfavorable economic policies imposed by the major Western European powers (and in China's case, Japan) at the point of many cannons. The drive of China and India to build formidable military forces to command their immediate environments and ensure the security of vital resource routes from Africa, Indonesia, and the Middle East can also be properly understood only within this historical context.

This book has argued that a major U.S. conflict with China, while unfortunately all too possible, is not inevitable. The United States and China have both benefited greatly from their growing interdependence over the past generation. Any conflict would have devastating negative effects on both countries. In the event of war, China's internal stability and its essentially peaceful economic and industrial growth would be capsized by a wave of virulent xenophobia. The United States, too, would suffer devastating economic consequences, even if it emerged victorious militarily.

The wild pendulum swings of Chinese history over the past 145 years that have been documented in this book are not common knowledge for most Americans. Their significance remains lost on most U.S. policymakers. Thoughtful consideration of these historical patterns is vitally necessary to temper both wide-eyed optimism and unalloyed hostility toward Beijing. U.S. policymakers should engage Beijing, but the engagement must be careful and clear-eyed.

The more American thinkers, reporters, politicians, and visionaries obsessed over China through the 20th century, the less they seemed to understand it and the more problems they wrought. Conversely, the simultaneous U.S. neglect of India proved generally benign. India maintained its vibrant democracy and stability despite having been largely ignored by Washington.

For Americans, Indian history and politics, like those of China, are full of surprises. Most U.S. policymakers and media pundits failed to anticipate China's extraordinary economic liberalization and its rapid industrialization launched by Deng Xiaoping. In a similar vein, the most enthusiastic advocates in Washington of the new U.S.-Indian strategic relationship were the people most taken by surprise by the victory of the Congress-UPA forces in India's 2004 general election. And they remain largely ignorant of the central role the Soviet Union played—and that Russia continues to play— as the centerpiece of India's global security strategy.

In Washington, there is a comfortable consensus that India has largely moved into the U.S. camp as a long-term strategic ally. Republicans focus on nuclear cooperation and the war on terror. Democrats rest their assumptions on commonly shared democratic values. Yet India's reliance on Russia as its main source of Sukhoi combat aircraft, aircraft carriers, supersonic BrahMos cruise missiles, naval frigates, and T-90S main battle tanks increased dramatically after the Bush administration took office and launched its strategic initiative toward New Delhi. This Russo-Indian partnership shows no sign of abating under President Obama.

The complexity of India and China counsels caution in our dealings with them. It is safer and far more advantageous for U.S. national interest to seek peace and cooperation with Delhi and Beijing than to seek conflict with either of them. Experts often interpret the future of Asia as an impending clash of civilizations between India and China and their respective political systems. Such an apocalyptic outcome is certainly not imminent. Both nations have far more pressing domestic concerns than to obsess over an Asian cold war.

Even if a conflict between India and China were to eventually come about, through blind chance and bad luck, or through simple error and miscalculation, it may not occur for many decades. Any U.S. "zero-sum" policy that seeks to embrace India while isolating China will stumble in the face of complex realities.

Aristotle's principle of balance, following a middle path in all action, should serve to temper the attitudes of U.S. policymakers for India and China. It remains possible that a prosperous, confident, economically expansive China may develop toward democracy in the coming decades. But the prospects of that happening will be vastly reduced, or extinguished entirely, if Sino-American relations descend into a new cold war fought along the Pacific Rim.

And just as American fears of China need to be tempered, so do America's hopes for India. India's democracy is real, but so are its great power ambitions and strategic imperatives, including its ravenous need for energy sources. Anti-American or anti-democratic developments in Indian politics currently appear far less likely than they do in China, but they cannot be ruled out. A thermonuclear war with neighboring Pakistan is not inconceivable. Such a catastrophe could kill tens of millions of people in both countries and could transform India's peaceful democracy into a militaristic, expansionist Hindu-nationalist warrior state.

India and China entered the 21st century under conditions never before seen in either country's history. For the first time in hundreds of years, China was powerful, confident, and expanding. For the first time in half a millennium, it was looking outward and exploring new frontiers, even into outer space. But it also had to find the resources to maintain a rising standard of living for a population of more than 1.3 billion—the largest of any nation in the recorded history of the world.

India's population and the challenges it entailed were of comparable complexity. The more than 900 million Hindus that compose 80 percent of the nation's 1.2 billion people entered the new century more politically independent and powerful than they had been in over 1,000 years. These historic demographic changes mean the national policies being crafted in New Delhi and Beijing will be unprecedented too.

This book has argued that, outside of a handful of specialists, India and China have remained unknown countries to most Americans. Yet two nations with a combined population that constitutes more than 35 percent of the human race are rising to assert their power in the world. The challenges of the coming decades will force changes in both nations. These impending surprises should temper even the most confident policy predictions with a healthy dose of humility. For the future, after all, is the most unknown country of them all.

184

Notes

Introduction

1. In *The End of History and the Last Man* (New York: Free Press, 1992), Francis Fukuyama vividly caught and reflected the delusion of secular millennialism that swept so many American conservative thinkers in the years immediately after the collapse of communism. See also Charles Krauthammer, *A New Moment in America? (After the Cold War and the Gulf War)* (Washington: Freedom House, 1991); and Krauthammer, "The Unipolar Moment Revisited," *The National Interest* 70 (Winter 2002–3): 5–17.

2. Chalmers Johnson, *Blowback: The Costs and Consequences of American Empire* (New York: Metropolitan Books, 2000).

3. *The National Security Strategy of the United States of America* (New York: William Drenttel, 2003). See also Lawrence J. Korb, *A New National Security Strategy in an Age of Terrorists, Tyrants, and Weapons of Mass Destruction: Three Options Presented as Presidential Speeches* (New York: Council on Foreign Relations Press, 2003).

4. See especially David Frum and Richard Perle, *An End to Evil: How to Win the War on Terror* (New York: Random House, 2003).

5. Some, such as Francis Fukuyama, have retreated from such a confident position. Others have not. See especially, Fukuyama, *America at the Crossroads: Democracy, Power and the Neoconservative Legacy* (New Haven, CT: Yale University Press, 2006).

6. Paul Kennedy, *The Rise and Fall of the Great Powers: Economic Change and Military Conflict from 1500 to 2000* (New York: Random House, 1987). Kennedy's book enjoyed a great vogue when it came out, but in the heady years after the collapse of communism it fell out of fashion, helped by fierce attacks from neoconservative writers. The economic as well as military dilemmas of strategic overstretch that the United States stumbled into during President George W. Bush's administration were straight out of Kennedy's original work.

7. See David E. Sanger, "The Global Dance Card," *New York Times*, September 18, 2005.

8. For an Indian perspective on the U.S.-Indian engagement, see C. Raja Mohan, *Crossing the Rubicon: The Shaping of India's New Foreign Policy* (New York: Palgrave Macmillan, 2004).

9. See Orville Schell, *Mandate of Heaven: The Legacy of Tiananmen Square and the Next Generation of China's Leaders* (New York: Touchstone, 1995); Willy Wo-Lap Lam, *The Era of Jiang Zemin* (New York: Prentice Hall, 1999); and Minxin Pei, "Political Change in Post-Mao China," in *China's Future*, ed. Ted Galen Carpenter and James A. Dorn (Washington: Cato Institute, 2000), pp. 291–315.

10. Hernando de Soto, "Beyond Bullets: Economic Strategies in the Fight against Terrorism," address at a New America Foundation conference, Washington, September 21, 2005.

11. Martin Sieff, "India Deals Blow to Bush, Neocons," United Press International, May 19, 2004; see also discussion in chapter 6, "India and China Today."

12. Martin Sieff, "India Looks to China, Not Just U.S.," United Press International, May 27, 2005.

13. See Barbara W. Tuchman, *Stilwell and the American Experience in China: 1911–1945* (New York: Macmillan, 1970).

14. The assumption that a world dependent on American goodwill in the heyday of U.S. industrial, financial, and military power would remain that way when these forces were exhausted and overstretched was eerily reminiscent of the British public and ruling elite's failure to comprehend in the 1930s why their own globally challenged and overstretched empire could no longer count on the fear of its mere displeasure to keep once obedient vassals and former allies in line. See Correlli Barnett, *The Collapse of British Power* (New York: William Morrow, 1972).

15. Tuchman, *Stilwell and the American Experience in China: 1911–1945*.

16. Bob Woodward notes how Deputy Defense Secretary Paul Wolfowitz, previously a hawk on dealing with China, switched within 24 hours of the 9/11 attacks into trying to convince President Bush to attack Iraq instead of Afghanistan, using the extraordinary argument that it would be an easier target. See Bob Woodward, *Bush at War* (New York: Simon & Schuster, 2002), p. 84.

17. Jephraim P. Gundzik, "Roadmap to a Nuclear Test," *Asia Times*, September 3, 2005, http://www.atimes.com/atimes/Korea/GI03Dg01.html. For China's weapons sales policies to North Korea, see Bill Gertz, *The China Threat: How the People's Republic Targets America* (Washington: Regnery, 2000).

18. For an excellent account of the many Bush administration bungles and misassessments in Iraq, see Anthony H. Cordesman, *The Iraq War: Strategy, Tactics and Military Lessons* (Washington: Center for Strategic and International Studies, 2003). Developments in the years since the book was published have only confirmed Cordesman's prescient critique.

19. Barnett, *Collapse of British Power*.

Chapter 1

1. See Sunil Khilani, *The Idea of India* (New York: Farrar Straus Giroux, 1998). Khilani makes the important point: "In India, democracy was constructed against the grain. Both of a society founded upon the inequity of the caste order, and of an imperial and authoritarian state."

2. On the East India Company, see John Keay, *Honorable Company* (London: Harper-Collins, 1991). On Britain's benevolent empire, see Niall Ferguson, *Empire: The Rise and Fall of the British World Order and the Lessons for Global Power* (New York: Basic Books, 2004); and Arthur Bryant, *Macaulay* (London: Weidenfeld and Nicholson, 1979).

3. This discussion draws heavily from Christopher Hibbert, *The Great Mutiny: India 1857* (London: Allen Lane, 1978).

4. For a recent overview, see Saul David, *The Indian Mutiny* (New York: Penguin Books, 2003).

5. For an overview, see Michael Edwards, *British India, 1772–1947: A Survey of the Nature and Effects of Alien Rule* (London: Sidgwick & Jackson, 1967).

6. Romesh C. Dutt, *The Economic History of India in the Victorian Age* (London: Routledge & Kegan Paul, 1956).

7. S. D. Mehta, *The Cotton Mills of India, 1854–1954* (Bombay: F. K. Ved, 1954).

8. Stephen P. Cohen, *India: Emerging Power* (Washington: Brookings Institution Press, 2001), pp. 66–68; and Cohen, *The Indian Army: Its Contribution to the Development of a Nation* (New York: Oxford University Press, 1990).

9. Philip Mason, *A Matter of Honor* (London: Cape, 1974).

10. Cohen, *India: Emerging Power*, pp. 15–17.

11. During the 31-year period from 1914 to 1945, the Indian Army played a key role in occupying and subduing all or key regions of Iraq on behalf of Britain, not once, or twice, but three times: in the conquest and occupation of 1917–18; in suppressing the massive Shiite-led nationalist rising of 1920; and in securing the key oil fields of southern Iraq in 1941.

12. See Martin Gilbert, *Winston S. Churchill: The Prophet of Truth, 1922–1939* (Boston: Houghton Mifflin, 1976); and William Manchester, *The Last Lion: Winston Spencer Churchill, Alone 1932–40* (Boston: Little, Brown, 1988).

13. Stanley Wolpert, *A New History of India*, 7th ed. (New York: Oxford University Press, 2004), p. 301. The historiography on Gandhi is, understandably, enormous. See, for example, Jo Anne Black, *Gandhi—The Man* (San Francisco: Glide Publications, 1972); William L. Shirer, *Gandhi* (New York: Simon & Schuster, 1979); Ved P. Mehta, *Mahatma Gandhi and His Apostles* (New York: Viking Press, 1983); and Judith Brown, *Gandhi's Rise to Power* (Cambridge: Cambridge University Press, 1972). For an astringent but insightful view, see V. S. Nailpaul, *India: A Wounded Civilization* (New York: Knopf, 1977). Anyone seriously pursuing the subject should start with D. G. Tendulkar's respectful but monumental *Mahatma: Life of Mohandas Karamchand Gandhi*, 8 vols. (New Delhi: Publications Division Ministry of Information and Broadcasting, 1960–63).

14. The surprise victory of Congress in the Indian parliamentary elections of May 2004, unanticipated by the sophisticated urban elites of New Delhi, Mumbai, and Bangalore, showed that Gandhi's heirs still remembered this crucial lesson.

15. R. C. Majumdar, *History of the Freedom Movement in India*, vol. 3 (Calcutta: Firma K. L. Mukhopadhyay, 1971).

16. See also the relevant section of the excellent bibliographical essay in Khilani, *The Idea of India*, pp. 221–22.

17. In *The Collapse of British Power* (New York: William Morrow, 1972), Correlli Barnett discusses the insurrection in the Punjab that led up to General Dyer's infamous massacre at Amritsar.

18. See K. K. Aziz, *History of the Partition of India: Origin and Development of the Idea of Pakistan*, 4 vols. (New Delhi: Atlantic Publishers, 1995); B. N. Pandey, *The Break Up of British India* (New York: Macmillan, 1969); and Leonard Mosley, *The Last Days of the British Raj* (London: Weidenfeld & Nicolson, 1961). For a particularly striking eye-witness account of the searing horrors of those days, see H. K. Suchdeva, *Blood and Tears* (Mumbai: Bharatiya Vidya Bhavan, 1996).

19. See portrait of Mountbatten in Andrew Roberts, *Eminent Churchillians* (New York: Simon & Schuster, 1995); see also Edward Behr, *The Last Emperor* (New York: Bantam, 1987).

20. Prashant Bharadwaj, Asim Ijaz Khwaja, and Atif R. Mian, "The Big March: Migratory Flows after the Partition of India," HKS Working Paper no. RWP08-029, John F. Kennedy School of Government, Harvard University, http://ssrn.com/abstract=1124093.

21. Under pressure from Nehru's daughter, Indian Prime Minister Indira Gandhi, the people of Sikkim formally voted to join the Indian Union in April 1975. China still refuses to recognize that change.

22. A. H. Hanson, *The Process of Planning: A Study of India's Five Year Plans 1950–64* (London: Oxford University Press, 1964); George Rosen, *Democracy and Economic Change in India* (Berkeley: University of California Press, 1967); and Myron Weiner, *The Politics of Scarcity* (Chicago: University of Chicago Press, 1962).

23. Selig Harrison, *India: The Most Dangerous Decades* (Princeton, NJ: Princeton University Press, 1960); and Cohen, *India: Emerging Power*, pp. 37–52.

24. Francine R. Frankel and Harry Harding, *The India-China Relationship* (New York: Columbia University Press, 2004), p. 27.

25. For the full official history of the war from the Indian side, see http:// www.bharat-rakshak.com/LAND-FORCES/Army/History/1962War/PDF/ index.html. See also George D. K. Palit, *War in High Himalaya: The Indian Army in Crisis, 1962* (New York: St. Martin's Press, 1991); and V. K. Singh, *Leadership in the Indian Army: Biographies of Twelve Soldiers* (New Delhi: Thousand Oaks, 1992). For a study of the Chinese side of the buildup to the war, see Roderick MacFarquhar, *The Origins of the Cultural Revolution*, vol. 3, *The Coming of the Cataclysm, 1961–1966* (New York: Columbia University Press, 1974). For the argument that Mao was reacting defensively only, see Neville Maxwell, *India's China War* (London: Cape, 1970). This author remains unconvinced by Maxwell.

26. The literature on Nehru is almost as enormous as that on Gandhi. See Savepelli Gopal, *Jawarhalal Nehru: A Biography*, 3 vols. (Cambridge, MA: Harvard University Press, 1976–84); M. Chalapathi Rau, *Jawarhalal Nehru: Life and Work* (Delhi: National Book Club, 1966); and Shashi Tharoor, *Nehru's Invention of India* (New York: Arcade Publishing, 2003). Of especial importance among Nehru's own voluminous writings are Jawarhalal Nehru, *An Autobiography* (New York: Penguin Books, 2004) and *The Discovery of India* (New York: Penguin Books, 2004). See also Stanley Wolpert, *Nehru: A Tryst with Destiny* (New York: Oxford University Press, 1996); Walter Crocker, *Nehru: A Contemporary Estimate* (London: Allen & Unwin, 1966); M. J. Akbar, *Nehru: The Making of India* (New York: Viking Press, 1989); and Michael Brecher, *Nehru: A Political Biography* (New York: Oxford University Press, 1959).

27. Walter Isaacson and Evan Thomas, *The Wise Men: Six Friends and the World They Made: Acheson, Bohlen, Harriman, Kennan, Lovett, McCloy* (New York: Simon & Schuster, 1986); David S. McClellan, *Dean Acheson: The State Department Years* (New York: Dodd, Mead, 1976); and Ronald McGlothlen, *Controlling the Waves: Dean Acheson and U.S. Foreign Policy in Asia* (New York: W. W. Norton, 1993).

28. Wolpert, *New History of India*, p. 404.

29. See Katherine Frank, *Indira: The Life of Indira Nehru Gandhi* (New York: Houghton Mifflin, 2002). Also D. Rankekar and Kamla Manjkekar, *Decline and Fall of Indira Gandhi* (New Delhi: Vision Books, 1977); and S. K. Ghose, *The Crusade and End of Indira Raj* (New Delhi: Intellectual Book Corner, 1978).

30. Ian and Jenifer Glynn, *The Life and Death of Smallpox* (New York: Cambridge University Press, 2004); and Lawrence B. Brilliant, *The Management of Smallpox Eradication in India: A Case Study and Analysis* (Ann Arbor: University of Michigan Press, 1985).

31. Lennard Bickel, *Facing Starvation: Norman Borlaug and the Fight against Hunger* (New York: Reader's Digest Press, 1974); and Norman Borlaug, *Norman Borlaug on World Hunger*, ed. Anwar Dil (San Diego: Bookservice International, 1997).

32. M. S. Venkatarami, *Bengal Famine of 1943* (New Delhi: Vikas Publishing House, 1973); and Wolpert, *New History of India*, pp. 336–37. John Keay, *A History of India* (New York: HarperCollins, 2000), p. 504, has a short but succinct account of the horror and conveys how greatly it exacerbated the bloody conflict between Hindus

and Muslims that tore Bengal apart only four years later during the nightmare of partition.

33. U.S. intelligence assessments cited by intelligence community officials to the author. See also, G. Parthasarathy, "Watch Out for Rising China," *Daily Pioneer*, November 28, 2007.

34. The parallel was not hyperbole. By the summer of 2005, there were more computer scientists working in Hyderabad than in Silicon Valley. See remarks by Lt. Gen. Robert M. Shea, J-6 and director of command, control, communications and computer systems for the Joint Staff of the U.S. Armed Forces at the August 2005 Directors of Information Management/Army Knowledge Management Conference, Fort Lauderdale, Florida, reported by the author for United Press International on August 23, 2005.

35. See, for example, William J. Clinton, press conference, White House lawn, Washington, September 15, 2000.

36. Shahid Javed Burki and Craig Baxter, *Pakistan under the Military: Eleven Years of Zia Ul-Haq* (Boulder, CO: Westview Press, 1991); Khalid Mahmud Arif, *Working with Zia: Pakistan's Power Politics: 1977–1988* (New York: Oxford University Press, 1995); and Sayyid Ghulam Mustafa, *General Zia, His Winged Death and the Aftermath* (Karachi: Shah Abdul Latif Cultural Society, 1994).

Chapter 2

1. *The Shu King, or the Book of Historical Documents*, trans. James Legge (Bexhill-on-Sea, UK: LongRead Books, 2004).

2. The great scholar Joseph Needham in the middle decades of the 20th century stunned the Western world with his recovery of the technical achievements that China had pioneered over the centuries. See the monumental Needham, *Science and Civilization in China*, 4 vols. (Cambridge, U.K.: Cambridge University Press, 1954).

3. Mark C. Elliott, *The Manchu Way: The Eight Banners and Ethnic Identity in Late Imperial China* (Palo Alto, CA: Stanford University Press, 2001).

4. Peter C. Perdue, *China Marches West: The Qing Conquest of Central Eurasia* (Cambridge, MA: Harvard University Press, 2005).

5. Jack Beeching, *The Chinese Opium Wars* (New York: Harcourt Brace Jovanovich, 1976); and W. Travis Haines and Frank Sancllo, *Opium Wars: The Addiction of One Empire and the Corruption of Another* (Naperville, IL: Sourcebooks, 2004).

6. There is a now a huge bibliography in English as well as Chinese on this extraordinary and, in the Western world, all too little known, episode. The best introduction by far, along with a masterly bibliography, remains Jonathan D. Spence, *God's Chinese Son: The Heavenly Kingdom of Hong Xiuquan* (New York: W. W. Norton, 1996).

7. Catherine Lamont, *The Second Opium War* (London: Allen Lane, 1974).

8. E. Backhouse and J. O. P. Bland, *China under the Empress Dowager: The History of the Life and Times of Tzu Hsi* (London: William Heinemann, 1911); and Marina Warner, *The Dragon Empress: The Life and Times of Tzu Hsi, Empress Dowager of China, 1835–1908* (London: Cardinal, 1974).

9. Diana Preston, *The Boxer Rebellion: The Dramatic Story of China's War on Foreigners That Shook the World in the Summer of 1900* (New York: Walker & Co., 2000); and Peter Harrington, *Peking 1900: The Boxer Rebellion* (Westport, CT: Praeger, 2005).

10. Frederic Wakeman, *The Fall of Imperial China* (New York: Free Press, 1977); and Barbara W. Tuchman, *Stilwell and the American Experience in China: 1911–1945* (New York: Grove Press, 1985).

11. C. R. Hensman, *Sun Yat-Sen* (London: S. C. M. Press, 1971); and Lyon Sharman, *Sun Yat-Sen: His Life and Its Meaning: A Critical Biography*, reissue 1991 (Palo Alto, CA: Stanford University Press, 1934). For an execrably simplistic hagiography, see Pearl Buck, *The Man Who Changed China: The Story of Sun Yat-Sen* (New York: Random House, 1953). The worship of Mao by the likes of Edgar Snow and Anna Louise Strong is even worse.

12. Ernest P. Young, *The Presidency of Yuan Shih-K'ai: Liberalism and Dictatorship in Early Republican China* (Ann Arbor: University of Michigan Press, 1977); Jerome Chen, *Yuan Shih-K'ai* (Palo Alto, CA: Stanford University Press, 1972); and Phillip Jowett, *Chinese Civil War Armies 1911–1949* (Oxford: Osprey Publishing, 1997).

13. Franz Schurmann and Orville Schell, *Republican China: Nationalism, War and the Rise of Communism, 1911–1949* (New York: Random House, 1980).

14. Chui-Liang Chui, *Democratizing Oriental Despotism: China from 4 May 1919 to 4 June 1989 and Taiwan from 28 February 1947 to 28 June 1990* (New York: St. Martin's Press, 1995); see also Schurmann and Schell, *Republican China*.

15. The bibliography on Jiang is, of course, vast and contentious. For an outstanding distillation of the most recent scholarship, see Jonathan Fenby, *Chiang Kai-Shek: China's Generalissimo and the Nation He Lost* (London: Free Press, 2003). For an unconventional but very useful discussion on the politics and intrigue behind Jiang's rise to power, see David Bergamini, *Japan's Imperial Conspiracy* (New York: William Morrow, 1971), pp. 360–62.

16. J. A. G. Roberts, *A History of China* (New York: Palgrave Macmillan, 2006), pp. 223–24; Jung Chang and Jon Halliday, *Mao: The Unknown Story* (New York: Knopf, 2005), pp. 44–45; and Paul Johnson, *Modern Times* (New York: HarperPerenial, 1992), pp. 196–97.

17. See David Bergamini, "Part Four, Rubicon Manchuria," *Japan's Imperial Conspiracy*, for a detailed guide through the labyrinthine intrigues of the period.

18. Fenby, *Chiang Kai-Shek*; and Bergamini, *Japan's Imperial Conspiracy*.

19. John King Fairbank, *The Great Chinese Revolution, 1800–1985* (New York: Harper & Row, 1986); Schurmann and Schell, *Republican China*; and Jean Fritz, *China's Long March* (New York: Putnam, 1988).

20. Its author, Yan-Jun Yin, concluded that in the 1937–45 period "21 million Chinese were injured and among them 10 million were killed" by Japanese forces. He concluded that "930 Chinese cities were occupied. Direct economic loss is $63 billion and indirect economic loss comes to $500 billion." From Yan-Jun Yin, *Chunichi Senso Baisho Mondai—Chogoku kokuminseifu no senji/sengo tainichiseisaku wo chusin ni* (Japan: Ochanomizu Shobo, 1996), p. 12. See comprehensive account in Iris Chang, *The Rape of Nanking* (New York: Penguin Books, 1997), pp. 35–60, 81–104. See also Bergamini, *Japan's Imperial Conspiracy*, pp. 3–49.

21. Bergamini sees Matsui as a tragic figure who tried ineffectually to prevent the horror. Bergamini, *Japan's Imperial Conspiracy*, pp. 22–24, 40–45, 47–48. Chang acknowledges the case for this and agrees that "the tubercular general was guilt-stricken over the entire episode" but concludes that on trial for his life "he waffled between lies and occasional self-denunciation" Chang, *Rape of Nanking*, pp. 274–75. Of all the great crimes against humanity committed during World War II, Nanjing remains to this day the least understood and least examined by Western historians.

22. For the most comprehensive recent biography of Jiang, see Fenby, *Chiang Kai-Shek*.

23. Barbara Tuchman, *Stilwell and the American Experience in China* (New York: Grove Press, 1985), pp. 455–61. Critics of General Marshall's postwar mission and of President Harry S Truman's skepticism toward Jiang pay no attention to this military fiasco of 1944 and the role it played in shaping the attitudes not merely of Marshall and Truman, but of senior U.S. Army generals and policymakers in the Pentagon at the time. For Mao's takeover, see Jonathan D. Spence, *The Gate of Heavenly Peace: The Chinese and Their Revolution* (New York: Viking Press, 1981); and Harrison Salisbury, *The New Emperors: China in the Era of Mao and Deng* (New York: Avon Books, 1993).

24. In 1998, the Japanese Health and Welfare Ministry estimated that 575,000 Japanese prisoners of war were taken to labor camps throughout the Soviet Union, of whom 65,000 died during their internment. Kyodo news agency report, March 7, 1998.

25. Tuchman, *Stilwell and the American Experience in China*, pp. 526–27. Stilwell by then was dead. Truman's contempt for Jiang and the China Lobby never abated and was forcefully expressed in his 1961 conversations with Merle Miller. See Miller, *Plain Speaking: An Oral Biography of Harry S Truman* (New York: Berkley Books, 1985), pp. 282–83, 288–89.

26. Harrison E. Salisbury, *War between Russia and China* (New York: Bantam Books, 1970), pp. 81–85; and Li Zhisui, *The Private Life of Chairman Mao* (New York: Random House, 1994), pp. 115–18. On Mao's takeover, see Chang and Halliday, *Mao: The Unknown Story*, pp. 320–32; and Salisbury, *The New Emperors*, pp. 54–61.

27. David Halberstam, *The Coldest Winter: America and the Korean War* (New York: Hyperion, 2007); T. R. Fehrenbach, *This Kind of War* (New York: Macmillan, 1963); Michael J. Varhola, *Fire and Ice: The Korean War, 1950–53* (Cambridge, MA: Da Capo Press, 2000); Clay Blair, *Forgotten War* (New York: Times Books, 1987); and Max Hastings, *The Korean War* (New York: Simon & Schuster, 1987).

28. See exhaustive account in Halberstam, *The Coldest Winter*.

29. The last two years of the war are generally overlooked even by professional American historians. See, for example, Varhola, *Fire and Ice*. For a useful corrective, see Donald Knox, *The Korean War: An Oral History*, vol. 2: *Uncertain Victory* (San Diego: Harcourt Brace Jovanovich, 1985). On Ridgway, see George Charles Mitchell, *Matthew B. Ridgway: Soldier, Statesman, Scholar, Citizen* (Mechanicsburg, PA: Stackpole Books, 2002); also, Ridgway's own superb and remarkably outspoken memoir *The Korean War: How We Met the Challenge* (New York: Da Capo Press, 1986).

30. Most scholars deny any U.S. dimension to the Chinese halt in operations in Assam, and it is certainly the case that correlation does not prove causation. However, as will be seen in this book's examination of the 1962 Indian–Chinese conflict in chapter 4, the remarkably close coincidence in dates between the resolution of the Cuban missile crisis and Mao's sudden halt order to his forces in Assam is too striking to be ignored.

31. Chang and Halliday, *Mao: The Unknown Story*, pp. 436–38. See also Salisbury, *The New Emperors*, part 4; Roderick Macfarquhar, *The Origins of the Cultural Revolution: The Great Leap Forward, 1958–1960* (New York: Columbia University Press, 1987); and Frederick C. Teiwes and Warren Sun, *China's Road to Disaster: Mao, Central Politicians, and Provincial Leaders in the Unfolding of the Great Leap Forward, 1955–1959* (Armonk, NY: East Gate Books, 1998).

32. Chang and Halliday, *Mao: The Unknown Story*, pp. 475–77.

33. Luo Zi-Ping, *A Generation Lost: China under the Cultural Revolution* (New York: Avon Books, 1991); William Hinton, *Turning Point in China: An Essay on the Cultural Revolution* (New York: Monthly Review Press, 1972); and Salisbury, *The New Emperors*, part 5.

34. See Henry Kissinger's insightful discussion of Mao's dilemma in Henry Kissinger, *White House Years*, vol. 1 (Boston: Little, Brown, 1979), pp. 1063–66. For a somewhat strained effort to find positive aspects of the Cultural Revolution on China's industry and education, see Roberts, *A History of China*, pp. 279–81. For an account of the basic measures Deng Xiaopeng and his allies had to take to stabilize China's economy after Mao's death and that also addresses the havoc caused by the Cultural Revolution, see Richard Evans, *Deng Xiaopeng and the Making of Modern China* (New York: Penguin Books, 1995), pp. 223–26.

35. See the excellent account and analysis of Nixon's visit in James Mann, *About Face: A History of America's Curious Relationship with China, from Nixon to Clinton* (New York: Vintage Books, 2000).

36. Kissinger, *White House Years*, vol. 1, pp. 733–87. See also Walter Isaacson, *Kissinger* (New York: Simon & Schuster, 2005), pp. 333–45; and Patrick Tyler, *The Great Wall: Six Presidents and China* (New York: Century Foundation, 1999), pp. 105–80.

37. Strobe Talbot, ed., *Khrushchev Remembers: The Last Testament* (Boston: Little, Brown, 1974), p. 269.

38. Mao Zedong, "Talks at the Chengdu Conference: On the Problem of Stalin," March 1958, in *Chairman Mao Talks to the People*, ed. Stewart Schram (New York: Pantheon Books, 1975), pp. 98–99.

39. Chang and Halliday, *Mao: The Unknown Story*, p. 464. Immediately after the Bucharest visit, Khrushchev ordered the withdrawal of more than 1,000 Soviet advisers from China, and also ordered the suspension of aid for some 155 industrial projects. Salisbury, *The New Emperors*, p. 157.

40. Arkady Shevchenko, *Breaking with Moscow* (New York: Knopf, 1985), pp. 165–66; Tyler, *The Great Wall*, pp. 47–103; and Chang and Halliday, *Mao: The Unknown Story*, pp. 548–51. See also Salisbury, *The New Emperors*, pp. 292–94.

41. Richard Evans, *Deng Xiaoping* (London: Penguin Books, 1995), gives an excellent overview of this crucial figure. See also a first-class discussion of the complex, fateful Mao-Deng relationship in Salisbury, *The New Emperors*, pp. 124–40; and Chang and Halliday, *Mao: The Unknown Story*, pp. 611–29. For an excellent discussion of the strains and ambiguities during China's great transformation, see Nicholas D. Kristof and Sheryl WuDunn, *China Wakes: The Struggle for the Soul of a Rising Power* (New York: Times Books, 1994).

42. Andranik M. Migranian, *Rossiia v poisakh identichnosti: 1985–1995* (Moscow: Mezhdunar, 1997); and Migranian, "The Authoritarian Perestroika Debate," *Telos*, no. 84 (Summer 1990): 115–25.

43. "An Overview of China's Foreign Direct Investment in 2005," Invest in China, Ministry of Commerce, Beijing, September 6, 2006, http://www.fdi.gov.cn/pub/FDI_EN/Statistics/AnnualStatisticsData/AnnualFDIData/FDIStatistics2005/t20060906_61535.htm.

44. Tong Hao and Liu Jie, "Private Companies Playing a Bigger Role," *China Daily*, January 29, 2008, http://www.chinadaily.com.cn/bizchina/2008-01/29/content_6428007.htm.

45. See Kristof and WuDunn, *China Wakes*, p. 86; Roberts, *A History of China*, pp. 291, 294; and Susan L. Shirk, *China: Fragile Superpower* (New York: Oxford University Press, 2007), pp. 35–39. Patrick Tyler notes that George H. W. Bush took seriously the possibility that Deng might be overthrown or killed by military leaders and their political allies; see Tyler, *The Great Wall*, pp. 360, 361–66. Harrison Salisbury, who was in Beijing covering the Tiananmen demonstrations and crisis, had no doubt that Deng gave all the crucial orders. Salisbury, *The New Emperors*, pp. 418, 468.

46. For the generational transition in leadership following Tiananmen, see Orville Schell, *Mandate of Heaven: The Legacy of Tiananmen Square and the Next Generation of China's Leaders* (New York: Touchstone, 1995); and Willy Wo-Lap Lam, *China after Deng Xiaoping: The Power Struggle in Beijing since Tiananmen* (New York: John Wiley, 1995).

47. "Major Foreign Holders of Treasury Securities," U.S. Treasury, September 2008, http://www.treas.gov/tic/mfh.txt.

48. Charles Krauthammer, "The Unipolar Moment," *Foreign Affairs* 70, no. 1 (Winter 1990–91): 23–33.

49. *Annual Report to Congress: Military Power of the People's Republic of China 2006* (Washington: Office of the Secretary of Defense, 2006), p. 32.

50. Lt. Gen. Xiong Gunakai, at the time deputy chief of staff for People's Liberation Army intelligence, in comments to Charles Freeman of the U.S. State Department that were later widely reported. Edward Timperlake and William C. Triplett, *Red Dragon Rising* (Washington: Regnery, 1999), p. 155.

51. David Shambaugh, ed., *Power Shift: China and Asia's New Dynamics* (Berkeley: University of California Press, 2006); and Avery Goldstein, *Rising to the Challenge: China's Grand Strategy and International Security* (Palo Alto, CA: Stanford University Press, 2005).

52. Eugene B. Romer, "China, Russia and the Balance of Power in Central Asia (Shanghai Cooperation Organization)," *Strategic Forum*, November 1, 2006.

53. Tun-Jen Cheng, Jacques Delisle, and Deborah A. Brown, eds., *China under Hu Jintao: Opportunities, Dangers and Dilemmas* (Hackensack, NJ: World Scientific Publishing Co., 2005).

Chapter 3

1. Stanley Wolpert, *A New History of India* (New York: Oxford University Press, 2004), p. 92.

2. Francine R. Frankel, "Introduction," in *The India-China Relationship: What the United States Needs to Know*, ed. Francine R. Frankel and Harry Harding (New York: Columbia University Press, 2004), pp. 19–20.

3. "Historical and cultural ties between China and India had already flourished between the first and 10th centuries AD, thanks to the arrival of Buddhism in China . . . via the Silk Road. . . . This cultural dimension helped shape Chinese civilization from the Han dynasty all the way to the Sui and Tang dynasties, the latter being considered the apogee, as well then decline, of Buddhism in China," *People's Daily*, February 24, 2005.

4. William H. MacNeill, *The Rise of the West: A History of the Human Community* (Chicago: University of Chicago Press, 1963), pp. 633–36, 640–43.

5. Frankel, "Introduction," pp. 20–22.

6. David Bergamini, *Japan's Imperial Conspiracy: How Emperor Hirohito Led Japan into War against the West* (New York: William Morrow, 1971), p. 354.

7. Frankel, "Introduction," p. 26.

8. Barbara W. Tuchman, *Stilwell and the American Experience in China: 1911–1945* (New York: Macmillan, 1970).

9. See William Slim, *Defeat into Victory* (New York: Cooper Square Press, 2000); Stephen P. Cohen, *The Indian Army: Its Contribution to the Development of a Nation* (Berkeley: University of California Press, 1971); Phillip Mason, *A Matter of Honour* (New York: Holt, Reinhart & Winston, 1974); and Bisheshwar Prasad, ed., *Official History of the Indian Armed Forces in the Second World War* (New Delhi: Orient Longmans, 1963).

10. Peter Fleming, *Bayonets to Lhasa: The First Full Account of the British Invasion of Tibet in 1904* (New York: Oxford University Press, 1986).

11. There was sporadic fighting between Tibetan and Chinese forces between 1910 and 1920 and then again in 1933.

12. Though it should be noted that this figure, while widely accepted, has been disputed by some scholars who believe direct casualties inflicted by Chinese forces to have been far lower. Tsering Shakya, *The Dragon in the Land of Snows: A History of Modern Tibet since 1947* (New York: Penguin Books, 2000); Melvyn C. Goldstein, *The Snow Lion and the Dragon: China, Tibet and the Dalai Lama* (Berkeley: University of California Press, 1999); Mikel Dunham, *Buddha's Warriors: The Story of the CIA-Backed Tibetan Freedom Fighters, the Chinese Communist Invasion and the Ultimate Fall of Tibet* (New York: J. P. Tarcher, 2004); and Robert F. A. Thurman, *Essential Tibetan Buddhism* (New York: HarperOne, 1996). For a much lower estimate of Tibetan losses, see Patrick French, "He May Be a God, but He's No Politician," *New York Times*, March 22, 2008.

13. See Steven A. Hoffmann, "Perception and China Policy in India," in Frankel and Harding, *The India-China Relationship*, pp. 36–37. For the full official history of the war from the Indian side online, see "Indian Army: War History of the Indian Army War in the Himalayas," Bharat-Rakshak, Consortium of Indian Military Web-Sites, http://www.bharat-rakshak.com/LAND-FORCES/Army/History/1962War/PDF/index.html. See also George D. K. Palit, *War in High Himalayas: The Indian Army in Crisis, 1962* (New Delhi: Lancer International, 1962); and V. K. Singh, *Leadership in the Indian Army: Biographies of Twelve Soldiers* (Thousand Oaks, CA: Sage Publications, 2005). For an excellent study of the Chinese side of the buildup to the war, see Roderick MacFarquhar, *The Origins of the Cultural Revolution*, vol. 3 (New York: Columbia University Press, 1974). For a very useful online summary of the war by Indian historian Col. Anil Athale, see "Remembering a War: The 1962 India-China Conflict," http://in.rediff.com/news/2002/nov/07china.htm. For the argument that Mao was reacting defensively only, see Neville Maxwell, *India's China War* (London: Cape, 1970). However, this author remains unconvinced by Maxwell.

14. See Harry Harding, "The Evolution of the Strategic Triangle: China, India and the United States," in Frankel and Harding, *The India-China Relationship*, p. 327. Harding makes the important point that even before Vietnam, Kennedy, like Lyndon Johnson after him, was not willing to sacrifice close U.S. ties with Pakistan, then seen as essential to preventing the spread of communism to the Indian Ocean and Iran. For a new and very revealing view of U.S.-Indian relations in the 1961–63 period, see Richard Parker, *John Kenneth Galbraith: His Life, His Politics, His Economics* (New York: Farrar, Straus & Giroux, 2005). Galbraith was Kennedy's ambassador to Delhi and exceptionally influential as the key link between Kennedy and Nehru.

15. See "Indian Army"; and Athale, "Remembering a War." See also Maxwell, *India's China War*; and J. P. Dalvi, *Himalayan Blunder: The Angry Truth about India's Most Crushing Military Disaster* (Dehradun: Natraj Publishers, 2003).

16. "Indian Army"; and Athale, "Remembering a War." Manekshaw, who died in 2007 in his 90s, was one of only two field marshals in the history of the Indian Army. He went on to command the exceptionally rapid and successful destruction of the Pakistan Army in East Pakistan, which then became the independent nation of Bangladesh, in the 1971 Indo-Pakistani war.

17. The most important reason for official U.S. myopia and incompetence was the systematic purging of veteran Asia experts in the Joe McCarthy era at the State Department who had correctly predicted the victory of Mao in the Chinese civil war. See David Halberstam, *The Best and the Brightest* (New York: Ballantine Books, 1993), pp. 323–25, 339–41, 369–92.

18. The best recent history of the 1947 Indo-Pakistani war and the partition of the subcontinent is Yasmin Khan, *The Great Partition: The Making of India and Pakistan* (New Haven, CT: Yale University Press, 2007). See also Richard Sisson and Leo Rose, *War and Secession: Pakistan, India and the Creation of Bangladesh* (Berkeley: University of California Press, 1991).

19. Outside India, Lal Bahadur Shastri is now almost totally forgotten. But despite his short time in office, he was responsible for momentous and lasting changes in world politics. He also played a crucial role in showing that Indian democracy could smoothly survive the death of its towering founding father, Nehru, and Shastri was the last, many would argue, the only, true heir of Mahatma Gandhi to rule India. See D. R. Mankekar, *Lal Bahadur Shastri: A Political Biography* (Bombay: Lalvani Publishing House, 1966).

20. Allen S. Whiting, "Sino-Soviet Relations: What Next?" *Annals of the American Academy of Political and Social Science* 476 (November 1984): 143.

21. "Memorandum of Conversation," President Nixon, Prime Minister Chou En-lai, and others, Tuesday, February 22, 1972, p. 18, http://www.gwu.edu/~nsarchiv/NSAEBB/NSAEBB106/NZ-1.pdf.

22. See Katherine Frank, *Indira: The Life of Indira Nehru Gandhi* (New York: Houghton Mifflin, 2002).

23. King C. Chen, *China's War with Vietnam, 1979: Issues, Decisions, and Implications* (Palo Alto, CA: Hoover Institution Press, 1987).

24. "Everything ever said to me, by any Chinese in any station during any visit, was part of an intricate design—even when with my slower Occidental mind it took me a while to catch on," Kissinger recalled in his memoirs. "And subjects were carried forward between meetings months apart as if there had never been an interruption." Henry Kissinger, *White House Years*, vol. 1 (Boston: Little, Brown, 1979), p. 778.

25. Bhabani Sen Gupta, *Rajiv Gandhi: A Political Study* (New Delhi: Konark Publishers, 1989); Ved Mehta, *Rajiv Gandhi and Rama's Kingdom* (New Haven, CT: Yale University Press, 1994); and T. N. Srinivasan, "Economic Reforms and Global Integration," in Frankel and Harding, *The India-China Relationship*, pp. 219–60.

26. Ahluwalia Meenakshi and Ahluwalia Shashi, *Assassination of Rajiv Gandhi* (New Delhi: Mittla Publications, 1991).

27. See, Wolpert, *New History of India*, pp. 426–51, for an excellent treatment of these troubled years. Note also V. S. Naipaul, *India: A Million Mutinies Now* (New York: Viking Press, 1991). Naipaul's work catches the atmosphere of the time, but is exceptionally misleading, reflecting the author's deep-seated contempt for India. With

the benefit of hindsight, India's democratic political stability and economic progress by any real benchmark were genuinely impressive during those years.

28. Russia's disenchantment with the corruption, chaos, and impoverishment brought by crash privatization and crash democratization alike in the early 1990s led even President Boris Yeltsin, the author of both, to view more cautious, authoritarian models of transition far more sympathetically. See Andranik Migranian, Igor Kliamkin, and Irina Zorina, "An Authoritarian Perestroika? A Roundtable," *Telos*, no. 84 (Summer 1990): 115–25.

29. Husain Haqqani, *Pakistan: Between Mosque and Military* (Washington: Carnegie Endowment for International Peace, 2005); Hassan Abbas, *Pakistan's Drift into Extremism: Allah, the Army and America's War on Terror* (Armonk, NY: M. E. Sharpe, 2004); Dennis Kux, *The United States and Pakistan, 1947–2000: Disenchanted Allies* (Baltimore: Johns Hopkins University Press, 2001); and Mary Anne Weaver, *Pakistan: In the Shadow of Jihad and Afghanistan* (New York: Farrar, Straus & Giroux, 2002).

30. Stephen P. Cohen, *India: Emerging Power* (Washington: Brookings Institution Press, 2001), p. 61.

31. Nicholas Kristof and Sheryl WuDunn, *China Wakes: The Struggle for the Soul of a Rising Power* (New York: Vintage Books, 1994), especially chapter 13, "Blood and Iron," pp. 376–77; and Willy Wo-Lap Lam, *The Era of Jiang Zemin* (New York: Prentice Hall, 1999), especially chapter 4.

32. China's ties with and support for Burma/Myanmar, and its interest in developing bases in the Andaman Islands, are of special significance in this regard and were regularly cited by Indian Defense Minister George Fernandes and his fellow hawks in the Vajpayee government.

33. On July 10, 2008, Sudha Ramachandran reported in *Asia Times Online* that "China's naval cooperation with Myanmar—the reported lease of [the] Coco Island[s] near India's Andaman Islands and its work in modernizing several Myanmar ports— has given the Chinese access to the Bay of Bengal and a presence near the vital Malacca Strait." Sudha Ramachandran, "India Chases the Dragon in Sri Lanka," *Asia Times Online*, July 10, 2008, http://www.atimes.com/atimes/South_Asia/JG10Df03.html.

34. Kristof and WuDunn, *China Wakes*, p. 81.

35. See James Mann, *The Rise of the Vulcans: The History of Bush's War Cabinet* (New York: Viking Press, 2004), for a description of the confident, hawkish, can-do worldview of the new Bush policymakers.

36. Ted Galen Carpenter, *America's Coming War with China: A Collision Course over Taiwan* (New York: Palgrave Macmillan, 2005).

37. Edward Timperlake and William C. Triplett II, *Red Dragon Rising: Communist China's Military Threat to America* (Washington: Regnery, 1999), chapter 10, pp. 151–72.

38. Muazzam Gul, "China's Growing Global Clout," United Press International, December 9, 2004. See also "China to Take Lead in ASEAN Trade Zone," United Press International, November 29, 2004.

39. Sonia Kolesnikov-Jessop, "China Seen Seeking Peaceful Rise," United Press International, April 6, 2005.

40. For Vajpayee's revealing efforts to improve relations with China a quarter century before while serving as foreign minister during the 1979 brief Sino-Vietnamese war, see Hoffmann, "Perception and China Policy in India," pp. 33–74.

41. For Vajpayee's efforts to improve relations with China in 2003–4, see Francine Frankel, "Introduction," in Frankel and Harding, *The India-China Relationship*, p. 13;

and Steven A. Hoffman, "Perception and China Policy in India," in Frankel and Harding, *The India-China Relationship*, pp. 64–65.

42. Indian policymakers were also acutely aware that the British Empire had used the Indian Army to put down the Shiite nationalist rebellion against the British in Iraq in 1920. At least 10,000 Iraqis died (some Iraqi estimates have claimed the death toll was 10 times as high) and so did more than 3,000 Indian troops.

43. Krishnadev Calamur, "Few Indian Gains in China Trip," United Press International, June 26, 2003. See also "India and China Announce New Pact," United Press International, June 25, 2003; and "India Recognizes Tibet as Part of China," United Press International, June 24, 2003.

44. C. Raja Mohan, "India Rethinks China Policy," *The Hindu*, February 26, 2004.

45. Ibid.

46. Ibid.

47. This began an ongoing trend. "India, China to Bolster Military Ties," United Press International, March 29. 2004. See also "India Seeks More China Naval Cooperation," United Press International, May 25, 2005; "India, China May Boost Border Ties," United Press International, May 25, 2005; Jawed Naqvi, "Chinese Team to Watch Indian War Games," *The Dawn* (Pakistan), May 1, 2005; and "India Looks to China, Not Just U.S.," United Press International, May 27, 2005.

48. C. Raja Mohan, "A New Asian Axis?" *The Hindu*, May 24, 2004.

49. Ibid. The use of the term "triangle" appeared to imply a balancing relationship between India, China, and Japan rather than an alliance.

50. Sultan Shahin, "India, Japan Eye New Axis," *Asia Times Online*, August 24, 2004, http://www.atimes.com/atimes/South_Asia/FH24Df03.html.

51. Feng Zhaokui, "China-Japan-India Axis Strategy," *People's Daily Online*, April 30, 2004, http://english.people.com.cn/200404/29/eng20040429_141908.shtml.

52. Ibid. By the time of the 2001 census, "India's population then had already passed 1 billion. Twenty-five years later it will exceed 1.4 billion, and will almost certainly pass 1.5 billion by mid-century." Tim Dyson, Robert Cassem, and Leela Visaria, eds., *Twenty-First Century India: Population, Economy, Human Development, and the Environment* (New York: Oxford University Press, 2004).

53. Ibid. See also David Shambaugh, *Power Shift: China and Asia's New Dynamics* (Berkeley: University of California Press, 2006), p. 65. "The recent (in 2001) China-India naval maneuver is an indication that the two countries do not see each other as an imminent threat." For a perspective on the growth of the Indian Navy in its first 40 years following independence, see Robert H. Bruce, *The Modern Indian Navy and the Indian Ocean, Developments and Implications* (Perth: Curtin University of Technology/Australian Institute of International Affairs, 1989).

54. Feng Zhaokai, "China-Japan-India Axis Strategy."

55. Jairam Ramesh, *Making Sense of Chindia: Reflections on China and India* (New Delhi: India Research Press, 2006); and Susan L. Shirk, *China: Fragile Superpower* (New York: Oxford University Press, 2007), pp. 115–18.

56. For the involvement of NGOs in developing grass-roots democracy in India and China see Manoranjan Mohanty, George Matthew, Richard Baum, and Rong Ma, eds., *Grass-Roots Democracy in India and China* (Thousand Oaks, CA: Sage Publications, 2007); and Jean-Jacques Dethier, *Governance, Decentralization and Reform in China, India and Russia* (Boston: Kluwer Academic Publishers, 2000).

57. Shirk, *China: Fragile Superpower*, pp. 52–64.

58. Cited in James Clad, "Convergent Indian and Chinese Perspectives on Global Order," in Frankel and Harding, *The India-China Relationship*, p. 286. See also Surjit Mansingh, *Indian and Chinese Foreign Policies in Comparative Perspective* (New Delhi: Radiant Publishers, 1998).

59. "The overall picture that emerges reinforces a view that globalization in the current era simply represents a continuation of exogenous forces prompting China and India to generate nationalist responses." Clad, "Convergent Indian and Chinese Perspectives on Global Order," p. 289.

60. "Emissions of Greenhouse Gases Report," Energy Information Administration, December 3, 2008, http://www.eia.doe.gov/oiaf/1605/ggrpt/.

61. It should also be noted that the balance of power in the Himalayas in the early 21st century is very different from what it was before the outbreak of the 1962 war. India's mountain divisions are now experienced, well trained, and well equipped. China has also extended its networks of railroads, roads, and air bases to maintain a strong military presence in Tibet.

Chapter 4

1. Dennis Kux, *India and the United States: Estranged Democracies* (Washington: National Defense University Press, 1993), is the best U.S. treatment of the relationship. See also William J. Barnds, *India, Pakistan and the Great Powers* (New York: Praeger, 1972) especially chapter 6, "The Soviet Union Chooses India," pp. 107–28, and chapter 10, "Tashkent and After," pp. 209–36.

2. See discussion in chapter 2. Also Stephen P. Cohen, *The Indian Army: Its Contribution to the Development of a Nation* (New Delhi: Oxford University Press, 1990); and Philip Mason, *A Matter of Honor* (New York: Holt, Rinehart & Winston, 1974). At the Versailles Peace Conference of 1919 and afterward, the U.S. focus on the Middle East was centered on British plans to retain control of Palestine, something President Woodrow Wilson and his officials were suspicious of, as well as ultimately futile thoughts of establishing U.S. mandates over the Kurds or the Turkish heartland itself. See David Fromkin, *A Peace to End All Peace: The Fall of the Ottoman Empire and the Creation of the Modern Middle East* (New York: Owl Books, 2001).

3. Stanley Wolpert, *A New History of India* (New York: Oxford University Press, 2000), p 301.

4. FDR's demand that Winston Churchill grant India immediate independence during the height of World War II is documented in Walter LaFeber, *The American Age: United States Foreign Policy at Home and Abroad since 1750* (New York: W. W. Norton, 1989). Churchill succeeded in fending off this demand, but Roosevelt's continued pressure on him over India was one of the biggest and most recurring strains between them. See James Macgregor Burns, *Roosevelt: The Soldier of Freedom, 1940–45* (New York: Harcourt Brace Jovanovich, 1970) pp. 219–22, 238–42, 379–81. See also Robert Dallek, *Franklin D. Roosevelt and American Foreign Policy, 1932–45* (New York: Oxford University Press, 1995); and Kux, *India and the United States*, pp. 9–19, 27–35. Kux also details the negative effect of Gandhi's "Quit India," campaign of 1942 on FDR and U.S. policymakers. See ibid., pp. 23–26, 37–38.

5. Dallek, *Franklin D. Roosevelt and American Foreign Policy*, pp. 325–26.

6. John T. McNay, *Dean Acheson: The British Accent in American Foreign Policy* (Columbia: University of Missouri Press, 2001); and James Chace, *Acheson: The Secretary of State Who Created the American World* (New York: Simon & Schuster, 1998).

See also Kux, *India and the United States*, chapter 2, pp. 47–90, especially Acheson's comments on Nehru, cited on p. 70.

7. David Fromkin, *In the Time of the Americans* (New York: Knopf, 1995), pp. 331–33; Thomas Fleming, *The New Dealers' War* (New York: Basic Books, 2001), p. 18; and McNay, *Dean Acheson*, p. 3 and chapter 5, pp. 101–28.

8. Nobody else expected it either. See, William Manchester, *American Caesar* (New York: Little, Brown, 1978), p. 234.

9. Galbraith resigned as ambassador and returned to academia in 1963 but retained very close ties to Kennedy and, at first, President Lyndon Johnson. But he never held any diplomatic or policymaking post again, and he broke with Johnson permanently over the Vietnam War, supporting Sen. Eugene McCarthy's anti-war candidacy in 1968 that ultimately convinced Johnson not to run for reelection.

10. See Theodore J. Burkett, *United States Foreign Policy toward Thailand in the Post-Vietnam Period* (Colorado Springs: U.S. Air University, Air War College, 1976); and Richard B. Burgess, *An Analysis of the Influence of Thailand on U.S. Policy in Vietnam* (Colorado Springs: U.S. Air War College, Air University, 1967).

11. The role of the CIA in enabling or encouraging General Suharto's military takeover is intensely debated. See in particular, Theodore Friend, *Indonesian Destinies* (Cambridge, MA: Belknap Press, 2003), pp. 118–19.

12. See ibid. For a heavily partisan, uncritically pro-Suharto account, see Tarzie Vittachi, *The Fall of Sukarno* (New York: Praeger, 1967).

13. See the outline in Wolpert, *A New History of India*, pp. 375–76. See also D. R. Mankekar, *Lal Bahadur Shastri: A Political Biography* (Bombay: Lalvani Publishing House, 1966).

14. P. R. Kumaraswamy notes that this policy in fact began under Nehru but was intensified by Indira Gandhi and her son Rajiv. P. R. Kumaraswamy, "India and Israel: Emerging Partnership," *Journal of Strategic Studies* 25, no. 4 (December 2002): 193, 195.

15. Barnds, *India, Pakistan and the Great Powers*, chapter 10, pp. 209–36. See also Kux, *India and the United States*, pp. 307–8, 338–39, 399–400; and Stephen P. Cohen, *India: Emerging Power* (Washington: Brookings Institution Press, 2001), p. 279.

16. For excellent accounts, see relevant sections of Kissinger's own massive but superbly readable memoirs. Henry Kissinger, *White House Years*, vol. 1 (Boston: Little, Brown, 1979); and Walter Isaacson, *Kissinger: A Biography* (New York: Simon & Schuster, 1992).

17. Jahanara Imam, *Of Blood and Fire: The Untold Story of Bangladesh's War of Independence*, trans. Mustafizur Rahman (New Delhi: Sterling Publishers, 1989); and Richard Sisson and Leo Rose, *War and Secession: Pakistan, India and the Creation of Bangladesh* (Berkeley: University of California Press, 1991).

18. See especially Kux, *India and the United States*, pp. 255, 259, 307–12. Ironically, Mrs. Gandhi, who had had a lonely and unhappy childhood, and who had been widowed early, won election as prime minister over the early Congress Party frontrunner Morarji Desai precisely because she was still, at age 48, so inexperienced and, apparently, diffident. However, once in office, she rapidly grew in confidence and in her ability to take decisive actions.

19. See Zareer Masani, *Indira Gandhi: A Biography* (New York: Thomas Y. Crowell, 1975), chapters 9, 10, and especially chapter 11. Particularly striking was Masani's prediction, two years before it happened, that Mrs. Gandhi would try to establish a

dictatorship. See Kux, *India and the United States*, pp. 335–39; and Stanley Wolpert, *New History of India* (New York: Oxford University Press, 2000), pp. 397–405.

20. Bhabani Sen Gupta, *Rajiv Gandhi: A Political Study* (New Delhi: Konark Publishers, 1989); and Ved Mehta, *Rajiv Gandhi and Rama's Kingdom* (New Haven, CT: Yale University Press, 1994).

21. Carter was the first U.S. president to visit India since Dwight D. Eisenhower in 1953, but Kux notes that the relationship soured during Carter's last year in office. See Kux, *India and the United States*, pp. 345–74.

22. Shahid Javed Burki and Craig Baxter, *Pakistan under the Military: Eleven Years of Zia Ul-Haq* (Boulder, CO: Westview Press, 1991); Khalid Mahmud Arif, *Working with Zia: Pakistan's Power Politics: 1977–1988* (New York: Oxford University Press, 1995).

23. For the effect of India's economic reforms, see Anne O. Krueger, ed., *Economic Policy Reforms and the Indian Economy* (Chicago: University of Chicago Press, 2002); and Bimal Jalan, *The Indian Economy: Problems and Prospects* (New York: Viking Press, 1992).

24. Joel Kotkin, *Tribes: How Race, Religion and Identity Determine Success in the New Global Economy* (New York: Random House, 1993). See especially chapter 7, "The Greater India," pp. 201–32.

25. With the exception of the late Ron Brown, secretary of commerce, it is hard to find any members of the Clinton cabinet who shared their president's obvious enthusiasm for a new special relationship with India. By contrast, although President George W. Bush at least at first did not share Clinton's vision, it was pushed by Secretary of Defense Donald Rumsfeld and his deputy Paul Wolfowitz and was later picked up by National Security Adviser and then second-term Secretary of State Condoleezza Rice.

26. For an analysis of Clinton's assessment of Bangladesh's potential, see C. Raja Mohan, "Clinton Discovers Bangladesh," *The Hindu*, February 6, 2000.

27. David Bornstein, *The Price of a Dream: The Story of the Grameen Bank* (Chicago: University of Chicago Press, 1997); and Muhammad Yunis, *Banker to the Poor: Micro-Lending and the Battle against World Poverty* (New York: Public Affairs, 2003). So strongly did Clinton feel about supporting the Grameen Bank that on his state visit to Bangladesh in March 2000, he insisted on scheduling a visit to a Grameen village project. The visit was canceled on the insistence of the Secret Service because of fears that Islamist extremists would try to shoot down the president's helicopter. This author was on the presidential press party for the trip.

28. "There are more software engineers in Bangalore than Silicon Valley," Lt. Gen. Robert M. Shea, J-6 and director of command, control, communications and computer systems for the Joint Staff of the U.S. Armed Forces speaking to the Army Knowledge Management Conference at Fort Lauderdale, Florida, August 23, 2005. Reported in "China Beats U.S. in Scientists 10 to One," United Press International, August 23, 2005.

29. James Mann, *The Rise of the Vulcans: The History of Bush's War Cabinet* (New York: Viking Books, 2004), pp. 321, 329.

30. For example, Wolfowitz made such comments at the opening reception of the Congress of Phoenix of the New Atlantic Initiative at the Biltmore Hotel, Phoenix, on May 16, 1997. The author attended that meeting.

31. See President George W. Bush's January 2005 second inaugural address. Bush's neo-Wilsonian enthusiasm for spreading democracy around the world by any means available, as quickly and energetically as possible, was eagerly embraced by the influential band of neoconservative intellectuals who had long advocated embracing India and confronting China on those grounds especially that China was authoritarian

whereas India was democratic. Ironically, democratically elected Indian leaders of the nationalist BJP and the center left United Progressive Alliance alike had no difficulty in renewing their traditional ties with Russia and energetically forging new ones with authoritarian China despite their genuine commitment to democratic values at home.

32. George W. Bush, "Second Inaugural Address," January 20, 2005, http://www.npr.org/templates/story/story.php?storyID = 4460172.

33. See Hassan Abbas, *Pakistan's Drift into Extremism: Allah, the Army and America's War on Terror* (London: M. E. Sharpe, 2004); Dennis Kux, *The United States and Pakistan, 1947–2000: Disenchanted Allies* (Baltimore: Johns Hopkins University Press, 2001); and Mary Anne Weaver, *Pakistan: In the Shadow of Jihad and Afghanistan* (New York: Farrar, Straus & Giroux, 2002).

34. For a most valuable and comprehensive account of all these episodes from the 1996–98 nuclear negotiations through the 2000 Clinton visit and the entire 2000–2004 Bush-Vajpayee honeymoon period, see C. Raja Mohan, *Crossing the Rubicon: The Shaping of India's New Foreign Policy* (New York: Palgrave Macmillan, 2004).

35. See, for example, Omar Khalidi, *Indian Muslims since Independence* (New Delhi: Vikas Publishing, 1995).

36. Mann, *Rise of the Vulcans*, p. 281. Harry Harding, "The Evolution of the Strategic Triangle: China, India, and the United States," in *The India-China Relationship: What the United States Needs to Know*, ed. Francine R. Frankel and Harry Harding (New York: Columbia University Press, 2004), p. 334. See also Robert Hathaway, "The U.S.-India Courtship: From Clinton to Bush," *Journal of Strategic Studies* 25, no. 4 (December 2002): 10–12.

37. Harding, "Evolution of the Strategic Triangle," p. 334. See also Hathaway, "U.S.-India Courtship," pp. 19–20.

38. Padam D. Sharma, *Inter Services Intelligence of Pakistan and Its Activities* (London: Minerva Press, 2004); Husain Haqqani, *Pakistan: Between Mosque and Military* (Washington: Carnegie Endowment for International Peace, 2005); and Abbas, *Pakistan's Drift into Extremism*.

39. For a valuable discussion of Musharraf and the diplomatic tightrope he has walked, see Owen Bennett Jones, *Pakistan: Eye of the Storm* (New Haven, CT: Yale University Press, 2003). Also Haqqani, *Pakistan: Between Mosque and Military*.

40. Gordon Corera, *Shopping for Bombs: Nuclear Proliferation, Global Insecurity, and the Rise and Fall of the A. Q. Khan Network* (New York: Oxford University Press, 2006); and Adrian Levy and Catherine Scott-Clark, *Deception: Pakistan, the United States, and the Secret Trade of Nuclear Weapons* (New York: Walker Publishing, 2007).

41. See John C. K. Daly and Martin Sieff, "India Sours on Intel Links with United States," *UPI Intelligence Watch*, November 1, 2004.

42. Sultan Shahin, "India in the Mood for Elections," *Asia Times*, February 4, 2004.

43. Ibid.

44. Mani Shankar Aiyar, "India File: More Growth, More Suffering," United Press International, February 23, 2004.

45. Alex Perry, "Subcontinental Divide," *Time*, February 16, 2004.

46. Eric D. Beinhocker, Diana Farrell, and Adil S. Zainulbhai, "Tracking the Growth of India's Middle Class," *McKinsey Quarterly*, August 2007; and Barney Gimbel, "The New New World Order," *Fortune*, July 14, 2008. See also Arvind Panagariya, *India: The Emerging Giant* (New York: Oxford University Press, 2008).

47. "The 'Bird of Gold': The Rise of India's Consumer Market," McKinsey Global Institute, May 2007.

48. "India's Congress Party Returns to Power," United Press International, May 13, 2004.

Chapter 5

1. For the assumptions that have guided U.S. foreign policymaking toward China over the past 33 years, see James R. Lilley and Jeffrey Lilley, *China Hands: Nine Decades of Adventure, Espionage and Diplomacy in Asia* (New York: Public Affairs, 2004). For overviews of U.S.-Chinese relations in recent decades see, James Mann, *About Face: A History of America's Curious Relations with China from Nixon to Clinton* (New York: Vintage Books, 2000); and Harry Harding, *A Fragile Relationship: The United States and China since 1972* (Washington: Brookings Institution Press, 1992).

2. See Mann, *About Face*. See also Patrick Tyler, *A Great Wall: Six Presidents and China* (New York: Public Affairs, 2000).

3. Nicholas Kristoff and Sheryll Wudunn, *China Wakes* (New York: Vintage Books, 1995), pp. 79–80.

4. See Yong Deng, *China Rising: Power and Motivation in Chinese Foreign Policy* (Lanham, MD: Rowman & Littlefield, 2005). For changing Chinese perceptions against America during the Jiang Zemin era and the Clinton presidency, see Peter Hayes Gries, *China's New Nationalism: Pride, Politics and Diplomacy* (Berkeley: University of California Press, 2004). For an overview of Jiang's domestic and foreign policies and priorities, see Willy Wo-Lap Ma, *The Era of Jiang Zemin* (New York: Prentice Hall, 1999).

5. The Chinese felt humiliated and toothless in the face of Clinton's move. Over the next decade, they devoted a major share of their conventional weapons budget to building up an arsenal to deter U.S. aircraft carriers from operating at will in the area in the event of any future conflict.

6. Clinton's own perspective on this can be found in his autobiography, Bill Clinton, *My Life: The Presidential Years* (New York: Vintage Books, 2005), pp. 1126–27.

7. See Ted Galen Carpenter, *America's Coming War with China: A Collision Course over Taiwan* (New York: Palgrave Macmillan, 2005), p. 124; and Edward Timperlake and William C. Triplett III, *Red Dragon Rising* (Washington: Regnery, 1999).

8. See Michael O'Hanlon and Mike Mochizuki, *Crisis on the Korean Peninsula: How to Deal with a Nuclear North Korea* (New York: McGraw-Hill, 2003); Joel S. Wit, Daniel B. Poneman, and Robert L. Gallucci, *Going Critical: The First North Korean Nuclear Crisis* (Washington: Brookings Institution Press, 2004); and Strobe Talbott, *Engaging India: Diplomacy, Democracy and the Bomb* (Washington: Brookings Institution Press, 2004).

9. Norimitsu Onishi and Edward Wong, "U.S. to Remove North Korea from Terror List," *International Herald Tribune*, June 26, 2008.

10. See discussion of this issue earlier in this chapter.

11. See Ted Galen Carpenter and Doug Bandow, *The Korean Conundrum: America's Troubled Relations with North and South Korea* (New York: Palgrave Macmillan, 2004), especially chapters 1 and 3, pp. 9–37 and 71–100.

12. Ross Terrill identifies North Korea as a "confrere" of China. Ross Terrill, *The New Chinese Empire* (New York: Basic Books, 2003), p. 340.

13. See, for example, Bill Gertz, "CIA Report Blames China, Russia for Massive Weapons Proliferation," *Washington Times*, September 10, 2001. As this story broke,

only a day before the al Qaeda 9/11 attacks on the World Trade Center and the Pentagon, it was rapidly forgotten. For critical assessments of China's weapons sales policies to U.S. enemies, see Bill Gertz, *The China Threat: How the People's Republic Targets America* (Washington: Regnery, 2000).

14. For an alternative theory that China's leaders want to encourage a united, nuclear-armed Korea following the collapse of the North that would be inherently hostile and threatening to Japan, see Richard Bernstein and Ross H. Munro, *The Coming Conflict with China* (New York: Knopf, 1997), pp. 180–82. However, Beijing's consistent policy of support for North Korea since then argues against this interpretation of Chinese policy.

15. For an outline of China's successful role in making itself the cornerstone of the six-nation nuclear negotiating process with North Korea since 2002, see Jephraim P. Gundzik, "Roadmap to a Nuclear Test," *Asia Times*, September 3, 2005, http://www.atimes.com/atimes/Korea/GI03Dg01.html.

16. "North Korea Hints at Nuclear Talks," Associated Press, March 22, 2005.

17. Ibid.

18. Carpenter, *America's Coming War with China*, p. 128.

19. For a study of Chinese negotiating behavior and diplomatic techniques, see Alfred D. Wilhelm Jr., *The Chinese at the Negotiating Table* (Washington: National Defense University Press, 1994).

20. When the Bush administration signed off on September 19, 2005, on an agreement with North Korea to defuse the nuclear issue in the context of the six-party talks in Beijing, it was fiercely attacked within days by Nicholas Eberstadt of the American Enterprise Institute. See Nicholas Eberstadt, "A Skeptical View," *Wall Street Journal*, September 21, 2005.

21. Susan Shirk, *China: Fragile Superpower* (New York: Oxford University Press, 2007), p. 254.

22. Carpenter, *America's Coming War with China*, p. 111.

23. Xinhua News Agency dispatch, December 5, 2004.

24. See Justin Logan and Ted Galen Carpenter, "Taiwan's Defense Budget: How Taipei's Free Riding Risks War," Cato Institute Policy Analysis no. 600, September 13, 2007.

25. William Arkin, "Early Warning," *Washington Post*, May 24, 2006; and Arkin, "U.S. Plan for Defending Taiwan Disclosed," *Taipei Times*, June 5, 2006.

26. Arkin, "U.S. Plan for Defending Taiwan Disclosed."

27. Arkin, "Early Warning."

28. "Military Power of the People's Republic of China 2007: Annual Report to Congress," Office of the Secretary of Defense, June 12, 2006, p. 17.

29. Kurt Campbell and Jeremiah Gertler, *The Paths Ahead: Missile Defense in Asia* (Washington: Center for Strategic and International Studies, 2006).

30. Ibid.

31. "Taiwan Deploys Missiles on Island off China," Agence France-Presse, July 25, 2004; Martin Sieff, "BMD Focus: The Missiles of Taiwan," United Press International, January 19, 2006; and "Production Set to Begin on Hsiung-Feng II-E Missiles," *Taiwan Times*, July 5, 2005, http://www.globalsecurity.org/military/world/taiwan/hf-3.htm.

32. For a discussion of how close Taiwan has come in the past to developing nuclear weapons, see David Albright, "Taiwan: Nuclear Nightmare Averted," *Bulletin of the Atomic Scientists*, January 1, 1998.

33. Figure from U.S. Department of Defense estimates. "Military Power of the People's Republic of China," p. 38.

34. Anthony H. Cordesman and Martin Kleiber, *Chinese Military Modernization: Force Development and Strategic Capabilities* (Washington: Center for Strategic and International Studies, 2007).

35. Bruce Klinger, "South Korea's Growing Isolation," *Asia Times Online*, August 5, 2006.

36. Ahn Mi Young, "Yankees, Don't Go Home Yet," *Asia Times Online*, August 15, 2006.

37. "Missile Defense Plans Have Their Skeptics," *Japan Times*, July 28, 2006.

38. Ibid.

39. In November 2008, a senior Chinese military official said that China was interested in acquiring or building an aircraft carrier, but that it would be used only for offshore defense. The same article refers to plans that China will build a carrier by 2010, but that seems unlikely. "Chinese Aircraft Carrier?" *Straits Times*, November 18, 2008.

40. "Major Foreign Holders of Treasury Securities," U.S. Department of the Treasury, 2009, http://www.treasury.gov/tic/mfh.txt.

41. The incident is recorded in Bob Woodward, *Plan of Attack* (New York: Simon & Schuster, 2004), pp. 24–27.

42. Harry Harding, "The Evolution of the Strategic Triangle: China, India and the United States," in *The India-China Relationship*, ed. Francine R. Frankel and Harry Harding (New York: Columbia University Press, 2004), pp. 108–11.

43. Siddharth Srivastava, "India-China Trade Reach New Trade Heights," *Asia Times Online*, January 22, 2006.

44. Figures from "Military Power of the People's Republic of China, 2008," Office of the Secretary of Defense, http://www.defenselink.mil/pubs/pdfs/China_Military_Report_08.pdf; "Taiwan Strait Military Balance, Air Forces," figure 12, p. 52; and "Taiwan Strait Military Balance, Naval Forces," figure 14, p. 54.

45. Ibid., pp. 24–5, and "China's Missile Force," figure 17, p. 56.

46. Ibid., p. 41; see also Carpenter, *America's Coming War with China*, pp. 9–23.

47. Judith Miller, "U.S. Imposes Sanctions on Companies Aiding Iran with Arms," *International Herald Tribune*, April 3, 2004.

48. See, for example, Ted Galen Carpenter, "President Bush's Muddled Policy on Taiwan," Cato Institute Foreign Policy Briefing no. 82, March 15, 2004.

49. Carpenter, *America's Coming War with China*, p. 99. See also Bernstein and Munro, *The Coming Conflict with China*, chapter 6, "Flashpoint: Taiwan," pp. 149–65.

50. Sergei Blagov, "Russian-Chinese War Game Meant to Boost Bilateral Partnership," *Eurasia Daily Monitor*, August 18, 2005, http://www.jamestown.org/publications.details.php?volume_id = 407&issue_id + 3441&article_id = 2370166; and "Taiwan Issue Clouds Russia-China Military Exercise," *Eurasia Daily Monitor*, March 22, 2005, http://www.jamestown.org/publications.details.php?volume_id = 407&issue_id + 3270&article_id = 2369454.

51. The exercises included a BDK-11 landing vessel, the Marshal Shaposhnikov anti-submarine vessel, and a Burny destroyer. Blagov, "Russian-Chinese War Game."

52. Martin Sieff, "Russia, China Prepare to Fight Wars," United Press International, August 22, 2005. See also *ITAR-TASS* dispatch, August 21, 2005.

53. Cohen cited in Sieff, "Russia, China Prepare to Fight Wars."

54. *Gazeta.ru* website, August 18, 2005.

55. Statement posted at *China Youth Daily*, July 18, 2005, cited in Sieff, "Russia, China Prepare to Fight Wars."

56. Martin Sieff, "Putin's China Visit Shifts Power," United Press International, March 22, 2006.

57. "Russia, China Sign Multibillion-Dollar Contracts during Putin's Visit," RIA Novosti News Agency, March 21, 2003; and "Russia Signs Gas Deal with China," BBC Online, March 21, 2006.

58. "Russia, China Sign Multibillion-Dollar Contracts during Putin's Visit."

59. "China, Russia More than Just Good Neighbours," *China Daily*, March 20, 2006.

60. Nikita Petrov, "New Defense Giant, Part 1," United Press International, December 11, 2007; and Petrov, "New Defense Giant, Part 2," United Press International, December 12, 2007.

Chapter 6

1. P. R. Kumaraswami, "India and Israel: Emerging Partnership," *Journal of Strategic Studies* 25, no. 4 (December 2002): 202.

2. Admiral L. Ramdas, cited in Praful Bidwai, "India Exposed by Missile Failure," Inter-Press Service, published in *Asia Times*, July 12, 2006.

3. See Sahibzada Yusuf Ansari, *Sonia Gandhi: Triumph of Will* (New Delhi: India Research Press, 2006); and Ravi Singaravarapu, *Sonia Gandhi through a Different Lens* (Palo Alto, CA: Fultus Corporation, 2005).

4. Raja Menon, "Burying the Past," *India Seminar*, April 2006.

5. Brahma Chellaney, "India Has Gone Far Enough," Rediff India Abroad, March 8, 2006, http://www.rediff.com/news/2006/mar/08bramhachat.htm.

6. Bharat Karnad, "Blighted Strategic Future," *India Seminar*, April 2006.

7. Amar C. Bakshi, "Professor Disappointed by U.S.-India Nuclear Deal," *Post Global*, June 30, 2007.

8. *People's Daily*, February 18, 2005.

9. Ibid.

10. Ibid.

11. Stephen Blank, *Eurasia Daily Monitor*, February 28, 2005.

12. Siddharth Varadarajan, "Rice Brings Reality Check on India-U.S. Ties," *The Hindu*, March 17, 2005, http://www.hindu.com/2005/03/17/stories/2005031707 951100.htm.

13. "Iran Says IPI Deal Not Closed," United Press International, July 25, 2006.

14. Cited in Blank.

15. Aiyar cited in Andrea Mihailescu and Martin Sieff, "Oil Needs Change Strategic Face of Asia," United Press International, March 5, 2005.

16. P. R. Kumaraswamy, "India's China Policy: Wishful Thinking Overtakes Harsh Realities," *Asian Tribune*, July 4, 2006.

17. Indrajit Basu, "Oil May Revive Indo-Russia Ties," United Press International, December 3, 2004.

18. Ibid.

19. Ibid.

20. Ibid.

21. "Gujarat Signs Agreement with Gazprom," *The Hindu*, July 9, 2006.

22. "Russia Woos India for IT Partnership," United Press International, December 5, 2004.

23. Ibid.

24. Harbaksh Singh Nanda, "Russia Won't Supply Nuke Subs to India," United Press International, December 2, 2004.

25. Ranjit Devraj, "India-Russia Alliance Turns Commercial," Inter-Press Service, December 7, 2004.

26. Subhash Kapila, "Russia-India Strategic Partnership Continues to Be Vibrant," South Asia Analysis Group, Paper no. 268, October 3, 2008. The Russia-India partnership is expected to deepen over the next few years with the updating of the IRIGC-MTC (Indo-Russian Inter-Governmental Commission on Military Technical Cooperation). This group is expected to further relations to a point described as "the transition from vendor and buyer to co-developers." Sandeep Dikshit, "India, Russia, to Step Up Strategic Ties," The Hindu, September 30, 2008.

27. Devraj, "India-Russia Alliance"; Krishnadev Calamur, "Analysis: India's Defense Sector," United Press International, November 7, 2007; Viktor Litovkin, "India Buys Russian Warplanes," United Press International, January 30, 2007; Nikita Petrov, "New Defense Giant, Part 1," United Press International, December 11, 2007; and Nikita Petrov, "New Defense Giant, Part 2," United Press International, December 12, 2007.

28. "India-Russia Stage Joint Naval Exercises," United Press International, October 17, 2005.

29. "Anti-Terror Naval Exercise in Sea of Japan," United Press International, April 24, 2007.

30. "Russia, India to Produce, Sell 1,000 Supersonic Cruise Missiles," Press Trust of India, July 21, 2006.

31. RIA Novosti News Agency report, April 24, 2007.

32. "Indigenous Aircraft Carrier on Its Way," Times of India, March 22, 2005.

33. Ibid.

34. Ibid.

35. Ibid.

36. See, for example, Christopher J. Pehrson, "String of Pearls: Meeting the Challenge of China's Rising Power across the Asian Littoral," Strategic Studies Institute, July 2006, http://www.strategicstudiesinstitute.army.mil/pdffiles/PUB721.pdf25.

37. Ibid.

38. Thom Shanker and Joel Brinkley, "U.S. Is Set to Sell Jets to Pakistan: India Is Critical," New York Times, March 26, 2004.

39. Editorial, Wall Street Journal, March 29, 2005.

40. Shanker and Brinkley, "U.S. Is Set to Sell Jets to Pakistan."

41. Anwar Iqbal, "U.S. Agrees to Sell F-16s to Pakistan," United Press International, March 25, 2005.

42. Shanker and Brinkley, "U.S. Is Set to Sell Jets to Pakistan."

43. Ibid.

44. Personal communication to the author from an Indian official speaking on condition of anonymity, July 2006. See also "India Concerned over U.S. Move to Sell Pakistan F-16s," Financial Express, July 4, 2006.

45. Ibid.

46. Martin Sieff, "Who Knew What Hu Would Do?" United Press International, January 25, 2005.

47. Willy Lam, "Hu's Campaign for Ideological Purity against the West," China Brief 5, no. 2 (2005).

48. Ibid.

49. Ibid.

50. James Mann, *The China Fantasy: How Our Leaders Explain Away Chinese Repression* (New York: Viking Adult, 2007).

51. Foreign direct investment in China in 2008 totaled $92.4 billion. "China's FDI Up 23.6% in 2008," Xinhua News Agency, January 15, 2009, http://news.xinhuanet.com/english/2009-01/15/content_10662757.htm. The United States was the sixth-largest source of foreign direct investment in China, totaling $2.6 billion, in 2007. "Forecast 2008: Foreign Investment in China," U.S.-China Business Council, 2008, http://www.uschina.org/public/documents/2008/02/2008-foreign-investment.pdf.

52. At that time, Japan was second with holdings totaling $573 billion. Anthony Faiola and Zachary A. Goldfarb, "China Tops Japan in Debt Holdings," *Washington Post*, November 19, 2008.

53. See Daniel Yergin, *The Prize* (New York: Touchstone, 1992), pp. 648–50.

54. Susan Shirk, *China: Fragile Superpower* (New York: Oxford University Press, 2007), p. 211.

55. Ted Galen Carpenter, *The Coming War with China: A Collision Course over Taiwan* (New York: Palgrave Macmillan 2005).

Index

About the Author

A prolific writer and commentor on world affairs, Martin Sieff was previously chief analyst for United Press International and was its former managing editor for international affairs. He has received three Pulitzer Prize nominations for international reporting and served as Soviet and Eastern European affairs correspondent and chief foreign correspondent for the *Washington Times*. Sieff has reported from 65 countries and covered more than 10 wars and conflicts. He has an M.A. from Oxford University and has been a regular contributor to the *American Conservative, National Review Online,* the *Globalist, Salon.com,* and the *Daily Beast.* He has appeared as an international affairs expert on Fox News, CNN, NPR, and the BBC.

Cato Institute

Founded in 1977, the Cato Institute is a public policy research foundation dedicated to broadening the parameters of policy debate to allow consideration of more options that are consistent with the traditional American principles of limited government, individual liberty, and peace. To that end, the Institute strives to achieve greater involvement of the intelligent, concerned lay public in questions of policy and the proper role of government.

The Institute is named for *Cato's Letters*, libertarian pamphlets that were widely read in the American Colonies in the early 18th century and played a major role in laying the philosophical foundation for the American Revolution.

Despite the achievement of the nation's Founders, today virtually no aspect of life is free from government encroachment. A pervasive intolerance for individual rights is shown by government's arbitrary intrusions into private economic transactions and its disregard for civil liberties.

To counter that trend, the Cato Institute undertakes an extensive publications program that addresses the complete spectrum of policy issues. Books, monographs, and shorter studies are commissioned to examine the federal budget, Social Security, regulation, military spending, international trade, and myriad other issues. Major policy conferences are held throughout the year, from which papers are published thrice yearly in the *Cato Journal*. The Institute also publishes the quarterly magazine *Regulation*.

In order to maintain its independence, the Cato Institute accepts no government funding. Contributions are received from foundations, corporations, and individuals, and other revenue is generated from the sale of publications. The Institute is a nonprofit, tax-exempt, educational foundation under Section 501(c)3 of the Internal Revenue Code.

CATO INSTITUTE
1000 Massachusetts Ave., N.W.
Washington, D.C. 20001
www.cato.org